SACRAMENTO PUBLIC LIBRARY

D0341207

# Deep State

# Deep State

## Inside the Government Secrecy Industry

MARC AMBINDER
AND
D. B. GRADY

**WILEY**

Copyright © 2013 by Marc Ambinder and D. B. Grady. All rights reserved

Cover Design: Wendy Mount
Cover Photograph: © Joe Raedle/Getty Images; Presidential seal © Sylvia Schug/
iStockphoto

Published by John Wiley & Sons, Inc., Hoboken, New Jersey
Published simultaneously in Canada

No part of this publication may be reproduced, stored in a retrieval system, or transmitted in any form or by any means, electronic, mechanical, photocopying, recording, scan-
ning, or otherwise, except as permitted under Section 107 or 108 of the 1976 United
States Copyright Act, without either the prior written permission of the Publisher,
or authorization through payment of the appropriate per-copy fee to the Copyright
Clearance Center, 222 Rosewood Drive, Danvers, MA 01923, (978) 750–8400, fax (978)
646–8600, or on the web at www.copyright.com. Requests to the Publisher for permission should be addressed to the Permissions Department, John Wiley & Sons, Inc., 111
River Street, Hoboken, NJ 07030, (201) 748–6011, fax (201) 748–6008, or online at
http://www.wiley.com/go/permissions.

Limit of Liability/Disclaimer of Warranty: While the publisher and the author have used
their best efforts in preparing this book, they make no representations or warranties with
respect to the accuracy or completeness of the contents of this book and specifically dis-
claim any implied warranties of merchantability or fitness for a particular purpose. No
warranty may be created or extended by sales representatives or written sales materials.
The advice and strategies contained herein may not be suitable for your situation. You
should consult with a professional where appropriate. Neither the publisher nor the
author shall be liable for any loss of profit or any other commercial damages, including
but not limited to special, incidental, consequential, or other damages.

For general information about our other products and services, please contact our
Customer Care Department within the United States at (800) 762–2974, outside the
United States at (317) 572–3993 or fax (317) 572–4002.

Wiley also publishes its books in a variety of electronic formats and by print-on-demand.
Some content that appears in standard print versions of this book may not be available
in other formats. For more information about Wiley products, visit us at www.wiley.com.

*Library of Congress Cataloging-in-Publication Data:*

ISBN 978-1-118-14668-2 (cloth); ISBN 978-1-118-22580-6 (ebk);
ISBN 978-1-118-23573-7 (ebk); ISBN 978-1-118-26378-5 (ebk)

Printed in the United States of America
10 9 8 7 6 5 4 3 2 1

"Sometimes, Tom, we have to do a thing in order to find out the reason for it. Sometimes our actions are questions, not answers."

— John le Carré, *A Perfect Spy*

*For Michael and Kelly*

# CONTENTS

# AUTHORS' NOTE

This is a book about secrets, and the authors feel an obligation to be transparent about a few things.

During his time in the military, author D. B. Grady (which is a pseudonym for David Brown) held a security clearance. No sensitive information he came across while serving in Afghanistan or in the United States made it into this book.

In September 2012, author Marc Ambinder began consulting for Palantir Technologies LLC, an analytics company that does work for intelligence agencies and the Department of Defense, among other clients. He was brought in to work on a specific project that did not require access to secrets or to classified information. There was no cross-pollination; the manuscript had already been completed, and nothing in this book comes from any material gathered at Palantir.

Finally, both authors wrote extensively about secrecy while writing this book. We've written tens of thousands of words on the subject, and have collectively written more than 20,000 posts to Twitter. If one compares our body of work to this book, it is possible that we have reused phrases or metaphors to describe certain subjects. If that is the case, it is entirely unintentional. Our brains don't compartmentalize the way that computers can. However, aside from some material about the U.S. Joint Special Operations Command that also appeared in *The Command: Deep inside the President's Secret Army*, the book is an original work in its entirety, the reporting is fresh, and the conclusions, we hope, are original.

While researching this book we stumbled across many things that we won't be able to write about. Though we have no legal obligation to submit our work to the government before publication, we have an ethical obligation as citizens to take extreme care when writing about sensitive subjects. We shared certain chapters with a number of former senior national security and intelligence officials, including several former directors of intelligence agencies. Our purpose was to learn if the publication of this book would truly jeopardize national security. After receiving the feedback, we asked ourselves whether there was a compelling reason to print the secrets in question anyway, and worked from there. We hope we've struck the proper balance.

# Asleep under Fire

On January 5, 2011, Mike Rogers, chairman of the House Permanent Select Committee on Intelligence, had dinner with the director of the Central Intelligence Agency, Leon Panetta, in a dining room at CIA headquarters in Langley, Virginia. After dinner, Panetta asked Rogers and his staff director, Michael Allen, to stop by his office. When they reached the seventh-floor office, Panetta shut the door. "We've got a bead on bin Laden," he told the two men. The CIA had tracked down Osama bin Laden's most trusted courier, and it turned out that the terrorist leader was holed up in an unusually constructed, well-crafted bunker-style house in a wealthy town in Pakistan just west of the Indian border. "Come back in a few weeks and we'll give you the full brief," he promised.

Panetta had divulged to the Republican chairman the nation's most precious secret at that time—and did so informally, and with a promise to provide more information. He did so without formally consulting the National Security Council. Over the next few months, he would find a way to make sure that the entire Gang of Eight, a group of eight leaders in the House and Senate, knew about the operation, the intelligence behind it, and the range of options the administration was considering. Rogers and Allen returned to Langley in February and took in two hours of discussion with the CIA's lead on the project. They pored over models of the compound and a variety

1

of other intelligence, much of which remains classified. A few weeks later, Panetta called Rogers to let him know that the White House had chosen the most dangerous, most potentially valuable option: a U.S. Joint Special Operations Command SEAL team would storm the compound and kill or capture bin Laden. On the Friday before the raid, Panetta telephoned Rogers on a nonsecure phone line.

"You know that thing I've been talking about?" he asked. "Well, there's going to be something on it soon." Rogers knew exactly what the director meant.

Because the raid was successful, it is hard to determine what the reaction from Congress would have been had things gone south. On one hand, congressional partisanship had frozen the Senate in place. On the other, Rogers came to trust Panetta. And Panetta had not hidden a thing from him.

Allen would later tell Jeremy Bash, Panetta's chief of staff, that Rogers was prepared to vocally defend the White House if the raid had gone bad. Even though the intelligence was equivocal, Panetta had the gumption and the foresight to share it with the Gang of Eight. A few weeks later, Rogers would get another call from Panetta, this one informing him about a more politically precarious secret: the United States had captured an al-Qaeda terrorist and was holding him on a U.S. ship in the Arabian Sea. Republicans refused to sanction any federal trial of terrorism suspects in the United States, but Panetta told Rogers that once the military and the intelligence community finished interrogating the suspect for knowledge about current al-Qaeda operations, he would be read his Miranda rights and transferred to the custody of the U.S. Department of Justice. Rogers could have squealed, or could have found some way to register his objections. But he did not. His interests and his institution's interests had been satisfied. In extending the umbrella, which risked compromising the administration's legal policy on terrorism, Panetta had instead depolarized the intelligence operation.

As a matter of course, the American government withholds information from the public. It's been this way since the beginning, and there's little likelihood that it will ever change. Accordingly, the public seeks to learn that information, both directly (through such mechanisms as the Freedom of Information Act) and indirectly (by purchasing newspapers with sensationalized details). The resulting tension is healthy and is essential to keeping the government honest in its classification authority. For example, in the 1940s, the United States began research into a secret "silent flashless weapon."[1] When this research began, someone recognized the danger of it falling into enemy hands, and classifying the material made it a criminal act to reveal any details. Today we know the truth. But if not for the continuing struggle between those who create secrets and those who expose them, we might never have learned about the "silent flashless weapon" of World War II—the bow and arrow.[2]

Few dispute that certain secrets are necessary to defend the Republic, but many secrets, like that one, are not. The line separating the two has never been clearly defined. In fact, there is no real agreement as to who, exactly, gets to draw that line. However, we can judge the quality of a democracy by the kinds of secrets it keeps. As long as there is debate on foreign policy, civil liberties, the national identity, and the morality of war, so too will there be a corresponding debate about the secrets generated by the national security establishment.

This book is about these government secrets—how they are created, why they get leaked, and what the government is currently hiding. We will delve into the key elements of the American secrecy apparatus, based on research and unprecedented access to lawmakers, intelligence agency heads, White House officials, and program managers, as well as thousands of recently declassified documents and interviews with more than one hundred authorities on the matter. Many of these interviews are on the record, remarkably candid, and thoroughly insightful. Whether driven by politics, paranoia, or cynicism, every citizen has wondered at some point, what terrible thing is the government hiding from us today?

Secrets are legion—impossible to count, challenging to oversee, and difficult to administer. They exist because the American people entered into an implicit bargain at the Republic's founding. The executive branch is permitted to protect its power and do things we don't know about, in exchange for keeping us safe and acting in a way that preserves our shared values while advancing our interests. As executive power has expanded, so have the mechanisms designed to protect it. At no time in American history has there been a proper set of checks and balances on secrecy powers, because Congress (especially since the Civil War) has been loath to limit the authority of the president as commander in chief. Indeed, much of the modern secret state is a creation of congressional legislation. The National Security Act of 1947 codified and upgraded the president's covert arsenal. It made "national security" a useful catchphrase for pretty much everything related to safeguarding the country from enemies foreign and domestic. In the process, it extended the secrecy umbrella to cover uncomfortable truths unrelated to our protection but politically untenable or simply embarrassing to make public.

There is no single unified intelligence budget, and Congress funds and oversees intelligence activities by way of an array of committees across an alphabet soup of budgets and agencies.* Once the intelligence budget is authorized, appropriated, and signed into law, most of the money is hidden from the public by way of a dense forest of line items in the annual defense budget, and further tucked away behind a series of programs with vague names.

The American deep state is not easily laid out on any organizational chart. It encompasses agencies you think you know about, like the CIA and the FBI, but also includes ones you likely do not, like the Defense Programs Activity Office, the Navy Systems Management Activity, the OSD's Special Capabilities Office or Special Collection Service. With the increase in terrorist threats, it's gotten harder to divide it into foreign and domestic operations. We can still divide secrets into four categories, however: what we've

---

*The planning for the 2013 budget started in early 2011, when the director of national intelligence (DNI) began asking program managers and agency directors for guidance and input, to defend their programs and projects to him. In early to midsummer, the Office of Management and Budget and the DNI issue broad planning guidance, which specify top-line numbers and include "wish list" programs from the White House and others. The office of the DNI then presents the adjusted budget to the rest of the intelligence community. After another round of reviews involving program managers defending their programs, the DNI issues "Director's Decision Documents"—his own version of the line-item veto—to the proposed budget. There is a lot of internal gamesmanship here, with contractors and agencies lobbying to get their favorite projects restored. This entire process is opaque to the oversight committees.

learned about enemies of the state, how we learned it, what we plan to do about it, and what new capabilities we've developed to manage any of these. Perhaps the most important distinction, the one people in Washington care most about these days, is: which secrets can be used for political gains, and which cannot?

In his touchstone text on this subject, *Secrecy*, the late Daniel Patrick Moynihan, U.S. senator from New York and chairman of the Commission on Protecting and Reducing Government Secrecy, wrote, "Eighty years from the onset of secrecy as an instrument of national policy, now is the time for a measure of definition and restraint."[3] Three years after the publication of Moynihan's book, however, terrorists hijacked four airliners and killed three thousand Americans. The restraints recommended by Senator Moynihan were quietly disregarded by the White House, which kept—and continues to keep—more secrets from Congress and from the public than anyone else had ever thought necessary, or even possible.

We know this because with all those secrets came an awful lot of leaks.

When asked whether the secrecy regime over which he now presides actually works, James Clapper, the director of national intelligence, sat back in his chair and stared off for a moment. An Air Force lieutenant general, Clapper has worked in intelligence at various levels since 1963. In that time, he has had access to practically all of the nation's secrets.

"I suppose," he answered, "it has to work."

Clapper calls himself "genetically antithetical" to the media, with which he works only under protest. He does not like testifying on Capitol Hill because his answers almost always drive the day's news agenda in a way they should not, and because to him, to speak of intelligence matters in an open forum is an oxymoron.

But eventually all secrets leak. They develop a motive force of their own.

The American people have an impoverished understanding of the state of secrecy and the implicit bargain. Misinformation is layered on top of myths and misunderstanding, and that's before you even get to the conspiracy theories about Area 51, or whether former vice president Dick Cheney ran a secret assassination ring. It takes a gross misunderstanding of the incentives in play to imagine the government could have had a hand, for example, in the assassination of John F. Kennedy without it leaking by now. In this book, we'll look more closely at a number of conspiracy theories; in most cases, it's clear that the original cover-up was of bungling and idiocy, the truth only revealed when it was in some insider's interest to let it out. Still, the impulse to believe that the government is up to no good has its roots in the real and terrible things have been done in the name of national security.

Last century, the government covered up assassination plots, secret coups, illegal acts, arms sales, and any number of activities that embarrassed the nation when revealed. In the interview with Clapper, which took place in a large conference room on the top floor of the Office of the Director of National Intelligence complex near Tysons Corner, Virginia, he allowed that the "record of the community isn't all that good" when it comes to the question of whether or not the government has shown itself capable of properly protecting secrets and not abusing its authority. Skepticism will always be warranted. "Our history is regretfully replete with abuse. There is some substantial basis for people to be suspicious," he said.

At the same time, Clapper and other members of the national security establishment contend that an unprecedented counterpressure has risen in tandem with the so-called American deep state. A *lot* of people see secrets. Clapper listed a few of the oversight mechanisms. "Congress. The PIAB [President's Intelligence Advisory Board], the GAO [Government Accountability Office], the IGs [inspectors general]—it's kind of endless."

Looked at a different way, there are more people with security clearances than ever before. Consequently, the political and temperamental demography of secret keepers more closely approximates the American mean. With the hundreds of thousands of new secret keepers come hundreds of thousands of new potential secret leakers. As Michael Morrell, the deputy director of the CIA, tells us, the gestation period between the time that a secret is established and the time that it is disclosed has narrowed significantly during his thirty-plus years of service.

Secrets tend to get out more quickly than ever before. The ability of those in power to wade only in the recondite waters of black budgets and black programs has degraded. As we will argue, this trend will eventually be the undoing of the deep state.

The volume of intelligence collected by the secrecy apparatus has grown exponentially, facilitated by the advances of the information age and driven by the threat of multinational terrorist networks. Because of the availability of sophisticated and once prohibitively expensive technologies, so too has the public's ability to mine databases for patterns that suggest examples of government secrecy. For example, using such tools as Google Maps, a legion of amateur sleuths and gadflies has identified the location of virtually every classified government facility in the United States. Imagery intelligence that was once inconceivably precise is now readily available to anyone with a computer or a mobile device. Today, secrets are easier to collect but harder to keep.

It's important to divide these leaks into good leaks and bad leaks, based on why the secret bearer let them out. It's nearly impossible to imagine in advance what the results of any particular leak will be, making motivation the key distinction to draw. Whistleblowing is generally considered to be a "good leak." It's a way for members of the intelligence community and the secrecy apparatus to expose illegal or self-evidently immoral activities, usually at some risk to their own careers or livelihoods. The Salt Pit prison in Afghanistan is a fine example. "Bad leaks" are often done for some kind of gain—it could be money, but is usually something less tangible. For example, the brave Pakistani doctor who helped the United States find and kill bin Laden is now in prison. That's a direct result of intelligence leaks. He did the world a service, and he's suffering because a government functionary wanted to impress a reporter.

During the Obama administration, we've had special focus on what the White House and related political operatives might be leaking, and why. The executive branch can declassify and reclassify at will, often selectively and for maximum political advantage. It claims the right not only to confirm or deny the existence of a program, but also to, plainly stated, lie about it. Senior officials can sometimes leak with impunity; White House staffers often act as though they have declassification powers extending from the president's penumbra.

Meanwhile, when lower-level members of the bureaucracy have no recourse but to leak wrongdoings to the press, they are punished when caught, even though their leaks rarely, if ever, bring harm to national security. Somehow, even as leaking has become epidemic among the appointed political class, it's not clear that it's any safer to be a whistleblower among the rabble.

We will also explore just how much sensitive material gets out entirely by accident—through the necessary transparency of flight patterns, for example, or through online job postings or pictures of friends on military bases. We will also examine the ill-conceived, though increasingly used, government practice of declaring a leak "unleaked"—in other words, to officially reclaim information that's already been declassified. For example, a soldier can have his memoir cleared for publication by Army officials, and only after it hits bookstores will the Defense Department find objectionable phrases in it that could "reasonably be expected to cause serious damage to national security." To solve this problem, the government buys back the remainder of the book's first run, rescrubs the manuscript, and authorizes a subsequent release.[4] The result: an inevitable comparison between the censored and uncensored versions, and a precise enumeration of those secrets that the Pentagon wanted to keep, now in the public record.

As an exercise in building trust in those who protect us, these practices leave much to be desired.

Journalists publish sensitive information every day, and the press is the primary vehicle through which leaks are conveyed to the public at large. Responsible reporting requires weighing the public benefit against possible harm to national security and providing accurate context in the form of a fully fleshed-out story. That is why there was such national outrage in 2010, when approximately 260,000 cables and 90,000 intelligence reports leaked. It was the largest such incident in the history of the world, and the public reacted with extreme and understandable hostility. It wasn't the content, but the principle. Before anyone could cognitively process the sheer volume of classified information unlawfully revealed, there was a gut response of violation and outrage. A *Washington Post*–ABC News poll conducted two weeks after the release found 68 percent of Americans agreeing that the cable release harmed the public interest, with 59 percent eager to see Julian Assange, who facilitated the leak by way of the transparency activist site WikiLeaks, in an orange jumpsuit.[5] Those between the ages of eighteen and twenty-nine were slightly more sympathetic to Assange and WikiLeaks—a not unexpected result from those comfortable with the stones that get thrown in the glass house of social networking. Surprisingly, however, overall opposition to the intelligence breach crossed party lines, with Democrats and Republicans in a rare moment of political alignment.

To manage the crisis, the White House put Deputy National Security Advisor Denis McDonough on point. He offered daily briefings to interagency officials in government. He contextualized information, prepared leaders to deflect incoming arrows, and helped mitigate residual fallout as diplomatic cables were processed. Meanwhile, the Department of Justice faced the unenviable task of determining exactly which laws were broken by Assange and how best to prosecute. Assange, briefly a fugitive for personal issues unrelated to the diplomatic cables release, warned of an encrypted "doomsday file" of the complete, unredacted database. He stated that should he be imprisoned or assassinated, WikiLeaks would release the file and password, thereby exposing the most sensitive names, locations, and operations of the American deep state.[6]

The source of the cables, Private First Class Bradley Manning, was an active-duty member of the U.S. Army and fell under the jurisdiction of the Uniform Code of Military Justice. Initially, Manning was charged with violating Articles 92 and 134 of the UCMJ. The first deals with general dereliction of duty, the second with bringing discredit upon the armed forces. Both charges stemmed from improperly accessing and disseminating classified material. The list of charges would expand over the course of an Article 32 investigation—the military equivalent of a grand jury—to include aiding the enemy. Although it is a capital offense, prosecutors declined to seek the death penalty.

Assange, meanwhile, became a target for politicians and political columnists in the literal sense. There were calls for his assassination. One prominent U.S. political figure deemed Assange's actions "treasonous," though because he is a citizen of Australia, it's unclear how such a charge might apply. Admiral Michael Mullen, chairman of the Joint Chiefs of Staff, went so far as to state, "Mr. Assange can say whatever he likes about the greater good he thinks he and his source are doing, but the truth is they might already have on their hands the blood of some young soldier or that of an Afghan family."[7] But according to Wendy Morigi, former spokesperson for the DNI, "It was much more of an embarrassment than a national security exposé." She adds, "Once you actually get into these things, so much of what is secret is already out there." With that in mind, tens of thousands of unreleased documents remain in wait.

The case of Bradley Manning is an inflection point for secrecy in the information age. Regardless of one's opinion of Manning (traitor or hero, disturbed or determined, ideological or idiotic), he put the entire apparatus to the test. A folder wasn't lifted from a locked filing cabinet in a subcontractor's office and passed to foreign intelligence for synthesis. Rather, Manning downloaded a perfect geologic slice of what we don't know—not merely from one office, but from a massive cross section of civilian and military agencies—and presented it to the world. He took the catastrophic loss of strategic information out of the theoretical and into the real world. He initiated the worst-case scenario.

We will examine the results and how the government managed the situation. Meanwhile, it's interesting to consider the larger nature of leaking state secrets. Manning now faces life in prison for his alleged crimes. But catastrophic leaks happen all the time. Days after the Osama bin Laden raid in Abbottabad, Pakistan, the Top Secret flight manifest of the mission's Black Hawks leaked to the press, which uniformly refused to run it. The leaker had nothing to gain by exposing the names of American commandos who were on the mission. (Indeed, *no one* had anything to gain, and the very idea of such an act is reprehensible.) Yet it was leaked all the same. Why? For what reason do secret keepers feel compelled to talk? Bradley Manning's lawyers credibly argue that their client suffers from psychological problems. That is not the case for everyone who goes to the press, even as they too risk arrest and imprisonment. Some leak to blow the whistle on immoral, unethical, or illegal behavior. Some leak for attention. Some leak to impress. The collective inability of the human species to keep secrets is hardly a modern phenomenon. Yet somehow enough secrets were held long enough for the American deep state to establish a nucleus, and then grow by orders of magnitude.

Those in power are often compelled to make political decisions about secrets, and these decisions are often choices between "very bad" and "even worse." The most obvious example is revelations of detainee abuse by members of the U.S. Army in Iraq. To press forward with a full accounting and admission of guilt puts the United States on the side of transparency and marks the first step in reconciliation with an abused people. On the other hand, full disclosure inflames otherwise dispassionate Iraqis and serves to recruit insurgents seeking retribution.

Many wonderful books have been written about Delta Force, Seal Team Six, the FBI, the CIA, the NSA, and even Area 51—agencies and organizations that live and die by the secrets they create. We owe those books and their authors a debt. We will look at the machinery of secrecy as a whole and how it's changed over the past century, especially in the last decade. It's time to assess the formal and informal mechanisms designed to protect Americans from abuses by the American deep state—and how they might be reformed.

David Foster Wallace puts the matter most succinctly in his book *Infinite Jest*: "The truth will set you free. But not until it is finished with you."[8]

# CHAPTER 1

# Need to Know

In 1912, the Department of State employed Herbert O. Yardley as a telegrapher, where he transmitted diplomatic cables to and from Washington, D.C. Infatuated with the methods of cryptography, he took it as a personal intellectual challenge to decipher the material crossing his desk every day. According to Gabriel Schoenfeld, author of *Necessary Secrets,* the defining moment of Yardley's life (and a pivotal moment in U.S. code breaking) would come when he deciphered a telegram sent from Germany to President Woodrow Wilson—in only two hours.[1] Yardley presented the findings to his paymasters at State, who were astonished and impressed. With the onset of World War I, Yardley was placed in charge of Military Intelligence, Section Number 8—the cryptography arm of the Department of War. Under Yardley's deft hand, MI-8 broke the codes of eight foreign governments.[2]

Interest in cryptography only heightened after World War I. Yardley, a genuine hero, was named chief of a new State Department agency responsible for codes and codebreaking. He called his new unit the American Black Chamber, after a secret program created by French royalty in the sixteenth and seventeenth centuries for snooping on the correspondence of their subjects.

The target of the new unit was Japan, a rising empire with ambitions for the conquest of Asia. The cryptography challenge was

NEED TO KNOW    13

beyond anything Yardley had anticipated, but the Black Chamber found only success. By 1920, through genius and diligence, Yardley had broken the *Ja*, the Japanese encryption. General Marlborough Churchill, head of Military Intelligence, called it "the most remarkable accomplishment in the history of code and cipher work in the United States."[3]

The Black Chamber stacked triumph upon triumph, formulating new methodologies for American encryption and deciphering even the most complex and impenetrable codes of the Japanese. In every instance, Yardley's work gave the United States an inestimable diplomatic advantage over Japan and an unobstructed view of their military objectives.

In his lifetime, Colonel Yardley earned two Distinguished Service Medals and upon his death, a plot at Arlington National Cemetery, induction into the National Security Agency Hall of Honor, and membership in the Military Intelligence Hall of Fame.

It would be great—for Herbert Yardley and for the United States as a whole—if that was the end of his story, but it is not.

President Herbert Hoover was no fan of clandestine operations. Henry Stimson, the incoming secretary of state, defunded and disavowed all actions of the Black Chamber. "Gentlemen," said Stimson, "do not read each other's mail."[4] This was in many ways a sentiment of the times and an echo of the British admirals who argued against establishing the Secret Intelligence Service (of James Bond fame), and who later spent decades fighting against its existence during peacetime.[5]

The most closely held secrets by the United States are what we know about *everyone else's* secrets and how we came to know them. The collection of communications between persons is called signals intelligence, or SIGINT, whether physically (communications intelligence, or COMINT) or electronically (ELINT).

By World War II, the U.S. Army and the Navy had reestablished fully staffed and highly effective interception capabilities. Like Hoover, President Harry Truman would later gut the intelligence community, reducing SIGINT by 80 percent. Listening posts were abandoned, as there was nobody left to listen, and in Truman's opinion, nobody left to listen to. As a result, cryptographers had no codes to crack.

This was a nontrivial problem. Cryptography is a cumulative science and a perishable skill. As a game of cat and mouse, it is imperative that codebreakers actively keep pace with codemakers, and vice versa. Historically, skilled cryptographers have enduring careers, and just as telegraphers once developed a knack for identifying their counterparts on the other side of the wire based solely on tapping style and cadence, so too do cryptographers crawl into the minds of their opposition. As a branch of academia, these techniques and methods are passed from one "generation" of cryptanalysts to the next.

At the same time, a counterintelligence strategy is employed in determining what decrypted information is acted upon, for fear of revealing what exactly codebreakers know. You never want your enemy to realize you've broken their codes.

For example, J. Edgar Hoover knowingly risked the acquittal of communist spies Julius and Ethel Rosenberg rather than reveal the existence of secretly intercepted and decoded Soviet files known as VENONA. The files contained information conclusively proving Julius Rosenberg's guilt and Ethel Rosenberg's complicity. At the time, however, it was more important to keep the Soviets from knowing that we had penetrated their cryptography.[6]

On October 29, 1948, the worst fears of the U.S. intelligence community were realized: the Soviet Union disappeared. As America dismantled its signals intelligence and cryptanalysis capabilities, the Russians were doubling down, and on that fateful Friday the Soviets implemented an entirely new communications grid and encryption methodology. Radio interceptions proved impossible, and what little remained was indecipherable.

In response, the secretary of defense ordered the creation of a Top Secret department known as the Armed Forces Security Agency (AFSA). Undermanned and underfunded, it suffered from early leadership woes, with the added stress of internal rivalries among its constituent branches in the U.S. military (almost to the point of a complete uncoupling) and an impossible mission of cracking a highly advanced Soviet system.

In this task, AFSA failed almost by design. But it did have some early success in monitoring plaintext, or unencrypted, low-level radio

communications by the Soviets. It also established a respectable traffic analysis capability. While transmissions were indecipherable, their
origins and urgency often painted a kind of residual image of Soviet
activity (much in the same way one might monitor a nation's flight
patterns to discover no-fly zones). This early form of Kremlinology
wasn't much, but it was something, and the American intelligence
and military communities leveraged it to the fullest.

AFSA had better luck during the Korean War, intercepting high-
level North Korean broadcasts. To the astonishment of SIGINT specialists, North Korea was broadcasting details of its most sensitive
military operations with no encryption. When the North Koreans
finally got wise, AFSA made short work of almost every cipher,
achieving what Matthew Aid, author of *The Secret Sentry*, called "one
of the most important code-breaking accomplishments of the twenti-
eth century."[7]

But there were also failures—three hundred thousand of them, to
be exact, when China inserted thirty divisions into Korea. For comparison, that is the equivalent of the entire U.S. Marine Corps, from
cooks to snipers, plus fifty thousand.

How did China do it? The same way Alexander, Caesar,
Washington, and Napoleon did it—without radios. When there are
no signals broadcast, there are no signals to intercept. Worse yet,
before the Chinese incursion in Korea, AFSA had almost entirely
neglected the Chinese military, and even if they had listening posts
diligently recording and decrypting SIGINT, they lacked linguists to
translate the intercepts.[8]

The year 1951 marked the beginning of a long stalemate in the
war, and during this time the Chinese helped upgrade North Korea's
encryption and transmission protocols. Chinese ciphers remained
a mystery for AFSA, crippling the American war machine, which
had become accustomed during World War II to an overwhelming
SIGINT advantage. The unbreakable codes of the Soviet Union
remained an alarming gap in U.S. national security. Reforms were
attempted, but internal turf wars among the Army, the Navy, and the
Air Force crippled the organization.

Affixing his signature to a revision of National Security Council
Directive No. 9, titled "Communications Intelligence" and dated
December 29, 1952, President Truman formalized and enumerated

the powers of a new National Security Agency (NSA), which would become one of the most secret organizations in the world: "The communications intelligence (COMINT) activities of the United States are a national responsibility, and they must be so organized and managed as to exploit to the maximum the available resources in all participating departments and agencies and to satisfy the legitimate intelligence requirements of all such departments and agencies." Its charter sought to address the failures of AFSA. The new agency's mission: "To provide effective, unified organization and control of the communications intelligence activities of the United States conducted against foreign governments."

The directive unambiguously decreed that the mission of the NSA is special, and that its activities require that

> they be treated in all respects as being outside the framework of other or general intelligence activities. Orders, directives, policies, or recommendations of any authority of the Executive Branch relating to the collection, production, security, handling, dissemination, or utilization of intelligence, and/or classified material, shall not be applicable to COMINT activities, unless specifically so stated and issued by competent departmental or agency authority represented on the [management] Board.[9]

To appease FBI director J. Edgar Hoover—always a pressing concern—the directive concluded with the statement, "Nothing in this directive shall be construed to encroach upon or interfere with the unique responsibilities of the Federal Bureau of Investigation in the field of internal security."

With three months left in office, President Truman, the man who loathed the activities of the FBI and the military's Office of Strategic Services—who in fact had once compared the organizations to the Gestapo—established the two most secret spy organizations in the history of the world: the Central Intelligence Agency (1947), which not only collected intelligence in foreign lands, but covertly worked to overthrow governments and reshape nation-states, and the NSA, an organization whose sole purpose is to listen to everyone in the world. Hoover's FBI worked in the gray. General Walter Bedell

Smith's CIA worked in the black. And the NSA worked invisibly, so much so that its abbreviation would be recognized unofficially as "No Such Agency."

Back to the matter of the Black Chamber. The end of World War I and the end of SIGINT operations meant national hero Herbert Yardley was soon out of a job. A man obsessed with puzzles and probability, he was also an accomplished poker player. But gambling takes money, and without his healthy government stipend, he did what every notable bureaucrat does when leaving federal service (especially those terminated with such casual disregard): he wrote a book.

*The American Black Chamber* was an instant best seller, compelling not only for its remarkable story but also for the information revealed. Yardley didn't hold back, exposing in detail the most important tools in the government's workshop. He didn't just pull back the curtain of the secrecy apparatus; he carefully aimed a spotlight at every key aspect of America's cryptographic capabilities. It should go without saying that the book was a blockbuster in Japan, for all the wrong reasons.

Yardley was threatened but never charged with espionage for fear that in prosecution he might disclose even more classified information. This is a recurring problem for prosecutors when deciding whether to bring traitors, double agents, and leakers to trial. Once on the stand, spies are obliged to tell the truth, the whole truth, and nothing but the truth. For the intelligence community, that's a bit too much truth for comfort.*

In the case of Yardley, the damage was done. Japan diverted massive resources to strengthening its cryptographic program, and the United States, now staring down the barrel of renewed hostility with the Japanese and a second looming world war, had to start from zero in its codebreaking operation. And Yardley's life had one more secret to reveal. After Japan's surrender in 1945, the United States seized Japanese Foreign Ministry documents for archival in the Library of Congress. In the late 1960s, the NSA took a hard look at Yardley's

---

*When used as a legal defense by members of the intelligence community, this is known as graymail.

activities and verified a suspected but never-confirmed bombshell: an "internal Foreign Ministry memorandum saying that the Japanese paid [Yardley] $7,000 for copies of deciphered Japanese messages and cryptanalytic techniques."[10] This was three years before the publication of *The American Black Chamber*.


One thing this story underlines is the importance of carefully choosing who holds a security clearance and has access to sensitive material. Not everyone with a clearance is susceptible to bribery or willing to betray his or her country out of spite. Some good men and women fall victim to blackmail. The SF-86 security clearance application, currently 120 pages in length, provides a penalty of "fines and/or up to five years of imprisonment" for lying. In addition, those caught making false statements on an application for clearance are candidates for disqualification. People who would risk jail time or their jobs to protect a personal secret might well reveal someone else's for the same reason. In that regard, background investigations are a way for the would-be handlers of state secrets to lay it all on the table—to tell the U.S. government everything there is to know, before foreign agents find out first and use it as leverage.

In many instances, even absolute transparency can result in a candidate being denied clearance. Before 1995, homosexuality was considered an immediate disqualifier for a perceived risk of blackmail.[11] Hard drug abuse can be an immediate disqualifier. (Former brewers of crank might take note that while many federal agencies require subjects to submit to a polygraph examination, the military does not.) The state's dogmatic pursuit of those pure in thought and deed sometimes comes at the expense of those well qualified but with a slip in judgment. It also costs federal agencies access to those with real-world connections or experience in the criminal underworld. This policy of "clean" sources notably redounded to the detriment of national security in 2001. Rare is the man with both Mullah Omar on speed dial and the clean hands for government clearance.

This mentality doesn't apply only to aspiring G-men in starched white shirts and conservative neckties. In 1995, it was taken to its natural endpoint when John Deutch, former director of central

intelligence, issued an order forcing CIA case officers to seek bureaucratic approval before fielding agents with significant criminal backgrounds.*,[12] While unsavory persons could still be hired for covert
activities, the policy (drafted in a period of relative peace) in effect
warned career officers away from taking unnecessary risks. In 2002,
Deutch defended the discredited policy, writing in *Foreign Policy*,
"Is the potential gain from the information obtained worth the cost
that might be associated with doing business with a person who may
be a murderer, rapist, or the like?"[13] Those desperate to infiltrate
and inveigle members of the Taliban would answer without hesitation: yes. In 2002, George Tenet, director of the CIA, rescinded the
Deutch order.[14]

Today there is no shortage of Americans with a security clearance.
According to *Top Secret America*, an investigation by *Washington Post*
reporters Dana Priest and William Arkin that charted the expansion
of secrecy after 9/11, 854,000 people hold a Top Secret clearance,
"nearly 1.5 times as many people as live in Washington, D.C."[15] In
2009, the Government Accountability Office reported a stagger-
ing 2.4 million people with some level of clearance.[16] This report
even excluded "some of those with clearances who work in areas of
national intelligence."[17] (Such a figure, as presented, would equal the
population of Chicago.)

With so many secret keepers, it is remarkable how well the secrecy
apparatus has kept classified material that might be devastating to
the state under wraps. The Bradley Manning WikiLeaks incident
of 2010 is heretofore a black swan event. Its execution and impact
was astonishing, yet in retrospect somehow obvious and inevitable.
More astonishing, perhaps, is that the U.S. government seemed
to have no contingency plans or response mechanisms in place.
Manning wasn't cashing in. He wasn't attempting to overthrow the

---

*Contrary to popular usage, an *agent* of the CIA is more or less equivalent to an
*informant* to the FBI. Along the same lines, the people we think of when we think
of the CIA are called case officers. At the FBI, they're called special agents.

Republic. He wasn't blackmailed. He wasn't an agent for foreign intelligence.

In fact, the direct intervention of foreign powers isn't the cause of most leaks, and foreign spies aren't where the information ends up. More often than not, the first place a leaked secret heads is the Internet.

# CHAPTER 2

# The Curious Case of Primoris Era

On Twitter, entire identities are forged with a single photograph, a biography of 160 characters, and witty banter. The press is especially drawn to the site because of its immediacy, and because it removes the barrier between the reporter and the reader. On Twitter, journalists and sources meet and mingle. Subject matter experts exchange thoughts on the news of the day, and because 854,000 people hold Top Secret clearances, when pressing events concerning national security strike, discretion often gives way to a certain James T. Kirk information swagger. Very few worked their charm, intellect, and access better than the mysterious Shawn Gorman, who wrote under the pseudonym Primoris Era.

She was a bombshell among missile defense experts, and over the course of two years she constructed an enviable personal narrative as an analyst for the Missile Defense Agency moonlighting for the Central Intelligence Agency. She punctuated pithy and insightful commentary on global events with tantalizing photographs revealing more than a little ankle. When the kind of men who fasten their top button scoffed, she ridiculed them and raised the stakes with shots in swimwear. The self-described "First Lady of Missiles" flirted shame-lessly and had the kind of body that inspired few complaints.

In espionage, a "honeypot" is a spy who uses his or her sexual appeal to lower the defenses of otherwise guarded secret keepers. If ever Twitter spawned a successful honeypot, she would probably look a lot like Primoris Era.

It's a certainty that a Twitter honeypot is recruiting online right now. His or her methods are as ancient as espionage itself, but on a scale impossible before social media. This is but one danger of many in a sprawling secrecy apparatus. Too many secrets require too many secret keepers—human beings with the human need for connection. And those connections can be exploited.

Question 5 on the Questionnaire for National Security Positions (SF-86) is, "Have you used any other names?" and specifies, "If 'Yes,' give other names used and the period of time you used them [for example: your maiden name, name(s) by a former marriage, former name(s), alias(es), or nickname(s)]. If the other name is your maiden name, put 'maiden' in front of it."[1]

But what does that mean in the realm of social media? If the purpose of the SF-86 is to disqualify unsuitable candidates from handling classified material, and the purpose of requesting aliases is to conduct a more rigorous screening, does it not stand to reason that online identities are just as much—and in some cases, even more—important than a maiden name? This is not so much to find a clearance petitioner's photographs in swimwear or less (though clearly blackmail material is abundant on such sites as Facebook), but also to cross-reference the candidate's online associations with known honeypots and persons of interest.

The question then becomes how deeply the government might delve into a candidate's parallel virtual life. There are thousands of online communities, e-mail lists, and social networks. Is membership in a *World of Warcraft* guild worthy of scrutiny, and why not? Should "Threr, Night Elf Mage of Drenden" be considered an alias? And how would the Defense Security Service, which processes security clearances, investigate such identities? How much burden should be placed on industry to ready their membership database, and how would such an interface for federal investigative cross-referencing spill over into law enforcement and domestic surveillance?

The more people in on secrets of national import, the more likely it is that such information leaks to the press, and then to the public. By means of social networking, the press is a middleman that can even be bypassed. As we have seen, on the Internet the difference between Top Secret and public domain is Edit/Copy, Edit/Paste. And once it's on the Internet, it's on the Internet forever.

To a young policy analyst for the Department of Defense—her first name is Robin—writing under the Twitter handle @FrostinaDC, Primoris Era's online life seemed a little too perfect. (Frostina's name is withheld at her request.) She worked for Michael Vickers, the chief special operations civilian at the Pentagon. She accused Primoris Era on Twitter of having a "fake persona" and set off a chain reaction of public correspondence that allegedly culminated with Primoris Era threatening Frostina's career and, obliquely, her life.

If the allegations had been true, they would have made Primoris Era—man, woman, or foreign intelligence agency—Twitter's first confirmed honeypot, and marked a new age in clandestine social engineering. A lot of men in the national security field who interacted with Primoris Era lost a lot of sleep over what they might have revealed through Twitter, instant messaging, e-mail, and Facebook. If they were in fact tricked, with their defenses let down they might have passed along very sensitive information on the state's most highly guarded secrets.

When the accusation was made, the press and the intelligence community began "crowdsourcing," or working collectively, to determine the nature of the perceived threat. Spencer Ackerman of *Wired* wrote, "Sometimes Shawna Elizabeth Gorman is Shawna Elizabeth Gorman. Sometimes she's Shawna Gorman. Sometimes she's Shawna Felchner. Sometimes she's Primoris Era. Sometimes she's Shawna1814. Sometimes she's Lady Caesar."[2] Naadir Jeewa, a student at Birkbeck College in London, added to the list a few other usernames with brow-raising similarities: VeritableSaint, Shad0wSpear, and ArchAngel_6.[3] (VeritableSaint was actually a different person—a U.S. Navy sailor.)[4]

The game to unmask Primoris Era was afoot.

•　•　•

In 2010, Thomas Ryan of Provide Security, LLC, launched a project to investigate just how deeply a constructed personality on the Internet could penetrate the secrecy apparatus. He created what he described as a "blatantly false identity" and joined Twitter, Facebook, and LinkedIn (a social network for industry professionals).[5] He chose as his avatar a striking young woman of vaguely Asian descent. He gave her ten years of experience as a cyber-security professional—which would have meant she entered the field at the age of fifteen. She was an MIT graduate, and her "present" job title was cyber-threat analyst for the Naval Network Warfare Command (a job that does not exist). He even named her Robin Sage.

The U.S. Army Special Forces training pipeline can last up to two years depending on a soldier's specialty, but every would-be Green Beret ends his training at the John F. Kennedy Special Warfare Center located at Fort Bragg, North Carolina. There, salty candidates are sent to the "People's Republic of Pineland" to engage in Robin Sage, a notoriously challenging three-week field exercise that puts years of Special Forces training to the test. Robin Sage is not a secret, and anyone with passing knowledge of special operations forces—certainly those in high-profile positions at the Department of Defense—would have heard the phrase a thousand times.

In the case of newly minted "Robin Sage," the counterintelligence red flags were everywhere. A possibly foreign female easy on the eyes with a fictitious job. An inexplicable résumé. An obvious pseudonym. An invented degree. According to Thomas Ryan's findings, presented in a paper titled "Getting in Bed with Robin Sage":

> By the end of this experiment, Robin finished the month having accumulated hundreds of connections through various social networking sites. Contacts included executives at government entities such as the [National Security Agency], [Department of Defense] and Military Intelligence groups. Other friends came from Global 500 corporations. Throughout the experiment Robin was offered gifts, government and corporate jobs, and options to speak at a variety of security conferences.[6]

It should be noted that not everyone fell for Robin Sage's electronic charms, and those who discovered her false identity did so by means available in the public domain. One industry professional asked a friend at MIT to look her up. No such person existed. One security specialist researched her National Security Agency Information Security Assessment Methodology credentials. (A listing of every NSA ISAM graduate is available to anyone.) But males dominate the national security industry, which "allows women to be a commodity in more ways than one."[7]

After Robin established a baseline of industry professionals, she grew her sphere of influence based on virtual association. Wrote one suitor, "I've never met you, but I saw you had Marty on your Facebook list, so that was good enough for me."[8] Her looks helped broaden her connections. Among the many photos she posted to Facebook was "one of her at a party posing in thigh-high knee socks and a skull-and-crossbones bikini captioned, 'doing what I do best.'"[9] Her job title suggested a Top Secret/Sensitive Compartmented Information security clearance, and thus enhanced her reputation. Government and industry leaders solicited her advice. "If the creator behind Robin had intentions other than to perform a social experiment, he would have had means to mislead experts in their studies and even steal their research."[10]

The similarities to the case of Primoris Era are striking. When Shawn Gorman first appeared on Twitter, she actively courted the friendship and confidence of national security policy wonks, journalists, and subject matter experts in the defense sector, many of whom work for the government and hold security clearances. Her reach extended even to Admiral James Stavridis, the Supreme Allied Commander of NATO.

Gorman, the "Doyenne of Air, Space, and Missile Defense," offered commentary and Internet links on the subject with clockwork regularity.[11] She debated experts on the START treaty, which concerns nuclear arms reductions between the United States and Russia (she spoke in vehement opposition), and flirted audaciously with many of her male audience. In both public and private, she reached out to journalists on the national security beat, occasionally responding to questions about technical issues in missile defense.

Before the incident with Frostina, several online followers noted what appeared to be inconsistencies in Gorman's career and life story. Her family lived in North Carolina—or maybe Hawaii. She was deployed overseas—or operated strictly in the Washington, D.C., area. She lived in Alexandria, but never appeared at the many informal national security happy hours put together by defense industry associates. (It was, in fact, at one of those drinking sessions in early April 2011 that doubts about her true identity first surfaced.)

When Frostina confronted Gorman, Gorman allegedly responded with a physical threat, and then deleted it. (According to one person who read the exchange in real time, the Primoris Era account suggested that Frostina was putting herself in peril, as Primoris Era knew the "right people." Gorman denies this.)

Frostina was indignant. "Seriously, you threatened me & then deleted it? At least I have the fucking balls to call you a sociopath to your face." She continued, "Your feed is riddled with lies about yourself & I can assure you sooner or later the house of cards will fall. You know the right people?? Ha, let me walked [sic] down to their offices & asked [sic] about you. They'll return blank stares."

Then came the bombshell from Frostina to the bombshell Primoris Era. "Just to be clear, I have intel that Primoris Era is a Honey Pot & if you're in my field you know what that means."

Frostina's purported proof stemmed from the Pentagon's master e-mail list. She allegedly checked the name Shawna Elizabeth Gorman against the database. There were no matches. The analyst concluded that Primoris Era was not who she said she was, and notified Frostina's superiors. Hours later, Frostina wrote on Twitter, "I have been informed that Primoris Era is asking people for programs to delete mass amounts of tweets. It's not real don't follow/engage."

Sam LaGrone, a journalist for *Jane's Defense Weekly*, investigated the back-and-forth and reported back to Twitter "after couple hours of digging [Primoris Era]. The woman's name attached to account has no record of being current [Department of Defense] employee."

Internet shorthand might seem to paint the dispute as a schoolyard fight. (Its prose certainly isn't Shakespearean.) But the consequences of an online spy, highly skilled in the art of social engineering and reaching the highest levels of the intelligence community, could prove to be catastrophic. It sounds like hyperbole, but our troops have already learned this lesson in Iraq and Afghanistan.

• • •

Mark Zuckerberg runs a giant spy machine in Palo Alto, California. He wasn't the first to build one, but his was the best, and every day hundreds of thousands of people upload the most intimate details of their lives to the Internet. The real coup wasn't hoodwinking the public into revealing their thoughts, closest associates, and exact geographic coordinates at any given time. Rather, it was getting the public to *volunteer* that information. Then he turned off the privacy settings.

"People have really gotten comfortable not only sharing more information and different kinds, but more openly and with more people," said Zuckerberg after moving 350 million people into a glass privacy ghetto. "That social norm is just something that has evolved over time."[12]

If the state had organized such an information drive, protestors would have burned down the White House. But the state is the natural beneficiary of this new "social norm." Today, that information is regularly used in court proceedings and law enforcement. There is no need for warrants or subpoenas. Judges need not be consulted. The Fourth Amendment does not come into play. Intelligence agencies don't have to worry about violating laws protecting the citizenry from wiretapping and information gathering. Sharing information "more openly" and with "more people" is a step backward in civil liberties. And spies, whether foreign or domestic, are "more people," too.

Julian Assange, founder of WikiLeaks, knows better than anyone how to exploit holes in the secrecy apparatus to the detriment of American security. His raison d'être is to blast down the walls protecting state secrets and annihilate the implicit bargain, yet even *he* is frightened by the brazenness of Facebook and other such social networking sites:

> Here we have the world's most comprehensive database about people, their relationships, their names, their addresses, their locations and the communications with each other, their relatives, all sitting within the United States, all accessible to U.S. intelligence. Facebook, Google, Yahoo — all these major U.S. organizations have built-in interfaces for U.S. intelligence. It's

not a matter of serving a subpoena. They have an interface that they have developed for U.S. intelligence to use.[13]

It's all there, and the Internet never forgets. But even if the impossible happened and the Internet did somehow develop selective amnesia, in the case of microblogging service Twitter, the Library of Congress has acquired every message ever posted by its two hundred million members.[14] As Jeffrey Rosen wrote in the *New York Times*:

> We've known for years that the Web allows for unprecedented voyeurism, exhibitionism and inadvertent indiscretion, but we are only beginning to understand the costs of an age in which so much of what we say, and of what others say about us, goes into our permanent—and public—digital files. The fact that the Internet never seems to forget is threatening, at an almost existential level, our ability to control our identities; to preserve the option of reinventing ourselves and starting anew; to overcome our checkered pasts.[15]

The U.S. government isn't the only institution to notice. Early in the military campaigns in Afghanistan and Iraq, soldiers of the social networking generation uploaded to their MySpace profiles pictures of camp life in the war zone. Innocuous photographs of troops horsing around in front of tent cities, bunkers, outposts, motor pools, and operations centers circulated freely on what was then described as "A place for friends."

The U.S. military soon realized that foreign intelligence services, sympathetic to America's enemies and savvy to the social revolution, could collect these photographs by the thousands and build detailed, full-color maps of American military bases. During the Cold War, this would have required the insertion of first-rate spies, briefcases filled with cash, and elaborate blackmail schemes. In the age of radical transparency, all it would take is a free MySpace account to know exactly where to fire the mortar rounds to inflict maximum damage on the United States. The Marine Corps confirmed this in a 2009 directive. "These Internet sites in general are a proven haven for malicious actors and content and are particularly high risk due to information exposure, user generated content and targeting by adversaries." The directive continued, "The very nature of [social networking sites] creates a larger attack and exploitation window, exposes unnecessary information to adversaries and provides an easy conduit for information leakage," putting operational security, communications security, and U.S. military personnel "at an elevated risk of compromise."[16]

This type of clever thinking on the part of America's enemies is not unique to this conflict. During the run-up to the Gulf War, foreign intelligence services had a pretty good idea that the U.S. war machine was preparing for its most substantial engagement since Vietnam. The U.S. military recognized a new kind of threat—one that didn't require foreign intelligence to insert an agent onto every base in the Republic. Open source information could be just as dangerous. Spikes in late-night orders from pizzerias near key military bases and an exceptionally busy parking lot at the Pentagon could tell hostile powers everything they needed to know.

In determining what should remain secret and what should not, the military—like each component of the American secrecy apparatus—is good at overreaction. The default answer: more secrets. To counter the MySpace problem, they banned blogs and social networks. This benefited base security but killed morale at home. No longer could parents see their young sons and daughters safe—and even happy—in the war zone. All that remained were breathless reports of intense combat on the cable news networks. And while the average supply clerk is probably safer in Baghdad than in Detroit, every parent and spouse saw the same thing: a son or daughter in a flag-draped casket. (In 2010, the Department of Defense revised and consolidated its ad hoc policy on social media.[17] On its official website it declared, "Service members and [Department of Defense] employees are welcome and encouraged to use new media to communicate with family and friends—at home stations or deployed," but warned, "it's important to do it safely.")[18]

Primoris Era was no honeypot, however. She did not obtain secrets about technical capabilities or troop movements. But she *was* a spy.

She was a serving member of the National Clandestine Service of the CIA. She joined Twitter while confined to a hospital in Germany, having had her legs nearly blown off by a vehicle-borne improvised explosive device in Gaza. When her identity was questioned, someone from the front company that the CIA was using to protect her identity tried to change her Wikipedia page. The Internet service provider of the editor was easily traced back to Dynetics, a small missile defense company based in Huntsville, Alabama. The company later provided the following statement for this book, which just about says it all:

> Dynetics would like to assure you that the company has had no involvement with the Twitter or other social media activities associated with Ms. Gorman that constituted the subject of your inquiry. While Ms. Gorman was an employee of Dynetics until the beginning of May, 2011, any Twitter, Facebook, or other social media activities were not a part of her work for Dynetics, and Dynetics did not authorize or have knowledge of such activities. Moreover, any social media activities, including social media updates to accounts associated with Ms. Gorman, were not done by Dynetics or authorized by Dynetics. Finally, Ms. Gorman's work at Dynetics had nothing to do with secret cover operations for intelligence agencies. While Dynetics doubts that any of the social media activities were more than a fantasy social media image, if there were any activities performed by Ms. Gorman, or others, in the realm of intelligence operations, Dynetics had no knowledge, did not authorize, and had no involvement in such activities.

Gorman denied the allegations leveled against her. "I have NEVER threatened her and I have NEVER given out classified or sensitive information nor have I EVER asked for it," she wrote (emphasis hers).[19] She added that her superiors were conducting an investigation into the incident and that she had been asked not to respond further.

The U.S. government "gave me a burn notice a week after that came out," she wrote. That meant, in essence, that she was unemployable. No one would hire someone who had been fired conspicuously. In the closed-off world of covert operations and secret contractors, a burn notice is equivalent to being declared persona non grata. However, within six months, she thought she would be back in a big way. She had been a superstar in the National Clandestine Service, and the intelligence community ignored her burn notice. General David Petraeus, shortly after the start of his (brief) tenure as director of the CIA, wanted to bring her on as a special assistant. That's where she ran into a different problem associated with disclosure: because her nonclassified posts to Twitter concerning missile defense and Obama administration policy were often critical, she had acquired some new enemies inside the administration, possibly (though we could not confirm this) even on the National Security Council.*

For months, Gorman languished in sort of a nether land. The CIA suddenly decided that Gorman was still "too hot" to bring on. Gorman couldn't get a job anywhere else because she had no unclassified resume. She couldn't provide a reporter with basic information like what CIA class she graduated from or whom she'd been deployed with. She refused to say who paid for her physical therapy and where she went for it. (We learned independently that the government is paying for her rehabilitation and that she travels to a health facility operated by the military in Maryland.) Her tormenters on the web continued to taunt her. Even though she was a U.S. citizen capable of exercising her liberties, finding a job, and searching for meaning in her life—she was a ghost.

To protect American forces in the field and what will invariably find its way to daylight, a philosophical shift will be required. Orange-bordered cover sheets for Top Secret material are no longer enough. Their quantity has diminished their power. Security clearances—no challenge to obtain—should no longer be sufficient grounds for access to computers with classified material. And to a large extent, military and intelligence personnel will need to police themselves. Presently, it is demonstratively easier to find the location

---

*Obama renamed his National Security Council the "National Security Staff," but the former term is still vernacularly in use and is one we think our readers will be more familiar with.

of CIA safe houses in the deserts of Iraq than it is to learn the features of the next Apple iPhone.[20] The information age is in its early days yet, and as demonstrated by the explosive popularity of social media, the public mindset is (for now, anyway) reoriented away from privacy and toward a sense of openness. Certainly some percentage of the 2.4 million people holding security clearances is part of that new way of thinking.

However, Bradley Manning was not driven by a would-be Primoris Era or a Robin Sage. What he did was intentional and systematic, and could only happen by way of the Internet. As information technology moves faster, packaged in smaller devices, it's only going to get easier from here to do exactly what Manning did, again and again. The bar for "need to know" must be elevated. Only a few people *need* to know a great many things.

CHAPTER 3

# From Inception
# to Eternity

The two most sensitive documents produced by the U.S. government are not stamped Top Secret, have never been leaked, and
have never found their way onto the Internet. One of these documents doesn't really have an official name, but rather an obscure
numerical designator that no one remembers. U.S. Secret Service
agents simply call it a "Site Post Assignment Log." Page 1 lists very
basic information. The day. The date. The name of the event. Then
it gets interesting.

Consider the atmospherics of the White House Correspondents'
Dinner on April 30, 2011. Present were the president and Mrs.
Obama, twenty-six members of Congress, the attorney general, the
treasury secretary, a half dozen governors, the mayor of the largest
city in the country, the director of the CIA, and the chairman of the
Joint Chiefs of Staff.

So far as sites go, this was a big one for the Secret Service. Forget
the symbolic resonance of the location: the Washington Hilton, also
known as the Hinckley Hilton—the place where Ronald Reagan was
shot in 1981. That irony is built into the price of securing an event
here. And though agents learn from the past, they don't dwell on it.
The only mission that matters is always the one under way.

At the Correspondents' Dinner, some of the most powerful people in the world are confined together in an underground ballroom for four hours on a date announced to the public months in advance. It is, in other words, assassin's bait. The site report, which meticulously lists the location of every Secret Service post-stander, his or her duties, the moment-by-moment schedule for the event, and the protocols in the event of an AOP (attack on principal), therefore becomes a remarkably dangerous weapon—a twenty-page, 14-point Times New Roman weapon of mass destruction.

Those who've seen it (and know what it is) admit to having their eyes drawn to it. You know you're not entitled to the information. You don't "need to know," but you really, really want to. And at any rate, events like these are as serious to the Secret Service as combat missions are to soldiers. It's no place for curiosity, and even *attempting* to somehow talk your way into the Secret Service security room is a good way to get questioned, if not arrested.

In language that a ten-year-old can understand, the site advance report meticulously describes the methods that the Service will employ that night to protect the president. One paragraph instructs the agent manning the "Charlie" frequency console in the security room—that's what the Service calls their command posts—to ensure that all post-standers are informed every time the president moves a few feet. "All posts on Charlie: Renegade and Renaissance are moving to the ballroom."

The agent on the Charlie frequency is responsible for a common operating picture. His counterpart is monitoring the Oscar frequency and the Presidential Protective Detail (PPD). His job is to keep the designated president site agent fully informed of developments that other agents report on Charlie.

If an agent fails to respond to a radio call, the Charlie operator will dispatch another agent to check on his or her welfare. The agent manning Charlie at the Correspondents' Dinner was on loan from the investigations division. Handsome, young, and easygoing, he looks a lot like Keanu Reeves. But he is one of the most ferocious polygraph examiners in the government.

About twenty minutes before President Obama's motorcade was scheduled to arrive at the Hilton, an agent radioed in that a White House staffer had lost the PIN that gave her access to sensitive areas.

Agent Keanu Reeves immediately radioed this out. "This is not good," he said to himself. He made a note on a log, and his counterpart telephoned the information to the PPD advance agent. One PIN might seem like nothing, but a bad guy could pick it up, and catastrophe could ensue. But ten minutes later, the agent radioed back. The PIN was in the pocket of the staffer. Keanu rolled his eyes. "Attention all posts . . ."

Those are two of the *least* sensitive job descriptions. A "homicide bomber response agent" has some pretty scary responsibilities. There is an agent inside a presidential bunker very close to the Hilton. (Don't bother looking for the bunker; you won't find it.)

That night, three specialists from the White House Communications Agency hovered around, changing out radios with drained batteries and rekeying working ones. They were distinguishable by their military bearing and high-and-tights and their bright red identification pins.

The final pages of the site report describe the procedures involved in evacuating the president during an emergency. There are multiple options. One is an emergency motorcade. Another provides instructions to get to a presidential safe house. A map includes a yellow-highlighted path to the "hard room" where the president will be taken if he needs to be secured on the premises.

A sidebar summarized the resources the Service was using that night: the number of agents assigned to posts; the presence of countersurveillance and intelligence division agents; the classified equipment that will magically appear if all hell breaks loose.

This document is well protected. Armed special agents carry them. Another document, given to a larger number of people, provides a moment-by-moment schedule of where the president will be at what time and who will accompany him. Even his elevator rides are premanifested. Joseph W. Hagin, the chief of White House operations in the Bush administration, calls this the most sensitive document there is, but too many people need to know the information it provides. It cannot be classified. So instead it is "Sensitive But Unclassified."

On the night of the White House Correspondents' Dinner, President Obama's poker face onstage hid an even bigger secret— the biggest he'd ever known. At most, a half-dozen guests knew what the president did: that seventy-nine members of three U.S. Joint Special Operations Command task forces were in the final stages of preparing the raid targeting Osama bin Laden. This secret didn't leak, which is remarkable for several reasons. Washington had recently seen its secrets revealed with strident disregard. And the *whole purpose* of the Correspondents' Dinner is for journalists to ferret confidential information out of their dinner guests. (A few of the more egotistical journalists brought celebrities. The smarter ones invited people with security clearances.)

There was a close call that night concerning the raid. William Daley, the White House chief of staff, was a guest of ABC News, as was actor Eric Stonestreet, who won an Emmy for his work on *Modern Family*. Stonestreet had apparently arranged for a tour of the White House that next day but was suddenly told that it was canceled. Over salad, Stonestreet turned to Daley and asked, "So I was wondering. Was there any reason they canceled my tour?"

George Stephanopoulos's head swung around, and he caught Daley's eye. "You got anything going on there, Bill?" Stephanopoulos asked teasingly. A veteran of the Clinton administration, Stephanopoulos knows how the White House works.

Daley began to sweat, by his own recollection, and blurted out an excuse. "It's something to do with the plumbing." He added, "You know what, Eric? Stop by Monday and I will personally give you the tour myself."

That answer satisfied Stonestreet, and more important, Stephanopoulos, who returned to his original conversation.

Why were there no leaks that night? Because no one involved had any reason to leak, and because the U.S. Secret Service has a decent record of handling classified material. But very often in Washington, carefully leveraged secrets can elevate one's status in social circles.

Leaks can be a deal with the devil, often nefariously targeted and driven by many motives not pure to principle. Since the dawn of formal journalism, or at least since the Progressive Era, when newspapers established their own counterestablishment voice, the public has generally trusted journalists to faithfully contextualize the common Faustian leak, understanding that the motives may be not be transparent.

This implicit trust ended with the Clinton-era collapse of faith in the notion of journalists as gatekeepers, though it arguably remains in place when it comes to disturbing leaks about the conduct of other corporations. We still recognize some categorical distinctions. The whistleblower remains an archetype that draws sympathy, although one's response to a whistle that has been blown depends on the partisan frame of reference of the hearer. We also react to official disclosures of classified information differently. The Bush administration had a case to make when they revealed some U.S. SIGINT capabilities in order to present a dossier to the United Nations in advance of the Iraq War. Likewise, in 1962, Adlai Stevenson's dramatic presentation of imagery intelligence gathered by U-2 overflights proved that the Soviet Union was positioning missiles on Cuban soil. This intelligence was rushed into the sunlight before the CIA had the chance to assess whether the damage was worth the policy benefit. (Clearly, in retrospect, it was.)

Big fish usually get away with leaks, and easily. Minnows have to fight.

Modern presidential press management traces its lineage to the failure of Woodrow Wilson to tend to the journalists who followed him as he crafted the League of Nations Treaty in Versailles. The Bob Woodward of the time was a bombastic dandy named Herbert Swope, who wrote for the *New York World*. This was Swope's first assignment, and he couldn't comprehend the restrictions the White House had placed on the press corps—and why the press corps seemed so damned compliant.

The president was secretly negotiating a treaty that had, as a core principle, the provenance of openness and honesty. This irony would prove to be the treaty's downfall. China knew about Wilson's secret talks with Germany about annexing Chinese territory to Japan and leaked this language to a Chinese-American journalist who worked for the *Chicago Tribune*. Upon publication, it caused an outcry in the U.S. Senate, which hardened suspicions that Wilson was not being forthcoming. The secrecy itself wouldn't have been a problem if Wilson had explained what he meant by "open covenants of peace, openly arrived at." It didn't really mean that every sensitive point of world diplomacy had to be in the open. Rather, according to the historian John M. Hamilton, Wilson meant that "no treaties would be created without citizens knowing that negotiations had taken place and having a chance to discuss the terms later."[1] Belatedly, as Wilson realized he was losing the battle of public opinion, he personally leaked a copy of the treaty provisions to Swope that involved reparations to Germany.[2]

Fast-forward to World World II. After the *Chicago Tribune* disclosed the Roosevelt administration's war plans—with no less a provocative headline than "FDR's War Plans!"—it was generally assumed that the press was flexing its independence. Daniel Patrick Moynihan, however, speculated that "the incident may have been the first instance of the executive using the power of secrecy for its own purposes by 'leaking' confidential information to the press."[3] (The authors would add "successful instance," given Wilson's ultimate failure.)

After intelligence confirmed the location of Osama bin Laden in Abbottabad, Pakistan, a Daisy Cutter dropped from an MC-130 aircraft at six thousand feet could have obliterated the terrorist mastermind. Instead, U.S. commandos stormed the al-Qaeda figurehead's compound and assassinated him with a "controlled pair" to the head. This decision was made in large measure to preserve photographic proof of his identity for the world.* Monitoring a live feed of the operation from the safety of the White House Situation Room, the Obama administration huddled in silence. A photographer captured the president's foreign policy team in what has become the public image of the operation.

The Obama administration later decided—over objections from Leon Panetta, leader of the operation and director of the CIA—to withhold all images of a lifeless bin Laden. The official reason: the images were too graphic for public consumption. This explanation does not survive scrutiny. After the assault, bin Laden's body was cleaned, autopsied, and given a proper Islamic burial at sea. At least one photograph of the most evil man in the world would have sufficiently sated a supposedly weak-stomached American public. After

---

*The White House claims a missile strike would have jeopardized the surrounding civilian populace, an admirable consideration, though more believable if such considerations were extended to the thousands of civilian neighbors to hundreds of terrorists who weren't Osama bin Laden.

all, the Republic somehow hobbled on after release of grisly imagery of the bullet-riddled bodies of Uday and Qusay Hussein and video footage of Saddam Hussein's hanging. By classifying photographs of a dead bin Laden, President Obama ensured that the defining image of the operation was his administration, resolute and astride armchairs. This politicization of secrecy will ensure a generation of bin Laden sightings, of conspiracy theorists, and of aggressive denial among the most hardened of Islamic terrorists.

When secrecy isn't used as a bartering tool of the bureaucracy, as Moynihan observed, it is used as a form of coercion. The CIA fell under a barrage of negative press for "enhanced interrogation techniques" in the aftermath of 9/11. Consequently, senior CIA officials leaked that it was, in fact, a top-secret military unit behind the lion's share of the dirty work. This type of selective leaking is often chosen advisedly, as black operations military forces and the CIA work closely together in the field. But on a management and strategy level, the agencies compete for turf and operations. When, for example, the CIA wants more resources or wants "in" to certain areas like Yemen, senior operations officers will leak details to the press about the military's large footprint there and the CIA's lack of presence. The desktop snipers of the Defense Department's black operations community are obliged to return fire. Within days, a competing newspaper will report how, for example, the CIA keeps corrupt members of the Afghan government on its payroll, completely undermining, at least in the eyes of the military, a counterinsurgency strategy that is predicated on building a transparent and viable government. Reporters work hard to get these stories, but timing and access to "senior administration sources" are almost always deliberate. Suddenly, intelligence community officials are willing to talk about previously off-limits subjects.

Many officials leak with an eye toward history. When things go right, nobody thinks of the intelligence community. When things go wrong, recriminations whisk by as though fired from machine guns, and good men and women who often did the right things and spotted the right signs and alerted the right people are drowned out of the conversation. These officials, hoping to set the record straight, sometimes find no alternative but to pass files to journalists. The CIA recognizes this as a dangerous game, and when certain officers and agents retire, they are given an office and kept on the payroll long enough to write classified memoirs for the agency archives.[4]

Leakers are not above manipulating the record for personal political gain or positive media coverage, especially after things get ugly. In his autobiography, former vice president Dick Cheney directly states that he pushed to have Secretary of State Colin Powell fired for leaking policy disputes to the press corps. "It was as though he thought the proper way to express his views was by criticizing administration policy to people outside the government."[5]

To circle the square, sensitive information is not always leaked to damage political opponents. It is sometimes *withheld* for the same reason. After being pilloried for the Bush administration's use of waterboarding and the failure of enhanced interrogation techniques against 9/11 mastermind Khalid Sheikh Mohammed, Cheney pushed for the complete declassification of the program so that its successes might also be revealed. This request was denied, and the political motivations for its denial (as well as its request) are obvious. One Bush administration official, upon learning that waterboarding had been used on "only" three detainees, wondered how much embarrassment they could have been spared if that information was disclosed earlier than it was.

It should be noted that WikiLeaks allegedly came into possession of several hundred classified files from Guantánamo Bay, Cuba, by way of Bradley Manning.[6] In an effort to discredit U.S. detention policies, it released a series of prisoner reports in May 2011. Ironically, one of these reports suggested that enhanced interrogation techniques provided a crucial "dot" connecting Osama bin Laden's preferred method of communication (courier) to his whereabouts (Abbottabad).[7]

The secrecy apparatus blocks daylight by design and therefore resists oversight and reform. Since Vietnam and Watergate, journalists have taken the position that they are institutionally compelled to force the issue. They are merely exercising their constitutionally protected First Amendment rights. The government cannot abridge speech rights unless there is a compelling reason to do so. Protecting national security information fits that criterion, and there is ample precedent for the executive branch to: (1) arrest people who use their speech to incite immediate violence; (2) forbid journalists who are embedded with U.S. troops from exposing the locations of those troops; (3) arrest people who provide classified information to a foreign government or an enemy of the state for the purposes of harming the state; and (4) prevent people who have signed nondisclosure agreements from publishing information about their work without a review by higher authorities.

Beyond those activities, however, there seems to be a bright red line. In general, people can say whatever they want, so long as it is true, and especially if it relates to "government affairs," as stated by the U.S. Supreme Court in *Mills v. Alabama* (1966). Importantly, this is not a right guaranteed only to the press. Courts have gone out of their way to deny that the press has any inherent right to exercise any more power than any other citizen. The difference, until relatively recently, is that the press has been the only entity with enough resources to compete with the government for access to national security information, while rarely being punished for doing so.[8]

Because the press and (for the most part) the press alone has this ability, it has developed into an informal privilege with its own boundaries and checks. The Supreme Court has even granted protection to something called "routine newsgathering," and has implied that journalists cannot be punished for engaging in the practice. This is why it is difficult to argue that if someone passes a stolen classified document to a journalist, the journalist should be prosecuted for theft.

Before publishing leaks—and classified material that appears in the press is usually the result of a leak by some official sworn to secrecy—responsible journalists try to balance the potential harm to national security against the public interest. Responsible journalism holds powerful interests to account, according to professors at journalism schools. Indeed, in many (but not all) instances, the "powerful interests" use the press as a mechanism to self-regulate.

A result of the WikiLeaks diplomatic cable release is that we have some idea of the gap between what we *think* and what we *know*. It's not so wide as anyone thought, or so malevolent. Accordingly, it would seem that most secrets are neither worthwhile nor particularly newsworthy and would rarely catch a second glance of a reader. In aggregate, foreign intelligence services obviously have a shot at puzzling out American motives and enterprises. But again, even when a thick slice of American secrecy is presented in its entirety (as was the case with WikiLeaks), our activities abroad are sometimes curious and surprising but rarely shocking. (Indeed, the most shocking revelations of WikiLeaks were the actions of other "hostile" governments, and their private cooperation and seeming friendliness with our own.)

As WikiLeaks demonstrated, the secret actions of the United States hardly muster general outrage or unrest. Even in the case of the National Security Agency and the terrorist surveillance program, the act of revelation by the press tends to provoke greater consternation than the programs and activities themselves.


Who decides (ultimately) where the boundary line must be drawn? In practice, as we shall see, journalists do. But who decides who, exactly, is a journalist?

When handling sensitive material, it falls to the journalist to follow lines of information from confirmed sources to the real-world consequences of publication, and, from the information gathered, determine the nature of that information. Investigative reporting of the secrecy apparatus is not unlike the work of intelligence analysts. It involves assembling a jigsaw puzzle while blindfolded, with little clue as to the puzzle's size and with thousands of extra pieces scattered about. Accordingly, journalists make decisions of astonishing import with little personal danger.

When Dana Priest reported, for example, the secret "Salt Pit" facility in Afghanistan, where a detainee was slain, buried, and erased from the books as a result of enhanced interrogation techniques, she exposed the American war machine at its worst and forced corrections (one hopes) to prevent future such atrocities. Another Priest article—a 2005 report in the *Washington Post* that exposed the locations of terrorist detention cells around the world—is less black and white. The white: the government was torturing people in our name, for little apparent benefit. The world was now aware of such prisons, and terrorist cells gained little material advantage (but, perhaps, for new targets). The black: this information undermined cooperating governments whose citizens are hostile to the "American Imperium," and endangered carefully orchestrated diplomatic partnerships, to say nothing of the soldiers and agents in the field.

In the past, it might have been worth debating if it was ethical of Priest to reveal both programs. That's still a worthwhile question for journalism classes and editorial meetings, but the truth is, if a leaker wants something out, he no longer needs Dana Priest or the *Washington Post* to alert the world. The Internet has moved the power and the ethical focus to the leakers themselves.

When the threat is still active, journalists are most obliged to act with an excessive degree of restraint. On the front page of the *New York Times* on December 16, 2005, in an exposé headlined, "Bush Lets U.S. Spy on Callers without Courts," reporters James Risen and Eric Lichtblau published the details of a Top Secret program in which the National Security Agency could monitor al-Qaeda telephone conversations without first arguing the wiretaps before federal judges. The entire program will be discussed later in this book. In short, the president authorized the Terrorist Surveillance Program in the post-9/11 bedlam. Expediency was key, as the terrorist organization was fast on the move and savvy to electronic communications. The laws in force at the time were antiquated at best, written thirty years before, when people still rented rotary telephones from the phone company and secrecy was essential for the program's success. The White House did not act unilaterally; congressional leaders had been briefed on the program's operational details no fewer than twelve times, as had the presiding judge of the Foreign Intelligence Surveillance Court.

Here, the *New York Times* ran presses at the expense of national security and alerted an active and agile enemy to an effective and efficient program. In *Commentary*, Gabriel Schoenfeld argued:

> If information about the NSA program had been quietly conveyed to an al-Qaeda operative on a microdot, or on paper with invisible ink, there can be no doubt that the episode would have been treated by the government as a cut-and-dried case of espionage. Publishing it for the world to read, the *Times* has accomplished the same end while at the same time congratulating itself for bravely defending the First Amendment and thereby protecting us—from, presumably, ourselves.[9]

Are these really two equivalent actions? It matters that the government employees leaked this to a newspaper because they thought the government was behaving unethically, and not to enemy agents for a paycheck. It matters that the reporters in question were informing the public of something a sizable portion of citizens would want stopped immediately.

The *Times* withheld details about the project at the government's request. It didn't publish what it knew for a year and then did so only because the report's author planned to publish a book with the revelations. But national security harm is national security harm, and the leakers and the journalists decided the ethical breach was more important than national security.

There is no independent arbiter here; the courts seem to be very reluctant to allow the executive branch's formal classification powers to be the final word on national security harm.[10] Basically, they want the tension to exist and work itself out.

The intent of the leaker can be very difficult to determine, because it's rarely as cut and dried as Bradley Manning handing documents over to WikiLeaks. Often, the person transmitting the information will not tell the journalist that it is classified and will often, if passing a piece of paper or an e-mail, redact information that would identify its provenance. A great deal of classified information is transmitted to journalists thirdhand.

A person, for example, with knowledge of a particular U.S. cyber defense program discusses an issue with a government consultant who is cleared to the level at which the program is classified but is not fully aware of the dimensions of the program. The consultant, who works at a public think tank, then engages with a journalist who is writing about cyber security and mentions some aspect of the program, though not nearly enough for the journalist to have a complete story. But the journalist, wise to the beat, starts to dig around, gathers up other clues, makes rational assumptions based on the probability of certain things being true, and soon he or she has a nearly complete and fairly accurate sketch of a classified program.

You may protest that this scenario is unlikely or hypothetical, but journalists in Washington and policy makers with security clearances will recognize it as the germ of just about every enterprising national security story. At some point in the process, the journalist becomes pretty sure he or she has acquired information that is classified but has no way of knowing for sure. The consultant, while not blameless, was not intending to transmit classified information. The person who discussed the program with the consultant—the original "leaker"—is almost completely blameless.

The journalist then calls other policy officials and says, "Aha! I have in my hand information about a program I think is sensitive. Yes I do! I'm bragging about it. So tell me what I should do about it." Or the journalist publishes the information and admits that he or she has obtained or been given access to classified information. The executive branch can huff and puff, but it has not found a way to establish a standard by which the journalist ought to be subject to prosecution. Instead, officials take the easier route: they try and figure out who the sources are and try to clamp down on the supply of secrets in the middle of the chain. But as we will see, successful leak prosecutions are rare. And the idea that they have a chilling effect on speech itself is not very well formed precisely because the secret keepers are inherently at a disadvantage.

In a remarkable amicus brief filed in the case of two employees of the American Israel Public Affairs Committee (AIPAC) accused of mishandling classified information given to them by a Department of Defense employee, six lawyers—including Viet Dinh, a former assistant attorney general in the Bush administration—make the plausible argument that Washington could not function without the routine, even casual transmission, of classified information to uncleared persons:

> Every day members of the press and members of policy organizations meet with government officials. The meetings are a vital and necessary part of how our government and society function. The Founders provided for them in the Bill of Rights. During the meetings information is exchanged and sometimes the government officials provide information about the state of internal policy deliberations. Sometimes this exchange occurs before government leaders are ready for official or formal pronouncements of the issues involved, and sometimes the government officials make the decision to recount information that may relate to such classified

information . . . . The practice of the media and others meeting with government officials and seeking information, the release of which some in the government might want to control, has gone on since our country was formed. This exchange is part of the very checks and balances on which the democracy has worked. This practice has become even more extensive through the lifetime of the Espionage Act. Until now, no administration has attempted to address what it may perceive as annoying or premature "leaks" by criminalizing the receipt and use of unsolicited oral information obtained as part of the lobbying or reporting process.[11]

There is a conspiracy afoot—a real one—that has kept laws that punish journalists who reveal classified information off the books; that has persuaded judges to read in to precedent exceptions for journalists that may never have been anticipated and perhaps even actively reviled by the Founders; that has given even the most rock-ribbed Republican member of Congress a pause before calling for actual sanctions.* Only once in fifty years has the federal government successfully prosecuted the unauthorized disclosure of classified information by someone who was not a spy.[12] Judges who grew up in the Watergate era have largely institutionalized the informal check provided by national security journalists. (This check remains strong, but it will atrophy over time; Watergate did not influence those now assuming positions of authority. Journalism no longer occupies a privileged status in society.)

The case of Wen Ho Lee, the scientist accused of leaking nuclear secrets to China, is an object lesson in how this special status can work against justice. The government officials who leaked his name to reporters were conspiring with the press, in essence, to frame an innocent man. A public interest defense cannot really be mounted here. As Michael Kinsley writes:

To say with a straight face that "only from confidential sources" could the public have been "informed about the issues" in this

---

*The New York Times's disclosure of the NSA wiretapping program resulted in some aforementioned huffing and puffing but no changes to the law.

"matter of great public interest"—about the Wen Ho Lee case! The matter of great public interest was imaginary. It was part of an organized effort to misinform the public. And the culture and rules of confidential sources are what made this campaign of misinformation possible. The real story was a government plot to destroy a man's reputation and violate his privacy. The culture of leaks was both central to that story and the reason everybody missed it.[13]

It's against our interests as journalists to admit that we can be used by a system that gives us special authority, but we are. This matters, because our ability to collectively report on national security will be jeopardized as we become more susceptible to dangerously politicized leaks of classified or sensitive information that, while not especially harmful to national security, are certainly not in the public interest. In that respect, we become more like WikiLeaks.

Julian Assange and his comrades are in good company when they decide to weaponize sensitive material to exact political change. Consider the case of former governor Gray Davis of California. Facing a recall and the end of his political career, he revealed intelligence pointing to a possible al-Qaeda attack on the Golden Gate Bridge, hoping for a halo effect. While the FBI had previously announced "uncorroborated information" of unspecified groups targeting unspecified bridges in an unspecified state, Davis pressed forward with everything he knew.[14] In the end, however, this ploy failed and the electorate rescinded his governorship.

President James Madison didn't publish notes from the Constitutional Convention until 1840—half a century after the fact.[15] Meanwhile, apocryphal stories of a drunken Benjamin Franklin regularly leaking select, encouraging details of the secret meetings in Philadelphia pubs each night are still taught in school. The twin strands of America's DNA, it seems, are and have always been opposite and irreconcilable.

CHAPTER 4

# Fairly Modest

By his own admission, Julian Assange's goal is to expose the United States (and other ostensibly oppressive regimes) as duplicitous and hypocritical—smooth-talking behind the State Department podium while orchestrating coups d'état and other malevolence in smoke-filled embassies. Assange's weapon, until it began to fall apart due to a lack of funding, government legal attacks, and personality conflicts within the organization, was an online database designed for anonymous officials, journalists, and whistleblowers to upload sensitive material for public consumption without fear of repercussions. His goal was the world stage. His method was laced with irony, which he has acknowledged. Nobody knows with certainty what secrets he possesses; his secrets are secret. And his modus operandi was to drip, drip, drip each classified document and government secret into the public record. Official denials and deflections are countered by evidence to the contrary. And by publishing these classified documents, Assange thought he could strike a shattering blow for transparency and accountability with such force as to jar loose the intellectually calcified philosophy whereby governments use secrecy to advance their nefarious, destructive agendas.

Using his stated criteria for success as a metric, in many ways Assange has achieved a measure of his goals. The publication of State Department cables revealed the extent of Tunisian president Zine El Abidine Ben Ali's corruption, and proved to be, if not a tipping point, then certainly a kind of fuel for public uprisings in the oppressed nation. Ben Ali's abdication of authority and escape to Saudi Arabia (the Argentina of the East) not only liberated a people with minimal bloodshed, but also ignited what has become known as the Arab Spring.

While Assange's associates at WikiLeaks see themselves as journalists on a political mission, their methods go where cable news talking-head partisanship cannot. By posting original documents provided by leakers, WikiLeaks activists empower citizens to make decisions for themselves without the mediating influence of a newspaper's editorial team or a news program's producers.

That's what makes their decision on April 5, 2010, so bizarre in retrospect.

On that day, WikiLeaks released a secret video recorded in 2007, marketing it as a "classified US military video depicting the indiscriminate slaying of over a dozen people in the Iraqi suburb of New Baghdad—including two Reuters news staff." The description continued, "The video, shot from an Apache helicopter gun-sight, clearly shows the unprovoked slaying of a wounded Reuters employee and his rescuers. Two young children involved in the rescue were also seriously wounded."[1]

The video, as edited, uploaded, and advertised, brought the site unprecedented attention. Military analysts were skeptical of the site's claims, however, and deconstructed the unedited thirty-nine-minute version. (Twelve minutes of context had been removed from the footage.) As Bill Keller of the New York Times wrote, "The video, with its soundtrack of callous banter, was horrifying to watch and was an embarrassment to the U.S. military. But in its zeal to make the video a work of antiwar propaganda, WikiLeaks also released a version that didn't call attention to an Iraqi who was toting a rocket-propelled grenade and packaged the manipulated version under the tendentious rubric 'Collateral Murder.'"[2] This context is crucial, as rocket-propelled grenades are a direct threat to military rotary-wing aircraft. Anthony Martinez, a former infantryman familiar with such aerial footage, wrote of the unedited version:

> Between 3:13 and 3:30 it is quite clear to me, as both a former infantry sergeant and a photographer, that the two men

central to the gun-camera's frame are carrying photographic equipment. This much is noted by WikiLeaks, and misidentified by the crew of [Apache helicopter] Crazyhorse 18. At 3:39, the men central to the frame are armed, the one on the far left with some AK variant, and the one in the center with an RPG. The RPG is crystal clear even in the downsized, very low-resolution video between 3:40 and 3:45 when the man carrying it turns counter-clockwise and then back to the direction of the Apache. This all goes by without any mention whatsoever from WikiLeaks, and that is unacceptable.[3]

Though Martinez, experienced in calling for air support, states that under the circumstances he likely would have recommended against Apaches engaging the targets, he takes special note that

> it has to be taken into consideration that there is no way that the Crazyhorse crew had the knowledge, as everyone who has viewed this had, that the man on the corner of that wall was a photographer. The actions of shouldering an RPG (bringing a long cylindrical object in line with one's face) and framing a photo with a long telephoto lens quite probably look identical to an aircrew in those conditions.[4]

In the instance of "Collateral Murder," as well as the massive diplomatic cable release that followed, it seems clear that Assange expected more than he got, or rather, saw what he wanted to see. Certain secrets held by the government—the order of battle for an Iranian conflict, contingency plans for a South Korean invasion by the North, response scenarios to a nuclear attack on a major U.S. city—are secret only to the extent that they're tactical and filed away. Once the trigger is pulled on any of those situations, and thousands more, the entirety of the plans become evident to the world. Likewise, should the Korean peninsula peacefully reunify, it stands to reason that the invasion contingency plans will eventually be declassified in the same manner as scenarios for nuclear war with the Soviet Union.

Less dramatic, perhaps, but no less important are the thoughts of U.S. ambassadors abroad and their interactions with foreign officials and informants. As a practical matter, intelligence generated is very important *today*, but has a relatively short half-life. Eventually, the information will make it into the footnotes of obscure political science dissertations and collect dust in university libraries.

All of this is to say that these secrets are certainly sexy and appealing to academics and enthusiasts (to say nothing of foreign intelligence), but should one of these plans or documents leak, it's unlikely to bring the Republic to its knees or force change in the way the United States does business. When they leak, it's really just a situation where they leaked illegally, but more to the point, leaked *too soon*.

There are secrets, however, both official and unofficial, that the government doesn't want to leak *ever*. In terms of foreign affairs, if it were discovered that the U.S. military intentionally poisoned a village's water well and blamed it on the Taliban, U.S. credibility would be annihilated. Likewise, if a well was accidentally poisoned, Americans knew but said nothing, and civilians died as a result, American credibility would suffer for the same reason. It's obvious why the government would want to keep such actions secret forever. But such secrets are now among the hardest to keep—both because the villagers can get their story out and because someone in the chain of secrets will have every reason to leak it and no reason to keep it.

In the material provided by Bradley Manning to WikiLeaks, Julian Assange expected to find a lot of poisoned wells. Instead, he found a lot of fairly banal and expected activities by State Department officials. Insofar as there were surprises, they generally came in the form of missing puzzle pieces and moments of "I knew it!"

When Assange set course to share tranches of his classified diplomatic cable cache with *Der Spiegel*, the *Guardian*, and the *New York Times*, he assumed that he would have more control over the documents' publications than he eventually did. Assange could have simply published the cables himself, but even he recognized the damage to WikiLeaks' credibility wrought by "Collateral Murder," and the inherent power of established and trusted journalistic entities (even entities he believed to be penetrated and corrupted by the system). Simply put, the *New York Times* still means something to Americans, and its stamp of approval confers legitimacy.

Assange's relationship with the *Times* soured very quickly when it became clear that the paper would not follow his calculated schedule for releasing the documents. (He has since publicly denounced the paper as a spineless pawn of the state and of falling victim to governmental pressure to accept an official spin.)[5] It is telling that Assange assumed the *Times* would abandon the traditional journalistic balancing act of revealing news on one hand while protecting national security on the other. By vetting its information with the U.S. government, the *New York Times* influenced what American readers learned from the cables and provided a crucial avenue for the German and London papers to learn the American government's perspective. Both the *Guardian* and *Der Spiegel* followed the lead of the *Times* on most redactions—and deliberately so. The *Times* was in a much better position to determine what was too sensitive to include.

The process deciding what, exactly, was fit to print closely mirrored the methods of the very secrecy apparatus targeted by Assange. The *Times* received the classified material directly from WikiLeaks and immediately set up the newsroom equivalent of a government special access program—that is, a "black" department that no more than a half-dozen people knew even existed. (This roster would expand to about forty before publication of the diplomatic cables, giving the *Times* employees a taste, most likely, of how hard it is to effectively keep your own secrets.) Bill Keller, then the executive editor of the *Times*, tapped the paper's longtime war correspondent Eric Schmitt to vet the documents so as to determine their legitimacy. ("Collateral Murder" put everything in doubt.) After careful scrutiny, however, Schmitt determined that the cache of documents was in fact the real thing.

The *New York Times* spent the next six weeks rifling through the most highly sensitive of the State Department cables and deciding which were most newsworthy. *Times* technicians devised a software algorithm to sort the cables by keyword, classification level, origin, and destination. (For example, cables intended for distribution to the National Security Council were more likely to be important, and were thus elevated in the priority queue.) This process identified approximately 150 cables of serious journalistic merit involving matters of national security. Included in the WikiLeaks revelations:

- A 2009 cable from the U.S. ambassador in Pakistan reporting on the state of Abdul Qadeer Khan's detention and observation. Khan is perhaps best known (or maybe *feared* is a better description) as the genius behind Pakistan's atomic bomb and the mastermind of an international proliferation network. After handing his Third World home a First World bargaining chip, Khan sought to establish a global turnkey operation for would-be nuclear powers, approaching such nations as North Korea, Iraq, Iran, and Libya—in other words, the Axis of Evil and Crazy. A national hero in Pakistan, he never faced criminal prosecution but was reported to have been placed under house arrest. According to U.S. ambassador Anne W. Patterson, however, Khan's house arrest has amounted to very little, "despite the [Pakistani] government's protestations to the contrary." The ambassador's warning to Washington: a mad scientist with legitimate claim on the title of Most Dangerous Man in the World generally roams freely, with popular expectation that he is "free to lead a more-or-less normal life."[6]
- A 2007 cable from the U.S. embassy in Pakistan warning of a certain shortsightedness in the previous year's agreement to sell F-16s to the nominal ally. Embassy officials noted that non-U.S. and non-Pakistani aircraft and personnel are forbidden on the same military bases as the F-16 aircraft. (This is a common precautionary move to prevent foreign nationals from gaining access to secrets of sophisticated American weaponry—in this case, a fighter jet.) The problem: "Pakistan's search and rescue helicopters are primarily of Russian and French origin." Additionally, Pakistan makes great use of European-manufactured Casa 235 "short takeoff and landing" airplanes. "If Pakistan cannot base these aircraft with the F-16s, Pakistani personnel (and U.S. trainers) could be unnecessarily endangered. At the very least, operational effectiveness would be hurt by lack of access to Casa 235 capabilities." Further, the embassy warned, the restrictions "prevent Pakistan from launching a unified strike package of U.S. and non-U.S. aircraft from a single air base. As pre-mission

briefings are essential to safety and effectiveness, this would be a serious handicap for the Pakistan Air Force."[7]

- A 2010 cable (scheduled for declassification in 2034) from the American embassy in Seoul. Within its pages, South Korean vice foreign minister Chun Yung-woo relayed word from China that nothing will stop the collapse of North Korea following the death of Kim Jong-il. According to Chun, North Korea has "already collapsed economically" and would last no more than three years beyond Kim's death. Meanwhile, and contrary to widespread belief, China has little control over North Korea, and Pyongyang "knows it." This is especially disconcerting as "the Chinese genuinely wanted a denuclearized North Korea, but the [People's Republic of China] was also content with the status quo." The message from China: if North Korea is determined to cultivate a nuclear program, they're going to continue, external influence be damned. The expectation over the long term, however, is the collapse of the North and a reunified peninsula, "anchored to the United States" in a "benign alliance." A nonaggressive partnership would satisfy China, which has little economic investment or incentive in North Korea, as well as Japan, which prefers a divided Korea but lacks the leverage to halt reunification.[8]

- A 2010 cable revealing that the Chinese government coordinated systematic intrusions into Google's network. Reportedly, "the closely held operations were directed at the Politburo Standing Committee level," and Google was not the only victim of such state-sponsored cyber crime. "Contacts in the technology industry tell [U.S. diplomats] that Chinese interference in the operations of foreign businesses is widespread and often underreported to U.S. parent companies." This is in accordance with China's goal of "exploiting the global economic downturn to enact increasingly draconian product certification and government procurement regulations." As part of its strategy, the cable reported, China appeals to the nationalism of its citizenry by accusing the U.S. government and its Internet cohorts of forcing China to accept "Western values." This strategy of information authoritarianism collapses under "Google's demand to deliver uncensored search results," which officials find "very difficult to spin as an attack on China." As a result of Google's stance, the heavily censored Chinese search engine Baidu "looked like a boring state-owned enterprise," while Google seemed "very attractive, like a forbidden fruit."[9]

- A 2007 message from the U.S. embassy in Berlin to the secretary of state, relaying ongoing discussions with German officials concerning Khalid El-Masri. In 2003, El-Masri—a citizen of Germany—was snatched as a suspected terrorist while vacationing in Skopje, Macedonia. (He was, in fact, confused with actual terrorist Khalid al-Masri.) A division chief at CIA headquarters in Langley approved extraordinary rendition for El-Masri. The innocent German greengrocer was beaten, bagged, and brought to the notorious Salt Pit just north of Kabul, Afghanistan. While at the "black prison" ostensibly operated by the CIA but kept off the books so as to allow for the most abusive of interrogations, El-Masri was tortured for information he did not and could not possess. Most damning, after CIA officers realized they had the wrong man, the spooks were spooked and kept El-Masri incarcerated. When George Tenet, director of the CIA, learned of this, he ordered an immediate release.

Still, El-Masri remained at the Salt Pit. It took two further demands by Secretary of State Condoleezza Rice for agents (including a German intelligence officer, it should be noted) to finally acquiesce. The CIA deposited the emaciated man on the Albanian border, five months after kidnapping him, without so much as an apology, to say nothing of remuneration.

Such a gross violation of the rights of an innocent vacationing citizen of Germany did not go over well with the German people or government, and calls arose for international arrest warrants against the field team. The possibility that an ally might drag the black operations of the global war on terror into the spotlight was similarly unwelcome in Washington, and diplomatic pressure was applied. In a suggestive statement as written in the leaked cable, "[U.S. deputy chief of mission John M. Koenig] pointed out that our intention was not to threaten Germany, but rather to urge that the German Government weigh carefully at every step of the way the implications for relations with the U.S." German officials pushed back with a weak hand, as one of its spies was on the ground at the Salt Pit. German deputy national security adviser Rolf Nikel assured Koenig that "the

Chancellery is well aware of the bilateral political implications of the case," but added that this case "will not be easy." Facing an outraged press and a hostile political environment, the Chancellery "would nonetheless try to be as constructive as possible." Koenig "hoped that the Chancellery would keep us informed of further developments" so as to "avoid surprises," and Nikel reiterated that he could not "promise that everything will turn out well."[10]

Though the New York Times would face scorn for publishing sensitive material, it never deviated from an internal compass that erred on the side of caution. Protecting the identities of soldiers, operatives, agents, and diplomats in the field remained a top priority. Before reaching out to the U.S. government, the Times of its own accord redacted or otherwise obfuscated all names and identifying details that might be traced to sources operating within the borders of oppressive regimes. If a cable noted that a Chinese industrialist visited the American embassy on a certain date, that date would also be excised as a precautionary measure, given China's predilection for routinely observing and recording the comings and goings of everyone from the American compound in Beijing. The New York Times therefore protected sources that might otherwise be identified by circumstance, as opposed to simply by name.

Keller and Jill Abramson, then managing editor and now the executive editor of the paper, agreed that the U.S. government should get a week's notice. This was decided as a measure to both protect the Times's competitive edge (as other papers would certainly print the cables with or without the New York Times on point) and give U.S. officials the opportunity to help contextualize the material revealed. It would also allow officials to backstop the Times's efforts to protect sources and highly sensitive intelligence programs and otherwise prevent the disclosure of information that might cause significant harm to the United States.

On the Wednesday evening before Thanksgiving 2010, after denials and outrage from the Obama administration, government officials finally came to the table.

Secretary of State Hillary Clinton designated William Burns, under secretary for political affairs, and P. J. Crowley, assistant secretary of state for public affairs, as team leaders of the ad hoc WikiLeaks response group. The State Department opened negotiations with an obviously overreaching request: that the *Times* redact all details of communication between American diplomats and foreign heads of state. Would they overlook, for example, the request by King Abdullah of Saudi Arabia for the United States to "cut off the head of the snake," referring, now famously, to Iran?[11] Similarly, would the *Times* withhold cables involving the king of Bahrain, who pleaded with General David Petraeus to deal with Iran "by whatever means necessary"?[12]

This opening bid was, of course, a nonstarter, and the *Times* never considered it. The State Department WikiLeaks response group argued that publishing these cables would rapidly destabilize regimes in such a way that would lead to riots, death, destruction, and carnage of the most abhorrent variety. (To a certain extent, the State Department was correct: regimes were destabilized, and several fell, as part of the Arab Spring.) Though representatives of the *New York Times* were fully aware that the cables would strain diplomatic relations, they determined that the government's request relied more on fears of embarrassment than on any legitimate, overriding threats to national security.

By the day of publication—November 28, 2010, under the banner "Leaked Cables Offer Raw Look at U.S. Diplomacy"—the U.S. government was actively working with the *Times* as a full partner in all but name. State officials vetted the cables for sensitive content in consultation with several government agencies, and the *Times* agreed to a number of the redactions requested. In fact, in most cases the paper had already independently decided to redact them. One involved a highly classified counterterrorism unit designated CTU—an abbreviation fans of 24's Jack Bauer might recognize. CTU had taken years to build, and was staffed by Yemeni, American, and British operatives, with the express purpose of intelligence sharing.[13] Though the Obama administration has publicly acknowledged an active footprint of U.S. special operations forces in Yemen training locals for counterterrorism, neither CTU nor multinational intelligence sharing had previously been revealed. Such a revelation would have been distinctly unpopular at home, with the rising threat of Yemen to U.S. security, and abroad, for obvious reasons.

A more interesting revelation of cooperation came not from a known front in the war, but from a hostile foreign power. On February 18, 2010, General Ali Mamlouk, the general intelligence director of Syria, attended a counterterrorism meeting "at the request of President Bashar al-Asad as a gesture following a positive meeting between [Under Secretary of State for Political Affairs] William Burns and the Syrian president the previous day." According to Imad Mustapha, Syrian ambassador to the United States, who translated for Mamlouk during the meeting, "Mamlouk's attendance at meetings with foreign delegations was extraordinary," and did not occur "even with friendly countries like Britain and France." This was a very personal gesture and a show of goodwill. The Syrian officials "were attentive during [Ambassador Daniel] Benjamin's presentation on al-Qaeda, foreign fighters, and other common threats, and reacted positively to his warnings that these issues presented challenges to both the U.S. and Syria." For his part, the Syrian spy chief extended the possibility of "security and intelligence cooperation" with the United States, so long as Syria was given point in regional actions, the bilateral relationship between the United States and Syria improved, and economic sanctions against Syria were alleviated. "In summary," said Vice Foreign Minister Faisal al-Miqdad, who was also present at the meeting, "President Asad wants cooperation, we should take the lead on that cooperation, and don't put us on your lists."[14]

By comparison, the WikiLeaks response group did not ask the *Times* to withhold publication of a cable where José "Pepe" Grinda Gonzalez, a Spanish National Court prosecutor, referred to Russia as a "mafia state," or the multitude of cables reporting tensions between Russian prime minister Vladimir Putin and Russian president Dmitry Medvedev.[15] (One of the more salacious reports by Russian insiders explores three branches of thought on the matter: that Medvedev is coming into his own as president; that Medvedev is "Robin" to Putin's "Batman"; that the two leaders coexist peacefully.)[16] These types of reports were trivial to the response group. Western intelligence sharing with terrorist states—a vital national security priority— triggered a blinking red light and barricades.

·   ·   ·

Interestingly, "Cablegate" has had but a limited effect on some areas of U.S. policy and has actually *strengthened* the president's governing agenda in others. As if in mockery of Julian Assange's loftiest ambitions, the release of State Department diplomatic cables has given ideological ammunition to those who believe that the entrenched state, methodically cloaked in secrecy, actually reflects the best interest of the polity.

Assange's Manichean view of the governing institutions of the United States arguably blinded him to the subtleties of foreign policy as revealed by the cable release. A clear-eyed reading of much of the classified material wrenched from the secrecy apparatus suggests a more accountable government than Assange—or anyone, really— ever imagined. Contrary to the initial alarmist reporting, the diplomatic cables make heroes out of American diplomats. For the most part, the puzzle pieces dumped by Assange (and patiently reassembled by outsiders) reveal an American government that indeed tries to do what it says it will do. And when the government is pressed to lie or obfuscate, it almost invariably does so to further a redeeming interest. The oppressive secrecy regime as perceived by Assange may be messy—yes—and abused—of course—but not altogether dysfunctional or objectively immoral.

Veteran investigative journalist Bart Gellman has outlined how this works in practice. The government competes with journalists on one level and cooperates with them on another. That is to say, the state labors to keep as much sensitive information out of the public square as possible. Once classified information has been compromised, however, the state works with journalists to facilitate its responsible publication, with context and elaboration.

Aside from threats of enforcing the Espionage Act—a rarely used sledgehammer in the government's toolshed—there is no legal or formal basis for the government to ask a reporter not to reveal classified programs, or the particulars of said programs. Indeed, in such cases the government's hands are often tied, as those requests would prove technically illegal. By asking for red pen authority over key classified details of a journalist's reporting, the government implicitly confirms those details. Because it is unlawful to share, suggest, or substantiate classified information with persons lacking clearance and "need to know" authority, the state is largely impotent when faced with the primed printing press. Blunt intimidation, therefore, is invariably ineffective.

None of the cable revelations, positive or negative, nullify the larger point: Julian Assange, and future Julian Assanges, are the direct result of the sprawling secrecy apparatus of the U.S government. Because so many matters of the state have been stamped Secret, the practice of illegally leaking to the press is not only considered acceptable, but oftentimes *necessary* for governance. Accordingly, lawmakers charged with crafting legislation to prevent future WikiLeaks scenarios are hamstrung by a situation they have created and a mechanism they have come to rely on. An overreaching law might prevent future Salt Pit–equivalent revelations, while anemic legislation would give tacit approval for similar illegal, unilateral, bulk declassifications. At the same time, politicians and the contemporary culture herald whistleblowing as an act of virtue. Well, Assange blew the whistle on King Abdullah of Saudi Arabia, who wanted the U.S. military to launch a preemptive decapitation strike on Iran.

Ultimately, Secretary of Defense Robert Gates—no stranger to the importance of state secrecy, having served as both the leader of a military at war and as former director of central intelligence—pointedly questioned the alarmists in Washington:

> Let me just offer some perspective as somebody who's been at this a long time. Every other government in the world knows the United States government leaks like a sieve, and it has for a long time. And I dragged this up the other day when I was looking at some of these prospective releases. And this is a quote from John Adams: "How can a government go on, publishing all of their negotiations with foreign nations, I know not. To me, it appears as dangerous and pernicious as it is novel."
>
> When we went to real congressional oversight of intelligence in the mid-70s, there was a broad view that no other foreign intelligence service would ever share information with us again if we were going to share it all with the Congress. Those fears all proved unfounded.

Now, I've heard the impact of these releases on our foreign policy described as a meltdown, as a game-changer, and so on. I think—I think those descriptions are fairly significantly overwrought. The fact is: governments deal with the United States because it's in their interest, not because they like us, not because they trust us, and not because they believe we can keep secrets.

Many governments—some governments deal with us because they fear us, some because they respect us, most because they need us. We are still essentially, as has been said before, the indispensable nation. So other nations will continue to deal with us. They will continue to work with us. We will continue to share sensitive information with one another. Is this embarrassing? Yes. Is it awkward? Yes. Consequences for U.S. foreign policy? I think fairly modest.[17]

Gates won few friends at the State Department for his candid remarks. He contradicted statements by Secretary of State Hillary Clinton, who had earlier called the WikiLeaks exposé "an attack on America" and on the international community, adding, "There is nothing laudable about endangering innocent people, and there is nothing brave about sabotaging the peaceful relations between nations."[18] The Department of Justice was apoplectic at Gates, fearing that such an unvarnished assessment by such a respected, experienced, and senior administration official—a man who by virtue of his career in government may well know more secrets than anyone—would undermine any future prosecution of Julian Assange.

The weeks and months following the WikiLeaks cable release have confirmed the statements of Secretary Gates. It *was* embarrassing. Some U.S. ambassadors found their telephone calls unreturned. Secretary Clinton, meanwhile, endured a public lashing in the press when cables emerged suggesting that the State Department had issued orders for diplomats to collect human intelligence. Never mind that such policies reach back to Thomas Jefferson, the first secretary of state, who instructed diplomats to gather "such political and commercial intelligence as you may think interesting to the United States."[19] Never mind that diplomats of the United States were not in fact conscripted into intelligence gathering. Rather, because the order was circulated to the entire State Department, Secretary Clinton's name appeared as the originator of the cable. This was and is standard procedure.

In 1990, Secretary of State James Baker found himself in similar tempest when reports surfaced that the American envoy to Iraq, April Glaspie, had tried to appease Saddam Hussein on the eve of the Iraqi dictator's decision to invade Kuwait. In fact, Glaspie's cable recounting events of the meeting noted that she had specifically warned the Iraqi leader *against* invading its neighbor. But higher-ups at the State Department didn't get the cable, or misplaced it, and it took the U.S. government some time to correct the record. Baker obviously couldn't know the situational specifics to defend Glaspie, and he wouldn't play the news media's game. "What you want me to do is say that those instructions were sent specifically by me on my specific orders," he scoffed, noting that 312,000 cables go out in his name each year.[20]

The cables related to Secretary Clinton's nonexistent spy ring involved guidelines set by analysts at the CIA's National Human Intelligence (HUMINT) Requirements Tasking Center. The HUMINT Tasking Center is charged with determining what types of intelligence the U.S. government requires for ongoing activities and how best to obtain it. In 2004, the CIA determined that in order to provide value-added insight to policy makers enmeshed in complex negotiations about war and terrorism, it needed additional raw data on foreign dignitaries, the United Nations, and various countries. The decision to send out a tasking was itself derivative of a 2003 presidential national security directive issued by President George W. Bush. The data would be used by many consumers: State's own intelligence branch; the National Security Agency, which has representatives in the center; the CIA; and the Defense Intelligence Agency, which compiles extensive intelligence and operations databases.

In 2009, the CIA updated its intelligence requirements and reissued the directive, which went to all members of the intelligence community, joint intelligence centers of combatant commands, and even to selected cleared personnel representing the Departments of Agriculture and Commerce overseas, as the 8,500-word cable itself makes clear. Once State got the order, Michael Owen, the acting

State Department intelligence chief, properly distributed the instructions with a gloss as to what his shop could use to provide the intelligence community with better information. Just as in the case of Secretary Baker, in all likelihood Secretary Clinton never saw the material, even though her name appeared as originator.

The leaked cable does, however, raise questions. Does the intelligence community spy on the United Nations? Yes. Does it spy on friendly African leaders? Certainly. Does the government want to collect sensitive and personal information on friendly international politicians, like the head of the World Health Organization? Somewhat uncomfortably, it does. But the State Department does not have the capacity to tap phones and collect data; Foreign Service officers aren't trained in tradecraft. They are not expected to gather intelligence for the sole purpose of feeding the CIA analytical beast.

Instead, there is an assumption made by every person who comes into contact with an identified member of the U.S. Foreign Service overseas that a representative of the U.S. government is going to act at all times in the interest of the U.S. government. Accordingly, every Foreign Service officer gathers information to some degree. The CIA HUMINT Tasking Center directive helps focus their efforts. There is no new, malevolent Clinton-directed blurring of lines; the lines were already blurred by design. Foreign officials understand the unofficial role played by diplomats and oftentimes use it as a means to send back-channel messages to the State Department.

Like every revelation by WikiLeaks made public so far, the furor subsided. The enticing narrative of a secret spy ring orchestrated by Hillary Clinton gave way to the more tedious reality of how paperwork is deployed in a bureaucracy. This is not to say, however, that nothing changed as a result of the scandal. On the contrary, it contributed to perhaps the most significant policy casualty of the WikiLeaks affair. Before the cable release, the CIA and the State Department were on the verge of finalizing an agreement designed to give thousands of intelligence analysts assigned to several agencies of State instant desk access to high-level diplomatic traffic. "That all went up in smoke," said an official who was brokering the announcement.

•  •  •

In the long run, this may prove to be a net positive for information security. The Secret Internet Protocol Router Network (SIPRNet) used by the Department of Defense is hardwired with no external points of entry so as to prevent illegal access by unauthorized personnel. During the first Bush administration, "authorized personnel" totaled five hundred users with security clearances. Today, several hundred thousand users have SIPRNet access. Many of them have only interim clearances—a mere signature on a nondisclosure agreement. With too many secrets come too many persons requiring access. That is how Bradley Manning, a troubled U.S. Army private at a forward operating base lacking even the slightest pretense of "need to know," gained access to the entirety of the State Department's secret files.

War fighting is measurably improved by such cross-agency data sharing, but the program was implemented at the expense of basic precautions. USB ports were not disabled. Nor were the write capabilities of CD and DVD drives. In a sense, the administrators of SIPRNet invited the security breach.

Post-WikiLeaks, interagency information sharing has been curtailed pending a reassessment of computer network security policies. The Office of Management and Budget (OMB) issued a directive ordering all federal agencies that handle sensitive information to review their internal security practices. In addition, the OMB has ordered that agencies build assessment teams composed of specialists in security and counterintelligence to establish new procedures and standards for training, access, and oversight. In the meantime, WikiLeaks has put a halt to intelligence community-wide efforts at declassification—the opposite of the organization's stated goal.

Whether or not WikiLeaks succeeded in revealing nontrivial overclassification, however, remains an open question. Certainly diplomatic cables consisting of compiled news summaries from the public press and stamped "Secret" are too much, though a fair argument can be made that even then a particular selection of newspaper columns reflects the priorities of the United States. But such cables' exposure does not equate with "significant" harm to national security. On other hand, those cables that would likely have imperiled the state were carefully redacted. The New York Times took the initiative and was soon assisted by the ad hoc State Department–*Times* partnership, and then followed by WikiLeaks itself. The organization did, in fact, redact the names of U.S. covert and clandestine operatives in the field.[21]

The WikiLeaks public relations effort certainly failed in one respect: by its publishing such a massive number of cables simultaneously, a kind of "security through obscurity" effect took place, with no one state secret able to astound and resonate before being stepped on by yet another. Although the WikiLeaks strategy attempted to steer media coverage with carefully timed revelations—the Khalid El-Masri horror in Germany, the innocent Iraqis killed during Operation Baton Rouge in Samarra, Iraq, the presence of U.S. special operations forces on the ground in Pakistan and working alongside Pakistani fighters—the WikiLeaks organization demonstrated for a second time a poor mastery of the dynamic between the press and the public.[22] (The first, of course, being the selectively edited "Collateral Murder.") In both instances, WikiLeaks itself became the story.

Still, with every passing day journalists and activists rifle through the ocean of secrets thrust into the public sphere by WikiLeaks, and it will take years before a full assessment can be made about the nature of U.S. diplomacy and the damage inflicted (or profits gained) by sunlight. But presently those with original classification authority in the U.S. government have been put on notice that embossing a document with "Secret" doesn't diminish its ability to be printed.

It's worth noting in closing that contrary to the darkest suspicions of the activists at WikiLeaks, the United States did not prove as a rule to be duplicitous and hypocritical in its dealings. As evidenced by tens of thousands of cables, American diplomats have proven to be a trusted and ardent force for good in the world. Similarly, the United States as a nation is not universally looked upon as an imperial beast in need of slaying, but rather is often seen as a benign force that friends, nominal allies, and public enemies alike turn to for guidance, protection, and leadership. These nations sometimes ask the impossible (decapitating Iran) or the awkward (support in secret and denunciations in public), but they do look to the United States. By that standard, America does not cleave the international community into segments for conquest, but rather binds them together for mutual benefit. Perhaps the most shocking and unintended revelation of WikiLeaks is that the United States isn't so bad at all.

It's worth reconsidering one other purported fact about WikiLeaks: though it may have been, in terms of volume, the largest leak in history, it was not the most damaging. Israel would say that nuclear technician Mordechai Vanunu's exposé of the country's nuclear weapons complex at Dimona was catastrophic; Britain had to deal with disorienting revelations in the biography of former MI5 assistant director Peter Wilson in 1987 containing leaks that led to a full-scale revision of the country's internal spying protocols.[23]

# CHAPTER 5

# Vital Information

The election of General Dwight D. Eisenhower brought the spy community a president of the United States who understood intelligence in both theory and practice. One of Ike's first orders of business was to provide encouragement to J. Edgar Hoover, who had eventually found acceptance but never comfort with Harry S. Truman. "Such was my respect for [Hoover] that I invited him to a meeting, my only purpose being to assure him that I wanted him in government as long as I might be there and that in the performance of his duties he would have the complete support of my office."[1]

Eisenhower thus unleashed Hoover and the FBI to pursue "security risks" in the federal government, a green light to hunt for communists on the payroll. The president further proved his devotion to Hoover by awarding the director the National Security Medal.

Eisenhower also empowered the CIA by promoting General Walter Bedell Smith, whose leadership by 1953 had reshaped the Company into a leaner, more focused institution of intelligence analysis and covert operations. (Concluded former case officer Samuel Halpern, "If it hadn't been for Bedell, I don't think there would be a CIA today.")[2] Smith, who was Eisenhower's most trusted, most capable associate during World War II, would become under secretary of state. The two men talked by phone "maybe several times a day."[3] Where everyone else in the administration referred to Eisenhower only as "Mr. President," Smith had no problem picking up the phone and saying, "Goddamn it Ike, I think..."[4] Though Allen Dulles, the new director of central intelligence, would work to limit Smith's influence in the State Department, Smith would soon become the president's closest adviser and chief overseer of covert operations.[5] Until his retirement, he continued working behind the scenes to protect and nurture the agency he once brought back from the brink.

With the Soviet bloc consolidating power in Eastern Europe, the CIA targeted every spot on the map where colonialism had flagged, from the Middle East to South America.[6] The objective was to prevent communist infiltration of collapsed states. Furthermore, so long as it could operate in complete secrecy, the CIA was empowered to conduct operations in any nation whose geopolitical sympathies were antithetical to those of the United States.

One of Eisenhower's highest priorities (and lasting achievements) as president involved imagery intelligence (IMINT). During World War II, he developed a minor obsession with IMINT, ordering pilots to fly him above the combat zone.[7] As president, he personally supervised the U-2 spy plane program, whereby a high-altitude reconnaissance plane equipped with the most sophisticated cameras of its time flew over Soviet soil, recording major infrastructure and tracking nuclear assets. The president signed off on every mission and closely studied each flight's findings with Dulles and other CIA officials.[8] He was no fool as to the risk such sorties entailed, however. "Well boys," he said when first presented with plans for the U-2. "I believe the country needs this information, and I'm going to approve it. But I'll tell you one thing. Some day one of these machines is going to get caught, and then we'll have a storm."[9]

That day almost came in 1958 when Hanson Baldwin, the military affairs correspondent for the New York Times, learned of the U-2 missions while visiting Germany. When Baldwin returned to Washington, he met Robert Amory, the deputy director of central intelligence, for lunch. Baldwin was giving the deputy director a heads-up that the U-2 story would soon appear in the Times, to which Amory replied, "Jesus, Hanson, no!"[10] Dulles would appeal successfully to Times publisher Arthur Hays Sulzberger to spike the story.[11]

That day of reckoning feared by Eisenhower arrived on May 1, 1960, when a Soviet missile hit but didn't destroy a U-2.[12] The plane landed mostly intact, though the pilot's fate was in doubt. (Survival was considered unlikely, and in any event the pilot was given a capsule of toxin to swallow in the event of capture.)[13] The Eisenhower administration kept the loss a secret in hopes that the Soviets would do the same.

Not long after, the U.S. ambassador was invited to an assembly of the Supreme Soviet, where he sat as a guest of honor. Premier Nikita Khrushchev presided over the 1,300-member Soviet legislature, conducting routine business before unexpectedly turning to darker matters:

> Lately, influential forces—imperialist and militarist circles, whose stronghold is the Pentagon—have become noticeably more active in the United States . . . . Comrade Deputies! On the instruction of the Soviet government, I must report to you on aggressive actions against the Soviet Union in the past few weeks . . . . The United States has been sending aircraft that have been crossing our state frontiers and intruding upon the airspace of the Soviet Union. We protested to the United States against several previous aggressive acts of this kind . . . . The aggressor knows what he is in for when he intrudes upon foreign territory . . . shoot the plane down! This assignment was fulfilled.[14]

"The pilot of the American plane," announced Premier Khruschev, "is alive and well."[15]

The diplomatic fallout was severe. The pilot, Gary Powers, spent nearly two years in a Soviet hard labor camp before being traded by the United States for a captured Soviet spy. Though the incident would prove embarrassing to the Eisenhower administration and devastating to international relations, it had the ironic effect of fast-tracking research and development of the U.S. Corona spy satellite, which would provide far more accurate image intelligence from the safety and security of space.[16]

For the record, the U-2 spy plane was flown from a secret CIA facility in Peshawar, Pakistan.[17]

•   •   •

When Eisenhower ordered the secret flights, he did so with the tacit approval of the public. The Soviet Union was a threat and had to be watched. His fear was not that the American people would learn of the missions and consider them criminal or immoral, but that the Soviets would learn of the missions and in some way retaliate. Still, whether a program is leaked, revealed post-conflict, or exposed by accident, sooner or later it's going to get out. The entire enterprise, therefore, is an effort at failing gracefully, or delaying political or historical approval.

Every president believes that the secret activities he orders or permits are both moral and in the interest of the nation. Sometimes he understands that the nation might not necessarily agree, and in such cases the hope is that the missions stay secret, lest they become a political concern as well as a security matter. Generally speaking, the worst effects of leaks (so far) have been the debates that result and the erosion of government trust by people who dislike having been kept in the dark.

A hypothetical example: An oil company executive tells the president that petroleum prices will double in six months. The president spends the next six months quietly working with hostile governments in oil-rich countries to prevent economic disaster. Her rationale for keeping the information and the negotiations secret is obvious. But after six months elapse, if prices remain stable and word leaks that the president in some way capitulated to an unambiguously wretched regime, public faith in the government erodes. Similarly, if the economy collapses and word leaks that *the president knew something*, public faith in the government erodes. In both instances, democracy feels like an illusion and the Republic suffers.

Another hypothetical: Immediately following a successful terrorist attack on the United States, authorities find and capture the mastermind. Intelligence suggests that another attack is imminent, but the terrorist isn't talking.

In that din of catastrophe, we should examine the limits of the faith we entrust to the government. Forty years after Eisenhower said, "I believe the country needs this information, and I'm going to approve it," the country again needed vital information, and the president again approved it. Only this time it didn't involve spy planes. It involved torture.

• • •

When the insurgency began in Iraq, it caused panic at the Pentagon. The lack of tactical intelligence about enemy combatants was a significant problem for war planners. In early June 2003, U.S. commanders in Iraq launched Operation Peninsula Strike, the first of its efforts to sweep away the underbrush that allowed the Fedayeen Saddam to survive. The operation was not a success. On September 12, as violence against coalition forces spiked, Secretary of Defense Donald Rumsfeld sent a memo to Stephen Cambone, the under secretary of defense for intelligence. "I keep reading [intelligence community] intel," he wrote. "It leaves one with the impression that we know a lot—who the people are, what they are doing, where they are going, when they are meeting, and the like. However, when one pushes on that information it is pretty clear that we don't have actionable intelligence." Furthermore, Rumsfeld didn't "have good data on the people we have been capturing and interrogating" in either Iraq or Afghanistan. "I don't feel I am getting information from the interrogations that should be enabling us as to answer the questions I've posed."[18]

It is not hard to see how, from this urgent need, a policy of enhanced interrogation techniques might develop, which in the frenzy of war might turn into torture. In 2004, according to a recently declassified memorandum written for Rumsfeld and three years after the start of the war, the U.S. Joint Special Operations Command (JSOC) now "operated from a reactive rather than a proactive posture, and was not structured for the complex, extended-duration operations they currently conduct." JSOC, it said, "lacked the 'find' and 'fix' and intelligence fusion capabilities essential" to the war on terrorism. Its intelligence capabilities, "particularly in human intelligence, were very limited."[19]

Such was the situation when Rumsfeld named then major general Stanley McChrystal as commanding general of JSOC. General McChrystal, the former commander of the 75th Ranger Regiment and a task force commander in Afghanistan, had just completed a Pentagon tour as vice director of operations on the Joint Staff. He had impressed Rumsfeld, who admired him for defending the Iraq War in pubic despite harboring private reservations.

McChrystal had, with the help of Marshall Billingslea, the Pentagon civilian in charge of special operations, painstakingly drafted the execute order that allowed JSOC to pursue terrorists in a dozen countries outside Afghanistan and Iraq, subject to various rules imposed by the National Security Council. (JSOC could not set foot in Iran; it had to jump through hoops to chase terrorists in Pakistan; Somalia was an open zone.) McChrystal, compact, intense, and stone-faced, was known for his Ranger high-and-tight, his minimal tolerance for bureaucracy, and his talent as a constant innovator. (To wit: before he put on his first star, he had rewritten the U.S. Army hand-to-hand combat curriculum.) He is at once disarming and intimidating in person. He struck some subordinates as a monk, largely because he was an introvert, and the nickname JSOC personnel give to their boss—the Pope—became synonymous with McChrystal, more so than with any JSOC commander before or since. (The Pope moniker traces its lineage to Janet Reno, the attorney general under President Bill Clinton, who once complained that getting information out of JSOC was like trying to pry loose the Vatican's secrets.)

McChrystal slept in tents with his men. Once, General Doug Brown, the commander of the U.S. Special Operations Command, visited a JSOC team forward-deployed in a war zone, expecting that McChrystal's office would befit a general officer's billet. It turned out to be an austere eight-by-ten-foot prisonlike cell. It wasn't for show that McChrystal accepted the designation of commander, Joint Special Operations Command Forward—he was always with his men. Indeed, under his command, JSOC's headquarters back in Fayetteville, North Carolina, often had little to do. McChrystal brought everything with him. But as a decorated Ranger recalls of the period, "We were cowboys in 2003 and 2004 . . . we were accountable to no one."

McChrystal inherited a command that included the military's brightest and boldest but also most overburdened. Indeed, his predecessor, Major General Dell Dailey, wanted to scale back JSOC's missions after Afghanistan in order to give the teams time to regroup. Rangers, in particular, had just finished Operation Winter Strike, clearing large swaths of territory in Afghanistan at the end of 2003. Task Force 1-21, JSOC's regional task force, followed. The demands on JSOC were prodigious, and it lacked a strategy or central focus for success. Even though the spigot of money for counterterrorism operations was open, the Command often had to beg to get a fixed-wing aircraft in the air. Simply put, JSOC lacked the resources, the structure, and the strategy to carry out its mission. McChrystal's first instinct was true to his infantry roots: he wanted more combined arms training for the units, but he quickly realized he had a much larger problem. As the war in Iraq turned ugly, no one really knew how to solve what in military terms was known as the "OODA problem."

An OODA loop is a term coined by the late military strategist John Boyd to refer to the way fighting organizations adapt: observe, orient, decide, and act. The challenge of fighting insurgencies is that smaller groups tend to outlast their larger adversaries because small groups have OODA loops measured in nanoseconds when compared with the lumbering decision chains of major world armies. The enemy is thus always a step ahead of even armies with the best technology and hardened soldiers.

Complicating matters was the existence of excess "blinks" between the development of a piece of intelligence and its use on the battlefield. Most of the actionable intelligence the United States received came from foreign sources (the Brits were particularly good in Iraq, as were the Kurds). The National Security Agency had yet to get a full read on Iraq's rudimentary but highly distributed cell telephone network. The U.S. intelligence community bickered over high-tech surveillance resources, and agencies refused to talk to one another. British journalist Mark Urban, writing in *Task Force Black*, a narrative history about U.S.-UK cooperation in Iraq, quotes a senior British officer as saying that the CIA's refusal to share information with even its own countrymen was "catastrophic."

Such confusion and desperation are two reasons harsh interrogations seemed morally permissible at the time. At the very least, enemy combatants would say something, which would set in motion kinetic operations. This at least gave the appearance of movement toward a goal.

•   •   •

In the early days of the chase for al-Qaeda and the Taliban in Afghanistan, the CIA and the U.S. Defense Intelligence Agency (DIA) did most of the interrogating. JSOC intelligence gatherers watched but did not participate. By October 2002, an internal JSOC assessment of interrogations at Bagram Airfield, Afghanistan, and Guantánamo Bay, Cuba, found that the resistance techniques of enemy combatants "outmatched" the interrogation techniques of U.S. forces. Higher headquarters was not satisfied with the results, and JSOC picked up the rope. The Command established a task force to determine whether its operators should directly interrogate the "designated unlawful combatants" they captured. One month later, U.S. military survival, evasion, resistance, and escape (SERE) instructors taught certain members of JSOC the finer points of harsh interrogation. (These operators, like all members of the special operations forces community, had previously attended SERE school as prisoners so as to learn how to effectively resist torture.) Around this time, some JSOC operators were read in to a classified program called MATCHBOX that included direct authorization to use certain aggressive interrogation techniques in the field (for example, the best way to throw a detainee against a wall).

Who chartered MATCHBOX (also known by the unclassified nickname COPPER GREEN, as revealed by journalist Seymour Hersh) remains a mystery. No one wants to take credit for it. Yet as a result of the program, JSOC adopted a standard operating procedure (SOP) for Afghanistan that included the use of stress positions, barking dogs, and sleep deprivation, among various other physical inducements.

When JSOC Task Force 6-26 set up operations in Iraq, it extended the practice, copying the SOP in its entirety, essentially only changing "Afghanistan" to "Iraq" on its letterhead. The primary mission of 6-26 was to hunt, kill, or capture high-value targets. At the top of the list: former senior members of the Baathist regime, followed by al-Qaeda and foreign fighters who flocked to the war zone en masse seeking a pound of Uncle Sam's flesh.

Just after the fall of Saddam Hussein, U.S. Army Rangers claimed a small Iraqi military base near Baghdad International Airport for use by special operations forces. Camp Nama, as it is called, was purposed to hold enemy combatants thought to possess actionable intelligence about the locations of 6-26 targets. The limits of enemy interrogation as defined in a revised, more humane SOP soon fell by the wayside. Personnel from Task Force 6-26 (with the participation of members of the DIA) subjected prisoners to intense physical, psychological, and occasionally lethal interrogation.

The Senate Armed Services Committee investigation into detainee abuse in Iraq includes several harrowing accounts of the interactions between conventional military officers and JSOC commanders. Reportedly, special operations officers acted as though they were above the law, and the Senate review later concluded that JSOC interrogators regularly brutalized their detainees. At the time, members of both the CIA and the DIA sent word up their respective chains of command that JSOC was possibly breaking the law. An effort by the Defense Department requiring JSOC to adhere to its own set of interrogation standards was ignored. One senior Joint Staff official testified that he would give 6-26 commanders a copy of the new SOP to sign every day. Every day, it would be "lost." It was never signed.

During numerous visits by outside personnel, higher-ranking non-JSOC officers halted interrogations midway. JSOC personnel seemed to be flaunting their harsh techniques with impunity. It got so bad that by late 2003 the DIA, the FBI, and British interrogation teams stopped all cooperation with JSOC.

The lack of accountability was startling to long-term military interrogators such as Lieutenant Colonel Steven Kleinman, who had been dispatched to Iraq to review and modify JSOC detainee operations. One Iraqi was picked up for allegedly knowing a lot about bridges. The bridges in question turned out to be of the calcium-and-enamel variety—he was a dentist. Kleinman later testified that he considered the JSOC facility to be "uncontrolled."

McChrystal commanded JSOC for more than a year before the harsh interrogations finally stopped. People close to McChrystal say that when he toured Camp Nama facilities, the interrogators would be on their best behavior and seemed to be following the classified SOP he had approved. By the end of 2004, however, it became clear that the abuses were habitual and institutionalized. According to Urban, the British Special Air Service (SAS) informed McChrystal that it would no longer participate in operations where detainees were sent to "black" sites, which now included a kennel-like compound near Balad, Iraq, and another at Bagram Airfield in Afghanistan. Up until that point, SAS units had been instrumental in helping JSOC uncover the rudiments of an intelligence railway that allowed al-Qaeda to penetrate Iraq so easily.

McChrystal ordered deputy commanding general Eric Fiel to quietly review the practices at Camp Nama. The review, which remains classified and locked in a vault at Pope Army Airfield, resulted in disciplinary action against more than forty JSOC person-nel. Several promising careers—including that of the colonel respon-sible for Nama at the time of the abuses—were ended. McChrystal has since told associates that he did not fully appreciate the degree to which interrogators at all levels lacked guidance and direction.

When the extent of the abuses at Camp Nama was made public, Under Secretary of Defense Cambone was furious at McChrystal, accusing the general of abusing the authority given to him. McChrystal, to put it mildly, did not appreciate being blamed for a program he had not created and by most accounts knew almost nothing about. A still-classified internal Pentagon investigation of McChrystal was initiated on Cambone's insistence. Its conclusions are not publicly available, but based on McChrystal's meteoric rise, one can extrapolate that the conclusions did not undermine confi-dence in the Pope.

In some ways, the detainee abuse scandals gave McChrystal a platform to clean house at JSOC, and by most accounts he did. He flew to JSOC operating locations around the world and insisted that the era of harsh interrogations—except in the direst of circum-stances—was over.

"My sense is that we just didn't know much about how to work or handle the detainees," said a senior military official whose service at JSOC spanned the Afghanistan and Iraq campaigns. "The mistakes that were made during our initial forays into detainee exploitation were more about ignorance and just trying to figure out this art, rather than any malicious attempt to violate any policies or regulations. We also suffered from a lack of trained personnel who didn't under-stand what was effective interrogation." But then, he added, "General McChrystal's leadership drove the need for a fix and professionalizing the force, and then general [Michael] Flynn drove the execution."

• • •

No doubt, when Bradley Manning turned his trove of secrets over to WikiLeaks, everyone involved assumed that they would find something scandalous on the scale of waterboarding, black sites, or Abu Ghraib. With conflicts as complicated and sprawling as the wars in Iraq and Afghanistan, those who were most skeptical of American military power were sure there must have been the murder of civilians, the corruption of foreign politicians, breaches of the Geneva Conventions, or at least collusion with some lesser of evils. When there wasn't anything grand enough, they worked to create something with the "Collateral Murder" tape.

This is not to claim the government is not currently engaged in morally or tactically questionable activities. Obviously, that's impossible to say definitively, and skepticism will always be warranted. At the same time, this is no longer Hoover and Eisenhower's national security state. So many people know about sensitive operations—people in lower levels of authority, with "civilian" mindsets and unlimited access to new ways to leak—that it's clear that Eisenhower's "someday" is now "someday soon." The period between the time that a secret is established and the time that it is disclosed has narrowed significantly, and those running operations of any sort can't depend on a thoughtful history judging them, but a heated and partisan present.

While this change owes a lot to the radical growth of the secrecy machine after 9/11 and the concurrent rise of the Internet, it really began in the 1970s. For the first time, that was when Americans really got a picture of what went on in the more secret corridors of power, and it wasn't always pretty.

# CHAPTER 6

# The Horrors Book

On December 22, 1974, Sy Hersh pulled back the drapes of the Central Intelligence Agency, and sunlight annihilated everything in its path. Under the headline "Huge C.I.A. Operation Reported in U.S. Against Anti-War Forces, Other Dissidents in Nixon Years," the *New York Times* reported that the CIA had engaged in widespread domestic spying in flagrant violation of its charter. Hersh's reporting was incomplete and distorted, but it was sufficient to light a fuse that ended in an explosion at Langley. According to the report, the Company had engaged in mass "break-ins, wiretapping, and the surreptitious inspection of mail." It had allegedly accumulated ten thousand files on U.S. citizens. The targets weren't necessarily spies or saboteurs; they were antiwar activists and members of Congress.

And for President Gerald Ford, that was the good news.

Two weeks later, in an Oval Office meeting with the president, Secretary of State Henry Kissinger would describe "the horrors book"—an accounting by William Colby, the newly appointed director of central intelligence, of Agency activities over the years. The litany of abuses, though ended years before and "undertaken in totally different circumstances than today's," left the president "concerned that the CIA would be destroyed."[1]

Among the legal violations by the Agency that most alarmed Colby:

- A two-year confinement and interrogation of a Russian defector. Because former director of central intelligence John McCone approved the defector's imprisonment on U.S. soil, which was highly unusual, the Agency had possibly violated kidnapping laws.
- The surveillance of investigative journalists Jack Anderson, Mike Getler, Brit Hume, Victor Marchetti, Robert Allen, and Paul Scott, among others.
- CIA plots to assassinate Fidel Castro of Cuba, Patrice Lumumba of Congo, and Rafael Trujillo of the Dominican Republic. (The Agency had no active involvement in the deaths of the latter two, and no success against Castro.)

And Colby was still digging.[2]

That day, the president signed Executive Order 11828, establishing a commission led by Vice President Nelson Rockefeller to "ascertain and evaluate any facts relating to activities conducted within the United States by the Central Intelligence Agency which give rise to questions of compliance with the provisions of [law]." Furthermore, the commission was charged with evaluating the legal mechanisms designed to keep the CIA in line, and advising the president as needed. It was to be a White House end run around those calling for a full-scale investigation.

Congress, by and large, was not impressed.

On February 20, 1975, the White House national security team gathered in Secretary of State Kissinger's office. The secretary opened the meeting by noting that "the nature of covert operations will have a curious aspect to the average mind and out of perspective it could look inexplicable." Kissinger didn't have the same problem in mind that Eisenhower did when he said there'd be a storm; the negative reaction he was predicting was entirely domestic and entirely political. The result of open congressional investigations, Kissinger predicted, "could be the drying up of the imaginations of the people on which we depend if people think they will be indicted ten years later for what they do."[3]

In Kissinger's office were the men who knew where the bodies were buried. There was little love lost among one another, and since they had been tempered under Nixon, there was little doubt that should the hammer drop, no one in the room could trust anyone or one another. Already, Colby sat squarely in Kissinger's crosshairs for having gone to the Justice Department to set matters straight. Colby, more than anyone else in the room, not only knew the secrets but lived them as a highly decorated U.S. Army paratrooper, a CIA case officer, CIA station chief in Saigon, and overseer of the paramilitary Phoenix Program. Where Kissinger wanted entrenchment, Colby immediately and unilaterally embraced transparency, offering Justice a forthright assessment of the CIA's "family jewels."

Executive privilege would allow the White House to resist congressional subpoena authority and control what got out. This would protect not only the men in power, but also secret geopolitical alliances. Said Kissinger, "We have to demonstrate to foreign countries we aren't too dangerous to cooperate with because of leaks." (Thirty years later, the Obama administration would fret over the same concern in the aftermath of WikiLeaks.)

J. Edgar Hoover had died three years before, after putting in a full day at the office. His beloved Bureau, whose image he had spent a lifetime protecting, was now imperiled. Up to the end, however, the director proved to be the most effective operator in Washington. He sensed change in the air, and by 1965 he had discontinued electronic surveillance, garbage searches, and involvement with the Postal Service.[4] By 1971, he had ended the Bureau's blackest of black operations—the COINTELPRO (Counter Intelligence Program) investigations—whose techniques, initially designed to destroy the Communist Party of the USA in the 1950s, would later spread into such activities as exposing homosexuals and extramarital affairs and planting false evidence in order to have suspected communists arrested by local law enforcement.[5] By February 20, 1975, the FBI was fully divested of its misadventures.

The most telling exchange of the meeting was between Phillip Areeda, deputy counsel to the president, and Kissinger. Areeda explained that Senator Frank Church planned to look "into the legal, moral and political cost-effectiveness aspects of [covert operations]."

"Then we are in trouble," responded Kissinger.

•  •  •

From the outset, skeptics doubted President Ford's rationale for appointing the Rockefeller Commission. It was either defensive posturing in a post-Watergate environment, designed to mitigate political damage (the investigation was limited to CIA operations on U.S. soil), or something more insidious was at play. In 1975, *New York* magazine reported that many observers believed that "Ford may have moved in order to fend off accusations of a more serious kind against the CIA—even more serious than domestic snooping in contravention of the agency's charter."[6] The suspicion, of course, was assassination. At any rate, Congress didn't waste time waiting for the executive branch to investigate itself. Senate leadership granted Frank Church a committee with full authority to investigate the whole of the intelligence community and its activities both foreign and domestic.

The hearings were brutal for the intelligence community. When Church's final report was released in April 1976, few had trouble predicting its conclusion: "Domestic intelligence activity has threatened and undermined the Constitutional rights of Americans to free speech, association and privacy. It has done so primarily because the Constitutional system for checking abuse of power has not been applied."[7]

The tragedy of the final report of the Church Committee is that it was right: the intelligence community was in dire need of reform and legal guidance. But the committee's gleeful partisanship undermined an otherwise worthy goal. It was the first time the nation—indeed, the world—was given access to the machinery of tradecraft, and some evenhandedness was merited. Many people didn't like what they saw, which was the point, but was to some degree an injustice.

The government had been spying on citizens for quite some time. During World War II, all telegrams sent to and from the United States were screened by the Office of Censorship and its chief client, the FBI. The program collected intelligence on persons of interest and potential threats to national security. With the end of hostilities came the end of censorship, and consequently an immediate cessation of telegram cable intelligence. That wouldn't do at all.

•   •   •

On August 18, 1945, the Army Signal Security Agency (SSA) sent representatives to "make the necessary contacts with the heads of the Commercial Communications Companies in New York, secure their approval of the interception of all Governmental traffic entering the United States, leaving the United States, or transiting the United States, and make the necessary arrangements for this photographic intercept work."[8]

International Telephone and Telegraph (ITT) "very definitely and finally refused" to play any part in the obviously illegal program.[9] Officials found a warmer reception with Western Union Telegraph Company, which agreed to cooperate under the condition that the attorney general sign off on the project. The SSA representatives then returned to ITT. In a meeting with a vice president, the SSA offered the veiled threat that "his company would not desire to be the only non-cooperative company on this project."[10] ITT relented, under the same proviso as Western Union. RCA was equally amenable, but again, only with authorization from the attorney general.[11] As the CIA Center for the Study of Intelligence would later report:

> Two very evident fears existed in the minds of the heads of each of these communications companies. One was the fear of the illegality of the procedure according to present FCC regulations. In spite of the fact that favorable opinions have been received from the Judge Advocate General of the Navy and the Judge Advocate General of the Army, it was feared that these opinions would not hold in civil court and, as a consequence, the companies would not be protected. If a favorable opinion is handed down by the Attorney General, this fear will be completely allayed, and cooperation may be expected for the complete intercept coverage of this material. The second fear uppermost in the minds of these executives is the fear of the ACA which is the communications union. This union has reported on many occasions minor infractions of FCC regulations and it is feared that a major infraction, such as the proposed intercept coverage, if disclosed by the Union, might cause severe repercussions.[12]

There is no evidence to suggest that either the president or the attorney general were ever briefed on the project, but not long after the SSA men visited the telegraph companies—and in spite of adamant internal resistance from each company's lawyers—Operation Shamrock went active. (Decades later, Louis Tordella, deputy director of the National Security Agency, would admit that "he did not know if *any* subsequent president or attorney general had ever been briefed on it.")[13]

One problem remained: physically transferring thousands of cables in secret. William Sidney Sparks, the traffic manager for RCA and a lieutenant colonel in the U.S. Army Signal Corps Reserve, worked closely with the SSA to find a solution. He swatted down ill-conceived schemes by his government counterparts on the grounds that "everybody and his brother would know just exactly what we were doing and why."[14]

According to James Bamford, author of *The Puzzle Palace*, "He told the officers that probably the most secure and efficient way to handle the problem would be to turn over to the agency all traffic entering, leaving, or transiting the company." The SSA couldn't believe their luck. Sparks initially stipulated that the SSA (soon renamed the Army Security Agency, or ASA) would receive only "header" information stating the origin and destination of each telegram. That policy soon fell by the wayside, and the agency began collecting hard copies of cables in their entirety.

For his part, Sidney Sparks understood that his actions were illegal, but also that the United States was staring down the barrel of a new kind of war. "I knew in my own mind that the Cold War was heating up at the time," he said, adding, "I was under no illusion at all that any responsible Government has to monitor, to some degree, the traffic of the other [foreign] Government agencies as far as it can get hold of them."[15] His superiors, as well as executives at Western Union and ITT, were equally cognizant of the criminal activities to which they were party and would remain terminally paranoid. General Dwight D. Eisenhower, then the Army chief of staff, sought to allay their fears, as would Secretary of Defense James Forrestal. Neither man, however, would prove particularly persuasive on this point. Shamrock was a military program; *of course* the defense secretary approved of industry participation. Meanwhile, neither the attorney general nor the president of the United States would ever directly convey any legal cover—or even any direct knowledge— of the program. Communications executives wondered, indeed, if Operation Shamrock ever reached their desks.

The ASA would eventually be absorbed by the Armed Forces Security Agency (AFSA), which would become the National Security Agency. The NSA thus inherited Shamrock and maintained tens of thousands of files on U.S. citizens.* As a practical matter, the AFSA and its successor acted as an information broker to the FBI and CIA. The intelligence agencies were even internally referred to as "customers." Initially, each agency (and a number of others) set up desks at Arlington Hall in Virginia, the nerve center of the AFSA. (The site was originally Arlington Hall Junior College for Women, a nonprofit girls' school seized by the Army Signal Intelligence Service in 1942 under the War Powers Act.[16] The fledgling NSA would later install itself in abandoned Army barracks at Fort Meade, Maryland.) These liaisons from every segment of the intelligence community rifled daily through the nation's cable traffic, forwarding useful data to their respective headquarters.[17] During the years that followed, each agency would submit watch lists of "persons of interest" for the NSA to be on the lookout for. In addition, NSA agents combed data in search of trigger words.[18]

Although Shamrock ostensibly searched only traffic originating and terminating on foreign soil, the project expanded to monitor perceived radicals susceptible to foreign influence.[19] For most Americans, this probably crossed the line between what was possibly illegal but benign and an absolute outrage.

The intelligence community, ever thirsty for more information and already operating outside of the law, would push the NSA as far as the agency would permit. Watch lists eventually became blanket requests. As Frank Raven, a former NSA official, later observed, "When J. Edgar Hoover gives you a requirement for complete surveillance of all Quakers in the United States, and when Richard

---

*Congressional hearings would eventually find no evidence indicating that the NSA used these files to monitor Americans, but rather that they were incidental to the NSA's foreign intelligence mission

Nixon is a Quaker and he's president of the United States, it gets pretty funny." (At the time, Hoover suspected that the Quakers were sending food to Southeast Asia. As for the FBI's involvement in illegalities, Hoover had requested and received permission for such activities from the attorney general in 1941.[20] This would suffice as legal cover for the Bureau.)

The NSA would also, in turn, act as a client of the FBI and the CIA. While the NSA had negotiated deals with the communications giants in New York, the Bureau dominated the Washington cable circuit and provided daily intelligence to the NSA. Furthermore, the Bureau, which had long mastered the art of infiltrating offices and installing listening devices, provided these services to the NSA, which was at its essence a stationary global listening post lacking an agile force on the ground. These so-called black bag missions saved the NSA time, money, and manpower. Deciphering encrypted calls and cables from foreign embassies in Washington might take the NSA months, if not years. The FBI's practiced special agents could plant a bug overnight.[21]

Meanwhile, the CIA performed similar operations on foreign embassies overseas, filching ciphers and codebooks. And when the NSA found itself in need of office space in New York City to process the massive collection of cable traffic, it approached the CIA for a "safe house." For seven years, the Company obliged the NSA's real estate needs.[22]

Operation Shamrock would run for thirty years, and at its height would collect 150,000 messages a month, illegally.[23]

On March 4, 1977, Robert Keuch, deputy assistant attorney general in the Carter administration, received a comprehensive summary of the illegalities of the intelligence community as gathered by Congress, and the names of those who should be prosecuted as a result.

The problem, according to the memorandum, was that domestic surveillance and intelligence collection was an evolutionary process and began with presidential authorization. Presidential national security power, it explained, "did not spring full grown from one source, such as the Constitution; rather, it started with an idea and grew steadily over the better part of four decades."[24]

Interestingly, as far back as the 1940s, J. Edgar Hoover sought secondary approval from the attorney general, writing that it would be "highly desirable that some definite decisions be made by the Department of Justice relative to the legality of the [wiretapping activity]." (Despite the aggressive campaign against Hoover since his death, even this "prosecutive summary" specifically notes that such a request for Justice Department guidance was "not really unusual in light of Director Hoover's strong dislike for wiretapping.")[25]

By the time the NSA had been created, surveillance authority of the executive branch was largely unrestricted. Indeed, with regard to communications intelligence, National Security Council Intelligence Directive 9 specifically stated:

> The special nature of Communications Intelligence activities requires that they be treated in all respects as being outside the framework of other or general intelligence activities. Orders, directives, policies, or recommendations of any authority of the Executive Branch relating to the collection, production, security, handling, dissemination, or utilization of intelligence, and/or classified material, shall not be applicable to Communications Intelligence activities, unless specifically so stated and issued by competent departmental or agency authority represented on the Board.... Other National Security Council Intelligence Directives to the Director of Central Intelligence and related implementing directives issued by the Director of Central Intelligence shall be construed as nonapplicable to Communications Intelligence activities... unless the National Security Council has made its directive specifically applicable to Communications Intelligence.[26]

Over the decades, the Department of Justice "had repeatedly sought (and invited) legislation from Congress which would both permit wiretapping and allow the use of the results or fruits of such surveillance at trial, but Congress, however, declined to act." In 1968, Congress would enact wiretap legislation—Title III of the Omnibus Crime Control and Safe Streets Act. Notably, however, a section of the act "expressly exempted the President's power from the coverage of the provisions of Title III."[27]

When you wonder why so many Americans doubt the trustworthiness of intelligence agencies, understand that from their respective inceptions, the FBI, the NSA, and telecoms would in fact violate aspects of the law with respect to wiretapping. That said, prosecution was difficult, if not impossible, because (as stated in the memorandum):

1. Prior Presidents and Attorneys General had notice of and, in at least once case, appeared to approve the operation;
2. Two Secretaries of Defense had tried to give the companies immunity;
3. Clause one of [section] 605 permits companies to disclose information "upon demand of lawful authority";
4. There was no divulgence outside the Executive Branch, so there was no divulgence within the meaning of [section] 605;
5. A use which benefits the Government is not the type of "use" contemplated by the statute;
6. It is not illegal to "ask" a company to give out copies of cables. If the company complies, it may be violating the statute but the recipient would not; and
7. The putative defendants acted in good faith, and they lacked the necessary intent to prove a violation of the law.

Further, "as it is clear from a review of an evolution of the President's power from its inception, the true scope of the President's power (with which the Bureau and the Agency were familiar) was unknown."

Congress did not escape scrutiny; by funding the initiatives, it had at least some notice of their activities, although very few members were equipped to understand them—a systemic imbalance that intelligence agencies continue to exploit. As for domestic surveillance by the CIA, again, Congress was not blameless. Again, according to the 1977 memorandum:

In July of 1973, William Colby testified before the Senate Armed Services Committee on his nomination to become

DCI. In response to a question specifically addressed to whether CIA was then engaged in assisting law enforcement agencies in addition to the FBI, Colby replied in the affirmative…. Since there was little doubt that at least some of CIA's information was governed by electronic surveillance, the Agency regards the lack of congressional objection as tacit approval of such dissemination.

Furthermore, National Security Council Intelligence Directive 5 delegated the CIA national security responsibilities abroad, and Title 50 U.S. Code Section 403 grants the Agency authority to perform "such additional services of common concern as the National Security Council determines can be more effectively accomplished centrally."

Perhaps the most important finding of the "prosecutive summary" is that in not a single instance was electronic intelligence used "for personal or partisan political purposes. The participants in every questionable operation, however oblivious or unmindful, appear to have acted under at least some colorable semblance of authority in what they conscientiously deemed to be the best interests of the United States."

The memorandum closes, "If the intelligence agencies possessed too much discretionary authority with too little accountability, that would seem to be a 35-year failing of Presidents and the Congress rather than the agencies or their personnel."

No one went to jail. In many ways, the hearings of 1975—the "Year of Intelligence," as Director Colby dubbed it—in fact emboldened the executive by infusing partisanship into the issue. Congressional oversight, already hapless at best, would further allow a certain permissiveness to intelligence activities depending on which party held the gavel. President Ford would fire Colby as director of central intelligence. In his autobiography, Colby wrote, "I believe I was fired because of the way I went about dealing with the C.I.A.'s crisis. My approach, pragmatically and philosophically, was in conflict with that of the President and his principal advisors." Colby's approach was sunlight—to cooperate with investigations "and try to educate the Congress, press, and public, as well as I could, about American intelligence, its importance, its successes and its failings."[28]

That simply would not do. The message was received, and thirty years later a new set of old problems would confront the intelligence community, the White House, and Congress.

Covert operations have inspired more acrimony between the legislative and executive branches than almost any other issue. Since the Year of Intelligence, Congress and the White House have furiously debated what information, exactly, Congress has the right to, and under what circumstances. It is an intragovernmental mirror of the wider secrecy debate.

In the earliest days of the Cold War, Congress showed little interest in the operational details of U.S. intelligence. There simply wasn't an appetite to know the nation's dirty secrets. As Leverett Saltonstall, senator from Massachusetts, explained in 1956, "It is not a question of reluctance on the part of CIA officials to speak to us. Instead, it is a question of our reluctance, if you will, to seek information and knowledge on subjects which I personally, as a member of Congress and as a citizen, would rather not have."[29]

Congressional attitudes toward executive power and the national security bureaucracy hardened in the wake of Watergate and revelations of controversial CIA actions at home and abroad. Standing over the festering remains of the Nixon administration, Congress had a gladiator's temperament. It asserted itself on the issue of covert actions in 1974 through the Hughes-Ryan Act, an amendment to the Foreign Assistance Act of 1961. Passed in 1974, Hughes-Ryan prevented the CIA from spending funds on covert activities unrelated to intelligence gathering unless the president "finds that each such operation is important to the national security of the United States and reports, in a timely fashion, a description and scope of such operation" to Congress.[30] The definition of "timely fashion" would be a matter of debate for decades. But at the time there was an understanding that briefings need not necessarily take place before a covert action had begun.[31]

As mundane as it sounds, the requirement for explicit presidential authorization of covert action was a significant reform. The "findings" stipulation meant that the CIA could not legally conduct its own freelance operations without the knowledge and consent of the president. This isn't to say that presidents weren't intimately aware of CIA operations, but rather that they always held a shield of plausible deniability. Hughes-Ryan was an attempt to force presidents to take responsibility for the intelligence community's activities.

Operations conducted in the context of a war declared by Congress, or executed in accordance with the War Powers Act, were exempted from the restrictions.[32] This was no small blessing, as at the time, the new law made for an onerous briefing arrangement given the scattershot congressional framework for intelligence oversight. Hughes-Ryan would eventually result in the requirement for the intelligence community to report to more than eight different committees: Armed Services, Foreign Affairs, Appropriations, and various intelligence committees in both the House and the Senate.[33]

Marathon committee appearances for covert action notifications proved unacceptable to the executive branch.[34] Shortly after Hughes-Ryan, the executive began restricting certain notification briefings to a "Gang of Four," consisting of the Senate and House intelligence committee leadership. It was a practice with no foundation in law but was tolerated by intelligence committee leadership.[35]

Today, journalists, whistleblowers, watchdog groups, and alert members of the intelligence community maintain a vigil so that mistakes of the past are not repeated. But are they successful, and is success even possible? Forty years after COINTELPRO, there are accusations that the government targets U.S. citizens who criticize policy. Glenn L. Carle, a former CIA case officer, has claimed that members of the Bush administration approached the agency "to get" Juan Cole, a University of Michigan professor and fierce critic of U.S. activities abroad.[36] The worst activities at Guantánamo Bay have ended, but Afghan government detainees incarcerated in a military prison at Bagram Airfield, Afghanistan, are often held without trial or timeline.[37]

These are the things we know about—the things that have been reported. But if an American public, inured to scandal and resigned to a kind of permanent shadow war, are no longer listening, will matters get better or worse? To ask the question is to answer it.

# CHAPTER 7

# Conspiracies

On August 2, 1964, three North Vietnamese torpedo boats engaged the USS *Maddox* in the Gulf of Tonkin. The *Maddox* had been collecting signals intelligence. When the PT boats entered attack formation, the *Maddox* fired warning shots, and when the boats launched torpedoes, the *Maddox* unleashed its main batteries. The incident ended with three crippled North Vietnamese vessels and no Americans harmed.

President Lyndon Johnson ordered the *Maddox* to resume patrols and gave a press conference warning the North against any further provocations. (The South Vietnamese government wanted total retaliation, but SIGINT suggested that the attack was a one-off by an overly aggressive North Vietnamese commander.) Meanwhile, the National Security Agency (NSA) was incensed at the attack on its ship and moved onto war footing. It directed all ears against North Vietnamese, and ordered priority status to any intercepts related to activities in the region.

Two nights later, a Marine signals intelligence team transmitted a warning that North Vietnamese PT boats were maneuvering in a way eerily similar to those of August 2. Meanwhile, the *Maddox* and the USS *Turner Joy* (sent to provide support) picked up a series of incomplete radar returns suggesting a North Vietnamese air and sea presence closing in fast, and received a priority alert from an NSA

listening post warning of an imminent attack. When sonar operators detected signals suggesting hostile vessels closing fast, the two
destroyers unleashed weapons on the radar blip for three and a half
hours. They reported two North Vietnamese boats destroyed.

Hours later, acting on the advice of the secretary of defense,
President Johnson authorized airstrikes against North Vietnam.
Meanwhile, the on-site commanders grew alarmed that no evidence
of an attack subsequently presented itself. Neither the *Turner Joy* nor
the *Maddox* took damage. There was never a visual confirmation of
North Vietnamese vessels; the attack was precipitated and directed
by radar and sonar, and bad weather may have confused instruments
and crew. The commander of the *Maddox* warned his superiors
against any further actions pending a review.

Pacific commanders began forwarding reports to the Pentagon
and the White House questioning the reliability of the contact report.
Signals intelligence that was initially certain now seemed ambigu-
ous at best. The most reliable confirmation available came from a
separate, classified SIGINT operation that had picked up a situation
report from the North Vietnamese describing an aggressive action it
had taken. The report was based on the translation of an intercepted
Vietnamese transmission, only parts of which were heard by the NSA.
And one key word was mistranslated: the North Vietnamese had said
that two "comrades" were lost, not two "ships." An error like this is
common in the din of battle, but with U.S. military leadership already
shifting to a war posture, here it would prove fatal.

The president can be forgiven for his response to the initial, erro-
neous report. Other mistakes can be attributed to the raw signals
intelligence forwarded to the White House; neither NSA nor CIA
specialists were consulted in the matter, and the SIGINT was never
properly analyzed. But either way, President Johnson, ready to widen
the U.S. footprint in Vietnam, presented the attack to the nation and
to Congress in the starkest possible terms.

In 1964, the NSA covered up its role in mistakenly reporting that
two U.S ships had been attacked. Through 2001, the NSA insisted
that a second attack did in fact occur two days later, and for years this
story didn't change. But it was a lie perpetuated by secrecy. As late
as the twenty-first century, the facts of the attack were classified and
marked as Secret/SI (which compartmented the material as secret

signals intelligence) as a means of perpetuating positive perceptions by Congress of the agency. Why would it do this? One agency historian suggests that it was embarrassed by its mistakes; that its leaders wanted to believe that a pattern of aggressive action by the North Vietnamese was emerging; and that the system set up to analyze the signals intelligence was confusing, compartmentalized, and unreliable.

The NSA did not create a lie to justify ensnaring the country in a tragic war, but when politics hardened some mixed intelligence into an unquestionable set of facts, they went along with it. The cumulative effect of the secrecy and cover-ups then fueled fantasies of conspiracy theorists and eroded trust in the government. It never seemed to occur to those in authority that using government power to punish political enemies, doing things to non–U.S. citizens that the general public would never approve of, and getting Americans involved in wars they didn't want can, and did, damage the ability of future presidents to protect the nation. Executive action in the post-Vietnam era is more tightly compartmented, and the latitude that the public often gives an executive during war has diminished over time. (Case in point: there will never be another military draft.)

History is replete with theories that the intelligence community and the military have used the power of secrecy to cover up covert actions so out of line with American priorities that it would shock our collective sensibility. The truth is less spectacular, though still troubling. The stovepiping of information—reporting secrets up the chain but sharing them with no one else, no matter how much the mission overlaps—is responsible for virtually every major intelligence failure of the modern age.

And there is a case to be made that the intelligence community as a whole is known more for its failures than its successes. This is the great burden that spymasters, analysts, and operatives in the field must bear. Arguably, the three most astounding failures of U.S. intelligence to protect the United States of America are the bombing of Pearl Harbor, the terrorist attacks of September 11, 2001, and the assassination of President John F. Kennedy.

Consider: Did the Navy or the FBI withhold an advance warning of the attack on Pearl Harbor from Roosevelt? No. Navy cryptanalysis had a field day with decrypts of Japanese diplomatic cable traffic. On documents sent to the White House, reports were labeled Top Secret/ MAGIC. (MAGIC being the compartment for communications intelligence on Japan.) Even though the FBI had become the country's de facto national intelligence service by 1940, the Navy did not share its MAGIC intelligence with J. Edgar Hoover or with the general and flag officers responsible for assessing the readiness of the Pacific fleet. Meanwhile, the FBI, focused primarily on Germans and communists, dutifully turned over every scrap of intelligence they collected about Japanese intentions to the White House—but not to naval intelligence analysts.[1] Collectively, the policymaking apparatus had a good sense of what Japan might do and had already begun preparations for an American entrance into the war. But intelligence (and thus the ability to derive value from it) was compartmentalized and dispersed. Secrets were properly kept; they just weren't properly used.

Before he died, Franklin D. Roosevelt had endorsed the policy of developing an atomic weapon for immediate employment. Astonishingly, Harry Truman was not briefed on the $3 billion doomsday project until twelve days after Roosevelt's death. When Henry Stimson, the secretary of war, and General Leslie Groves, director of the Manhattan Project, presented the bomb to the new president on April 24, it was as a fait accompli. The weapon would be ready in a few months, and it would be used to end the war.

Did the military deliberately manipulate the information available in order to ensure that Roosevelt's settled policy would not be altered? Many accounts of Truman's decisions subsequent to the revelation certainly suggest just such a thing. And if it were the case, it would represent one of the most egregious uses of secrecy in American history.

But in fact the opposite was true. Stimson and Groves were not of one mind about the wisdom of using the bomb. And Truman—a "decent, impulsive and simple man," was motivated as much by his own insecurity at his instant presidency as he was by any false picture of the war or any set of constricted choices presented by his advisers.[2] Truman knew what he was doing. And intelligence was rather incidental to his decision.[3]

Did the CIA keep information about plans for the Bay of Pigs invasion from President John Kennedy, afraid that he would balk if he knew the unlikelihood of insurgents successfully gaining a foothold in Cuba? No. Some charge that the Company had so much invested in the idea of regime change, especially following its successfully executed coup d'état in Guatamala, that it subordinated everything to the perceived menace from Havana.

But the truth is that the CIA's internal predictions were as optimistic as the ones that Allen Dulles, director of central intelligence, and his deputy Richard Bissell presented to Kennedy. For his part, Kennedy not only endorsed the goals of the plan, but also withheld details of it from advisers to the Joint Chiefs of Staff—all in the name of secrecy.[4] As the day of the invasion approached, Kennedy grew nervous about fallout from possible disclosures of U.S. involvement and yet was eager to show the Soviet adventurists exactly how unwelcome they were in our hemisphere. The president hedged his bets, pressing for "less noise" and cutting mission-essential air support. When Kennedy decided to move the landing point of the invasion eighty miles away from the Escambray Mountains—a political calculation—he neither asked nor was told by his military advisers that the Cuban exiles would have no place to hide with no mountains near their invasion site.[5]

The CIA held nothing back from Kennedy. Its own mistake was compartmentalization; the covert action staff never "read in" those CIA officers with the most strategic knowledge of Cuba. And the president, despite misgivings and suspicions, obsessed over keeping a project a secret until the very end. Using an exile force to overthrow Castro was not an implausible scenario when President Eisenhower signed a covert finding authorizing it. But by the time Kennedy had clipped the mission's wings to the nub, it was both implausible and became highly embarrassing.

Declassified CIA histories of the Bay of Pigs invasion that exonerate the Agency are predicated on knowledge gleaned from its failures after the fact. The Agency's covert operations division did everything well—which is of course beside the point. Compartmentalization and secrecy ensured that "everything well" was not nearly enough.[6]

• • •

Volumes have also been written about the Kennedy assassination. From November 22, 1963, to September 10, 2001, it was the go-to singularity for crackpots and conspiracy theorists. It's the shallow end of the insanity pool—a place where otherwise reasonable thinkers can wade in unreasonable ideas.

Here are the facts:[7]

Four years before Lee Harvey Oswald pulled the trigger of a Carcano M91/38 bolt-action rifle, the FBI opened a case file on him. The former U.S. Marine had defected to the Soviet Union, taking with him, according to his mother, his birth certificate. The G-men feared the Soviets might recruit Oswald as a spy, or return an impos- ter to the United States in his stead.[8] When Oswald returned four years later, special agents interviewed him, finding a man "cold, arro- gant, and difficult to interview." Oswald denied any wrongdoing, or that he had renounced his American citizenship. Two months later, the FBI again interviewed him and closed the file on him. Bureau sources in the Dallas Communist Party had never heard of the guy, and members of his family interviewed provided no actionable mate- rial. Notably, Oswald returned from the Soviet Union with a wife. The Bureau did not interview her, believing she could be adequately monitored in conjunction with her husband. Marina Oswald was, in fact, a point in her husband's favor: a foreigner living in Russia can- not marry without the permission of the Soviet government. It seems unlikely that the Soviet authorities would have permitted Oswald to marry and take his wife with him to the United States if they were contemplating using him alone as an agent.[9]

Again, Lee Harvey Oswald pinged the Bureau's radar when he sub- scribed to the *Worker*, a communist newspaper. The Dallas Field Office of the FBI noted this in Oswald's file and reopened the case the follow- ing year. At the time, agents did not interview Marina, because her hus- band "had been drinking to excess and beating [her], and the relevant FBI manual provision required that he allow a 'cooling off' period."*

---

*J. Edgar Hoover, for his part, considered this excuse "asinine," and James Gale, assistant director in charge of the Inspection Division, later wrote that, if anything, "Mrs. Oswald definitely should have been interviewed and the best time to get information from her would be after she was beaten up by her husband." Noted Hoover in the margin, "This certainly makes sense."

Oswald again found himself on the business end of the FBI after he moved to New Orleans to organize a pro-Castro organization. But for all of Oswald's strident Marxism and hostility, the interview yielded little new information for the file. It's not illegal to be a political malcontent or a jerk.

The Bureau wouldn't know that Oswald left New Orleans for Mexico until after he'd already returned to the United States, and then only after the CIA forwarded an intercepted cable stating that "Lee Henry Oswald" had been in contact with the Soviet embassy in Mexico City.

Oswald's next stop would be Texas, and national tragedy.

It should be very clear—it certainly was to FBI headquarters— that the Oswald case was mismanaged on an almost metaphysical level. After the president's assassination, J. Edgar Hoover intended to drop the hammer on vast swaths of special agents. "I do not intend to palliate the actions which have resulted in forever destroying the Bureau as the top level investigative organization," he noted. The Inspection Division, however, advised him that the Warren Commission would subpoena those agents, all of whom would be compelled to testify under oath that they had in fact been negligent. This would reflect poorly on the Bureau as a whole. Hoover's obsession with preserving the image of the FBI would, as always, be paramount in the director's agenda.

Occam's razor dictates that the president was slain by a deranged man, and that federal agents worked as federal employees often do: with minimum effort. Special agents with the New Orleans Field Office of the FBI had grown careless operating in an anti-Castro, anticommunist area. Dallas agents, meanwhile, either lacked the hard-charging spy hunter chops of those on the East Coast or were weary from decades of chasing phantom Texas commies. Likewise, the U.S. Secret Service let their guard down on a sunny day in Dallas, when adoring throngs surrounded the president.

What complicates matters is plain embarrassment by law enforcement and damage control by the Kennedy family. Whatever one's feelings of JFK, he was not shy about wielding executive power. He was stridently anti-Soviet. He ordered IRS audits with impunity. He micromanaged the CIA and developed a fascination with "wet" jobs—the kind of serious assassination missions only in the concept stages at the CIA. His brother, Attorney General Robert Kennedy, ordered (an agreeable) Hoover to illegally wiretap Martin Luther King Jr., for fear the civil rights leader might be a communist and thus an embarrassment to the party.

The Kennedy family had no interest in such matters being made public and did not ask for a sprawling investigation. Alan Dulles, Kennedy's former director of central intelligence, got himself installed on the Warren Commission, which was responsible for investigating the assassination. (As Lieutenant Colonel William Corson, a Marine Corps intelligence officer assigned to the CIA, noted, "Allen Dulles had a lot to hide.")[10] Meanwhile, President Johnson feared that the American political right would tie the Kennedy assassination to the Soviet Union (Johnson himself suspected Soviet involvement) and use the tragedy to start World War III. Every investigation pointed to Oswald, and no investigation found foreign involvement.

Still, the Johnson administration made it known to Hoover that any circumstantial evidence that might be used by politicians to stoke the flames of war was unwelcome. The Bureau issued multiple statements asserting Oswald's guilt, and did in fact launch a cover-up. Only Hoover wasn't hiding an X-Files–esque conspiracy; he was hiding red herrings. Simply put, everyone had something to hide when President Kennedy was killed, but it wasn't government complicity. It was government incompetence.

Over the years, the FBI has been accused of covering up its associations with Oswald (there were none), or of refusing to interview witnesses (virtually every witness who supposedly never talked to the FBI did in fact talk to the FBI), or even of complicity with the assassination itself. The FBI's first report on the investigation was thin, and the Warren Commission refused to rely on it, reinterviewing witnesses. This infuriated Hoover, who redoubled the Bureau's effort to track down every conceivable and even inconceivable lead. Still, despite the hard work put in by the Bureau (something even the agency's critics acknowledge), historians who follow the Kennedy assassination oeuvre blame the FBI for barely looking into Oswald's ties to Cuba, or at the mob's growing dislike for the Kennedy brothers, and the FBI's failure to deeply investigate the backgrounds of Oswald and Jack Ruby.[11]

Oswald was known to the FBI because of his defection to Russia and repatriation back into the United States. An agent named James Hosty was assigned to his case. In early November, Oswald showed up at the Dallas FBI Field Office with a note for Hosty, who was out conducting interviews. He was upset that Hosty, trying to figure out what Oswald was up to, had shown up at his home and harassed his wife. The Hosty note has been fodder—pretty much the only fodder—for conspiracy theorists since its existence was disclosed. His supervisor at the field office knew about it and asked Hosty to write a memo for the record about what happened. That memo was never sent to the FBI's internal registry, because it was theoretically embarrassing. (God forbid that Hoover find out.) But Hosty would testify fully and completely to the Warren Commission, and later to the House Select Committee on Assassinations. No evidence has ever challenged his story.

Because a local FBI office decided to cover up an incidental, indirect contact between a special agent and a recently repatriated U.S citizen who later killed the president, the specter of other malfeasance has simply been assumed by conspiracy theorists.[12] Had Hosty kept the note (which, because of all the cases he was working on at the time just didn't seem that important to him) and not destroyed the contemporaneous memo, there would be nothing in the record about the FBI's conduct before and after the assassination that would suggest anything other than candor in its dealings with independent investigators. The same can be said for the Secret Service, which was embarrassed by reports that a few agents had been drinking the night before the assassination (but nonetheless cooperated fully), and the CIA, which probably should have kept better tabs on Oswald overseas, but didn't. (The Agency's cooperation with the Warren Commission and later investigations waxed and waned in part because of the compartmented nature of intelligence operations.)

Many tangential connections with Oswald surfaced after the fact simply because they were only discovered later. Not once did the CIA ever refuse to provide the House Select Committee on Assassinations with a document on national security grounds.[13] If there was any erosion of faith that Americans had in their government as a result of the assassination, it was because the national security apparatus failed to prevent it.

There was no cover-up. There was no conspiracy.

And this is without considering the effects of social networks, instant information sharing, and the post-privacy age. As the World War II generation gives way to the next, papers and private files are passed onward. Considering the hundreds of people required to launch and maintain a conspiracy of assassination against the president, it's almost impossible to believe that someone hasn't turned up something—a smoking gun, so to speak. Yet nobody has posted a suspicious scanned document to Facebook, auctioned proof of government complicity on eBay, or simply handed files off to one of the thousands of reporters on Twitter. It defies credulity to claim a second generation of omertà-sworn LBJ loyalists.

But the nature of state secrecy ensures that there will always be conspiracy theorists. Kennedy is but one in a list that grows every day, despite the pesky meddling of the duo of logic and facts. And magic bullets are nothing—no conspiracy theory has defied logic and facts longer than the idea that the government has hidden proof of alien contact for the better part of a century.

## CHAPTER 8

# Inside the Enclave

R achel, Nevada, is an austere ranching town near the Groom Lake salt flat, with a friendly population of eighty, a small diner, a lone highway, and space aliens. (Well, nobody's actually *seen* the space aliens, though UFOs are a common occurrence.) Groom Lake adjoins one of the most protected sites in the United States, and indeed the world—the Air Force Flight Test Center (Detachment 3) of Edwards Air Force Base, better known as Area 51.

Privately owned land borders the perimeter of Area 51, but if the owners of those ranches decide to visit their inhospitable property, flight tests are canceled. The owners—private citizens—have signed nondisclosure agreements and are required by law to notify the Air Force of any visitors and to provide their names, dates of birth, and Social Security numbers to the U.S. Air Force Office of Special Investigations (OSI), which maintains a classified squad of agents devoted solely to the site and its counterintelligence needs. Visitors don't want to set off any sensors, and any attempts to photograph employees entering the Janet terminal at McCarran International Airport are likely to result in a not-so-friendly investigator from OSI making not-so-polite inquiries.

In theory and practice, any visitor lucky enough to catch sight of an odd-looking aircraft escaping at high speeds from Area 51, only to see it explode, seemingly shot down from nowhere, won't be allowed to stay to see government employees collect the remains.

That's bound to start some rumors.

The security and secrecy surrounding Area 51 has endured for more than sixty years. As we've seen, politics of varying sorts make sure the government isn't good at keeping secrets forever, and the shelf life of a secret is getting shorter and shorter. What, then, could stay so secret for so long, unless it was the worst of the worst, something no one must ever know, or something no one would ever believe?

The answer, of course, is that it is the least controversial kind of secret: new weapon systems. And many of the secrets created there, like flying drones, are no longer a secret. Theories of secret alliances with intergalactic governments aside, virtually anyone with a passing interest in aviation or defense is aware that the site is used to test secret programs. Commercial pilots know it as a restricted airspace—"the container"—where lethal force is used. Even the way that employees get to Area 51 is itself a part of popular culture. Janet Airlines, operated by EG&G, flies out of McCarran six times per day, its signature white jets with an ugly red stripe on the side being easily photographed by hobbyists. Microsoft Flight Simulator even uses the Janet flight to Area 51 to teach students how to turn a jet. As soon as the plane crosses into restricted airspace, an unidentified flying object whizzes by.

The U.S. Air Force's obsessive secrecy ensures that Americans remain confused about the site. Its program managers learned long ago, too, that mystique and money are related concepts. The more vital to national security Area 51 *seems* to be, the less vulnerable to the budget ax it will become.

But the impishness of engineers and program managers provides a glimpse into the current roster of projects. Historian Trevor Paglen managed to obtain unit and mission patches from crews that worked at the site as recently as 2008, publishing a coffee table book that contained numerous artistic references to highly classified projects. He noticed that many patches contain joking references to aliens. Others have six stars—usually five stars in one configuration and one star in another (5 and 1, or 51). Still others refer to their particular aircraft's unique stealth capabilities or high speeds. In their own way, using signs and symbols, they are bragging. Though the employees theoretically could not explain the meaning of the patches to outsiders, the fact that they exist (and they *are* real) is an outlet for the basic urge that accompanies most satisfying types of work. The employees want recognition for what they do. Because of this impulse, in many ways we know more about specific projects being tested at Area 51 than we do about the site itself. Also, a group of former Groom Lake engineers and employees operate an alumni website and regularly talk to journalists about their experiences, Air Force censorship be damned.[1]

The Air Force acknowledges that it has an "operating location near Groom Lake, Nevada," but that is the extent to which the public affairs officers are briefed, and that is the extent to which they are willing to share anything about the site with anyone.* It is hot and miserable in the desert, which is one of the reasons the location was chosen. It's a natural deterrent to visitors who might lurk and stumble onto things they are not supposed to see. Ironically, under the arms control Open Skies Treaty ratified by the United States, foreign countries can capture aerial images of anything they want. The United States has even provided Russia with an airport diagram of the facility.[2] But no photographs of the complex have entered the public domain since 1968; the National Archives segregates any imagery of the site that should have, under law, been automatically declassified. In 2000, John Pike, then director of the Public Eye program at the Federation of American Scientists (FAS), took advantage of the newly flourishing world of commercial satellite companies. In theory you could order images of whatever you wanted. And FAS wanted to see what would happen if they asked for pictures of Groom Lake.

Tim Brown, an imagery analyst who worked with Pike on the project, says, "There's nothing really normal about the place. It's a

---

*Something it was forced to admit when former employees sued the Air Force over the effects of alleged exposure to toxic fumes, prompting the Clinton administration to assert a state secrets privilege and order the Environmental Protection Agency to exempt the site from certain federal regulations.

ripple in the space of reality." In other words, it was the perfect subject to test whether the new commercial satellite technology could be used to shed light on long-held secrets like Groom Lake.

They placed an order with Space Imaging, a commercial satellite company, for a one-meter image of the area. "We said, 'Look, here are the coordinates, we want this facility, and that's that.' And then we waited. They said it could take weeks."

They waited. Weeks went by with no response. Then a different satellite company released a less precise two-meter image of Groom Lake from the Russian Aviation and Space Agency. When Groom's veil was pierced, Pike and Brown's order suddenly came through. "The day after, wouldn't you know, all of a sudden Space Imaging found our order behind a file cabinet and said, 'Oh yeah, here's your image.'"

When Pike and Brown finally got the photos, they found that Groom Lake was a hive of activity. The photographs showed numerous newly constructed hangars, a baseball field, and other recreation areas, as well as evidence of a recent runway expansion. It was vindication for Pike. "Highlighting the discrepancy between what the public knows, and what the government will acknowledge, is a key instrument in teasing out the absurdities of the security enclave," he wrote. "There is no better opportunity for such mirth than Area 51. The U.S. Government has only recently acknowledged the 'fact of the existence' of this facility, despite ample publicity and super-abundant speculation over the past decades."[3]

For Pike, this gap showed that government secrecy inhabited a bizarre alternate universe where the perpetuation of secret aircraft programs—programs generally designed to further the interests of defense industry and to promote an ideology that presupposes future military conflict—is the primary end, rather than secrecy to protect national security interests.

One irony of the photo release was that the Russian government surely had higher-resolution photos. The U.S. government had placed a restriction on the image resolution that commercial providers could sell to private customers. It also theoretically retained "shutter control" over releasable imagery of sensitive sites.[4]

•   •   •

The Air Force Flight Test Center's Detachment 3 manages operations at Groom Lake for all customers, including the CIA. Those who work there call it "the remote site," "the alternate site," or simply "the site." With the largest dry lake bed outside Edwards Air Force Base in neighboring California, it remains the place where the Department of Defense and the CIA test their secret aviation projects and exploit and test aircraft parts stolen from other countries.

About two thousand government employees and contractors touch ground there at least once a year. According to the résumés of several engineers who have served at the site, Detachment 3 services about one hundred continuing projects, a dozen of which are fully realized prototype aircraft.* Many—especially the unmanned aircraft—are managed by the Air Force's new Rapid Capability Office, which exists on paper as an acquisitions team, and by the Air Force's Big Safari Program Office, which for decades has overseen the acquisition, fielding, and testing of secret intelligence, surveillance, and reconnaissance planes.[5] Lockheed Martin and Northrup Grumman have a full-time presence on the site.

To protect the facility, the Air Force restricts all related information to a special access program known by the initials CD. In a four-hour session, initiates are "read in" to the basic purpose of the site, its history, its security procedures, and how the base is restricted even to those who are given permission to be there. Groom Lake's 350 security officers are contractors drawn from the same firm that manages the flights to and from the site: EG&G Technical Services. They actually went on strike after 9/11 because of too much overtime, the union steward told a Las Vegas newspaper.[6] The Air Force security squadron ostensibly assigned to the remote site (the 99th Security Forces Group) has no actual presence there.[7]

Initiates are also told that the neighboring Tonopah Test Range, a 336,000-acre site operated under Department of Energy cover (it used to be known as Area 52) is also not to be acknowledged, although the Department of Energy does so freely, as do contractors bragging about their projects there.[8] Formally, Lockheed Martin, under a DOE contract, uses the area to test the nuclear weapons

---

*On his LinkedIn profile, one such engineer wrote that he worked "on a DOD national electronic combat test and evaluation range for tri-service customers."

stockpile reliability (checking, for instance, whether fuses and elec-
tromagnetic pulse shielding work properly).* Informally, the Army,
the Air Force, and the Navy have program offices at the site (the U.S.
Army Threat Systems Management Office is one of them).[9] The Air
Force occasionally uses Tonopah Test Range as a cover for projects
that were actually tested at the Groom Lake site. Lockheed Martin's
once highly classified RQ-170 Sentinel drone was tested at Groom
Lake beginning in 2006; officially, the Air Force says it was tested
at Tonopah Test Range. It has also served as a forward staging base
for foreign aircraft parts that are due to be exploited by engineers
at the Groom Lake site. Often the two sites are used together for what
the government calls Foreign Material Exploitation (FME) Tactical
Material Exploitation missions. (First, figure out what the enemy aircraft is capable of. Then figure out how your pilots can effectively
counter the threat.)

In 2006, the government declassified a program called
CONSTANT PEG, revealing that the United States had acquired
numerous Soviet aircraft and brought pilots to the Tonopah Test Range
to fly these aircraft with other pilots to test their skills against actual
Russian jets. In 1984, the vice commander of the Air Force Systems
Command was killed at Groom Lake while flying a MiG-23 — something the government unsuccessfully attempted to cover up at the time.[10]

The Air Force implies that the end of the Cold War prompted
the end of such testing and reverse engineering, but the U.S. government continues to use Groom Lake and Tonopah Test Range for the
same purposes today. The cover-name conventions likewise remain
the same. In 2006, Groom Lake was used for testing Su-27 Flankers
(Russia's version of the F-15) that the United States had purchased
from one of the former Soviet republics. Flying the foreign aircraft
can be dangerous, and most of the FME data is used to create virtual
simulations of foreign fighters. Somewhere on base is a repository of

---

*According to the DOE, "Sandia Corporation (a subsidiary of Lockheed Martin
Corporation through its contract with the U.S. Department of Energy [DOE]),
National Nuclear Security Administration (NNSA), Sandia Site Office (SSO), oper-
ates the Tonopah Test Range (TTR) in Nevada. Westinghouse Government Service,
TTR's operations and maintenance contractor, performs most environmental pro-
gram functions."

foreign aircraft parts and systems, and the United States has billion-dollar procurement programs in place to find and steal them.

Groom Lake has to control its employee access somehow. As of 2008, its site badges were emblazoned with the crest of the Air Force Flight Test Center. AFFTC owns land abutting the complex, but officially (and unsurprisingly) has no presence in Nevada. Its home is at Edwards Air Force Base in California, but flight trackers have identified jets that regularly travel between Edwards and Tonopah Test Range, Nellis, and McCarran—and also, apparently, Groom Lake.[11]

Because flights out of McCarran are difficult to keep secret, the detachment's security team often brings employees in by bus. Some shuttles might be manifested for Site 1 but will deliberately go to Site 4, something that workers must know in advance, lest they get dropped off somewhere at the site that they're not supposed to be and see something they're not supposed to see.

When the site needs power lines replaced, it transports specially cleared personnel in blacked-out vans, although the workers are forced to wear frosted goggles, or "froggles," that provide an extra measure of visual obscurity. This may have been necessary when Area 51's existence wasn't acknowledged, but it's hard to imagine that the workers aren't aware of where they're headed now.

Getting time to test your secret project is difficult, and program managers sometimes find the site's security restrictions overly onerous. Security officers at the site's Range Coordination Agency often forbid offsite transportation of any data or telemetry transmitted to or from an aircraft that indicate the aircraft had been at the site. In practice, that means that the Air Force or the CIA has to create a separate security compartment for flight data recorders and instruments that are tested there, even though everyone involved in the particular program has been cleared at the Top Secret/Sensitive Compartmented Information level.

Remote sensor platforms (drones) are particularly hard to test. The aircraft are outfitted and launched by a ground unit at the site, and they're operated by pilots and technicians elsewhere—sometimes at nearby Creech Air Force Base in Nevada, or at Hanscom Air Force Base in Massachusetts. Site rules require that no latitude or longitude data be transmitted outside the airspace, so systems engineers have to create special software programs specific to the testing phase. The risk in this case is miniscule, given that the data is encrypted and the chances of it being intercepted, decrypted, deciphered, and exploited by a foreign government is nil. But the site makes the rules.

Anytime an alien hunter or curious passerby triggers a remote sensor, crews have to quickly push aircraft and equipment back into hangars. The Detachment receives intelligence from Air Force units tracking Chinese, Soviet, and Israeli satellites. If there's any chance that satellite (commercial or foreign) might be overhead during any given day, the site will be locked down.

There are several other areas inside the National Security Test Site where spooky things happen. The Air Force tests missile defense systems and new radars at the Tonopah Electronic Combat Range. The U.S. Joint Special Operations Command and the CIA maintain training facilities. The Defense Threat Reduction Agency also maintains a presence inside the container.

Even in our hypothetical opening example, the only thing hypothetical is that anyone would have seen it. When the Predator program began its tests at the site in the mid-1990s, Detachment 3 managers insisted on fitting the aircraft with special automatic detonation devices that would destroy the drones if they wandered out of the restricted airspace.* On the maiden voyage of one of the first test Predators, its operator increased its speed beyond allowable tolerances. This somehow sent bad data to the communication module on the detonation device, which sent an error message to a ground unit that had interrogated it. All of this resulted in a computer generated auto-destruct order. A $30 million prototype was destroyed—a victim of an obsession with operational secrecy.

Yet it is hard to fault the government for a zero-risk policy. GRASS BLADE was the developmental nickname for two Black Hawk helicopters built in secret by the U.S. Army Integrated Aviation Systems 21 group, working under the umbrella of the Applied Aviation Technology Directorate at Fort Eustis, Virginia. For three years beginning in 2007, engineers and technicians developed

---

*Officially, the Predator was tested at another range on the Nellis complex, the Indian Springs Auxiliary Airfield.

sound-dampening devices, mixed special resins and paints, and laboriously and rigorously subjected the resulting helicopter prototypes to radar and acoustic tests. Once assembled, the helicopters were transferred to Groom Lake in 2010 and given the operational nickname TRACTOR PULL. At Groom Lake, pilots from the U.S. Joint Special Operations Command Aviation Testing and Evaluation Group practiced flying them. To those who didn't know about TRACTOR PULL, the gray helicopters often seen at the Groom Lake looked like mechanical wolves and soon acquired the nickname "Air Wolves." Had the program been compromised, the military would not have had a way to clandestinely transport Navy SEALs to Abbottabad on the morning of May 3, 2011.

CHAPTER 9

# The Tip of the Spear

For the SEALs of Red Squadron, putting two bullets in a primary target wasn't asking much. The insertion aircraft were a little different, a little more crowded than standard Black Hawks, owing to some bolted-on stealth technology recently tested at Area 51. Destination X, a fair-weathered hill town only thirty miles from the capital of Pakistan and well within that country's borders, would make for a daring incursion. One blip on a station's radar would scramble Pakistani jets armed with 30 mm cannons, air-to-air missiles, and very possibly free-fire orders. Still, it wasn't anyone's first time in Pakistan, and it wouldn't be the last. When you're fighting shadow wars everywhere from Iran to Paraguay, quiet infiltrations with no margin for error are simply the expected way to do business.

Those men of the Naval Special Warfare Development Group (DEVGRU), better known as SEAL Team Six, had spent weeks (and, it later occurred to the them, months) training for the mission. That night, the aircrews of the U.S. Army 160th Special Operations Aviation Regiment (Airborne) piloted the one-of-a-kind stealth helicopters through Pakistan's well-guarded and highly militarized border. CIA paramilitaries acted as spotters on the ground and monitored the situation from afar. A ratlike RQ-170 Sentinel unmanned aerial vehicle operated from Nevada by the U.S. Air Force 30th Reconnaissance Squadron hovered about fifty thousand feet above

Abbottabad, equipped with a special camera designed to penetrate thin layers of cloud and down to a three-story compound below.

The drone was ordered by defense planners to provide a covert way to monitor nuclear weapons sites in Iran and North Korea. The National Security Council, however, had granted special permission for its use over Pakistan. To mitigate diplomatic fallout in the event the drone was to crash in Pakistan, the U.S. Defense Department disallowed nuclear-sensing devices from the aircraft, in opposition to the wishes of the CIA. Pakistan was incredibly sensitive about U.S. surveillance of their nuclear establishment; the CIA was obsessed with it.

Transmitters on this drone's wing beamed encrypted footage to an orbiting National Reconnaissance Office satellite, which relayed the signal to a ground station in Germany. Another satellite hop brought the feed to the White House and elsewhere.

The Sentinel had spent months monitoring and mapping the Abbottabad compound. The area had fallen under scrutiny after intelligence analysts learned that the high-value target in question communicated by courier. Captured enemy combatants—some subjected to enhanced interrogation techniques—fleshed out details. A name. A description. A satellite first spotted the courier's van, and the drone circled. Ground crews in Afghanistan attached sophisticated laser devices and multispectral sensors to the drone's underbelly, allowing the U.S. National Geospatial-Intelligence Agency to create a three-dimensional rendering of that little piece of Pakistan. Details were so precise that analysts managed to compute the height of the tall man in question they nicknamed "the Pacer." When it wasn't gathering imagery intelligence (IMINT), the drone would sometimes fly from Jalalabad, Afghanistan, to Abbottabad and back, on signals intelligence (SIGINT) operations, listening to the routine chatter of Pakistan's air defense forces so that U.S. National Security Agency analysts could determine patterns and alert configurations.

There was a scare just three weeks before the Abbottabad raid. While the drone was in transit over a Pakistani airbase, translators listening to the feed picked up Pakistani air controllers alerting crews to an orbiting American reconnaissance plane. Had the Sentinel— designed to evade detection and crucial to the operation—been outed? Moments later, when a Pakistani air controller ordered its fighter pilots to ascend to the altitude of "the EP-3," Americans could exhale. The Pakistanis were merely practicing for the possible straying of an EP-3E Aries surveillance plane from its permitted flight path from the Indian Ocean into Pakistan.

Among the list of units that participated in the Abbottabad mission—otherwise known as Operation Neptune's Spear—there are others still unknown but whose value was inestimable. Some entity of the U.S. government, for example, figured out how to completely spoof Pakistani air defenses for a while, because at least some of the U.S. aircraft in use that night were not stealthy. Yet at the core of it all were the shooters and the door-kickers of Red Squadron, SEAL Team Six, and a dog named Cairo. It took just forty minutes from boots on dirt to exfiltration, and although they lost one helicopter to the region's thin air (notoriously inhospitable to rotary-wing aircraft), they expended fewer rounds than would fill a single magazine, snatched bags of evidence, and collected a single dead body.

The team detonated the lost Black Hawk and slipped like phantoms back to Jalalabad, where DNA samples were taken from the body. They loaded into MH-47 Chinooks and again passed over now-cleared parts of Pakistan, then landed on the flight deck of the waiting USS Carl Vinson aircraft carrier. In accordance with Muslim rites, a short ceremony was held above deck (all crew members were confined below), and the body of Osama bin Laden was tossed overboard. The after-action report doesn't go into much more detail than that, but the story of Abbottabad, of seamless integration between elite special forces and the intelligence community, includes many more layers. Lost in the sparkling details of the raid is the immense logistical challenge of providing reliable communications. There was a contingency plan; military interrogators were in place on the Vinson, along with CIA officers, just in case bin Laden was captured alive. The 75th Ranger Regiment played an unknown role in the proceedings. And someone had to later exfiltrate the CIA officers who were on the ground.

The next day, the world changed, but perhaps for no one more so than Red Squadron, SEAL Team Six, and its parent, the U.S. Joint Special Operations Command (JSOC), the president's secret army. At the end of a ten-year American crucible of terrorist attacks and two wars, and as the psychic burden of its citizenry was made all the heavier by a collapse in the financial markets and a near-total dysfunction in government, Operation Neptune's Spear offered the tantalizing suggestion that something in government *could* work and *did* work. Here, government agencies worked together in secret, in pursuit of a single goal. No boundaries separated the intelligence community from the military or one military unit from another. In the parlance, it was the perfection of a process thirty years in the making—operations by joint military branches ("Purple") conducted seamlessly with multiple agencies of the intelligence community ("Gold").

It was the finest example of the apparatuses of state working in concert and probably the finest example of government secrecy approved of by the general public.

JSOC (pronounced "JAY-sock") is a special military command established in 1980 by a classified charter. Its purpose is to quietly execute the most challenging tasks of the world's most powerful nation with exacting precision and with little notice or regard. The Command is clandestine by design. When it makes mistakes, this often means that its singularly lethal techniques were applied to the wrong person, or that the sheer exuberance of being the elite of the elite dulled the razor-sharp moral calculus required of war fighters who have so much autonomy.

Before the terrorist attacks of September 11, 2001, JSOC spent twenty years quietly operating on the periphery of the armed forces, inventing tactics to do the impossible and succeeding in execution. It recruited some of the best soldiers and sailors in the world and put them through the most intense training ever developed by a modern military. The last ten years have witnessed JSOC transform itself and, in so doing, change way the United States and her allies fight wars.

This is not an exaggeration or some attempt to burnish the Command's mythos. Consider these two strategic objectives: suppressing the insurgency in Iraq so that conventional forces could regroup and mount a renewed counteroffensive, and degrading the capabilities of al-Qaeda. Without JSOC's aggressive fusion of intelligence with operations in real time, and without its warp-speed tempo in tracking high-value targets, the United States would very likely still be slugging it out in the trenches of Iraq, and al-Qaeda would still be a credible threat to U.S. security. Whatever your view of the Iraq campaign or of war itself, and whatever your tolerance for the often nebulous morality of special operations missions, it behooves you to understand how this type of unconventional warfare evolved and what it means as the U.S. military faces significant spending cuts.

The bin Laden assassination bore all of the hallmarks of a modern JSOC operation. It was *joint*, involving military elements both white and black from different branches of the armed forces. It was *interagency*, coordinated with the CIA and leveraging the assets of much of the U.S. intelligence community, largely without conflict. It was legal *enough*; the razing force was temporarily placed under the control of Leon Panetta, the director of the CIA, because JSOC isn't strictly authorized to conduct operations in Pakistan. It was also resource-intensive, involving millions of dollars' worth of secret equipment, significant satellite bandwidth, the attention of national policymakers, and a swath of military personnel belonging to various commands.

JSOC is the secret army of the president of the United States. But what does "secret" mean when it involves units virtually everyone has heard of? By the numbers, JSOC's cover has not changed, and its subordinate units must "study special operations requirements and techniques, ensure interoperability and equipment standardization, plan and conduct special operations exercises and training, and develop joint special operations tactics."[1] Although that's not a lie, it is to some degree obfuscation. JSOC does indeed plan and conduct special operations exercises, but it also conducts highly sensitive missions that require particularly specialized units. Many of those units have passed into American cultural legend.

In many ways, this mythologizing began with Colonel Charlie Beckwith, the father of Delta Force and its first commanding officer, who wrote a book about his unit. Journalist Mark Bowden later revealed in astonishing detail the operational effectiveness, bravery, and brutal efficiency of Delta operators in sustained combat against overwhelming numbers as exhibited in the Battle of Mogadishu. (Ridley Scott would later commit the operation to celluloid in the film *Black Hawk Down*.) Eric Haney, a former senior noncommissioned officer of Delta, produced a television show called

*The Unit,* based on a book he'd previously written. Years earlier, Charlie Sheen and a camera crew were inexplicably granted access to the actual SEAL Team Six compound in Virginia to film a movie about DEVGRU. And of course, the beat reporters in Fayetteville, North Carolina, where Delta is headquartered, and Dam Neck, Virginia, where DEVGRU is headquartered, know the names of the colonels and the captains responsible for the military's most daring forces.

So it's not quite right to say that the two principal counterterrorism units of JSOC are secret, per se. A better description might be that they are *officially unacknowledged.* And though he can't come out and say it, that's what Ken McGraw, a spokesman for U.S. Special Operations Command, means when he tells reporters he won't be talking about the "special missions units" with them.

Right now, with mostly successes visible to the public, we respect that this secrecy is for operational security. However, that respect may not last forever, because secrecy exists also to remove layers of accountability. JSOC doesn't want most of our elected leaders to know what it is up to, especially in cases where things go wrong. And most of our elected leaders would rather not know, for the same reason. The secrecy apparatus of JSOC is prodigious in scope, and the Command camouflages itself with cover names, black budget mechanisms, and bureaucratic parlor tricks to keep it that way. It is heavily compartmentalized; the commanding officer of Delta knew about Neptune's Spear only days before the operation. To get around Freedom of Information Act inquiries, JSOC security officers advise operators and analysts to "stick to paper and safes," as one intelligence operative describes, meaning that for sensitive conversations, nonmilitary cell phones are preferable to classified military computer networks where every keystroke is recorded for use by counterintelligence investigators. JSOC currently participates in more than fifty special access programs, each one designating a particular operation or capability. The programs are given randomly selected and always-changing nicknames and are stamped with code words such as Meridian and Principal that are themselves classified.

JSOC perfectly represents the two sides of the secrecy coin. Most of their secrets—new technologies, new targets, new techniques—will not be a secret from our enemies once the operation is carried out. However, there will be things—there are almost surely already things—that they hope no one outside JSOC ever learns about.

The Command's secrecy can intimidate outsiders, but such an operational culture is a necessity. Among its most sensitive tasks in recent years has been to establish contingency plans to secure the Pakistani nuclear arsenal in the event that the civilian government falls in a military coup d'état. Here, policymakers are given a welcome choice—a choice not to know, which allows senior administration officials to reliably and honestly explain to the public and to Pakistani officials that they are confident in Pakistan's ability to keep its arsenal safe without having to lie. Only a few political appointees and members of Congress need to know the nature of such contingency plans. Incidentally, JSOC is also a key part of the classified contingency plans to preserve the U.S. civilian government in the event of a coup from the military or anyone else.

It's clear, however, that the blankets of secrecy are fraying. "If you Google JSOC," Admiral William McRaven, the commander of the Special Operations Command (SOCOM), a former DEVGRU operator and the previous commander of JSOC, has said, "you can find out pretty much everything you want to know."

Yet JSOC has done a decent job of keeping to itself. The missions we hear about are but a fraction of those it completes. Likewise, JSOC has done a remarkable job of hiding from the public the incredible scope of the missions it is assigned and a fine job of preventing anyone outside the circle of trust from obtaining all but the slightest knowledge of its history, organization, function, and structure.

"Brian," the decorated Naval Special Warfare Development Group deputy commander who planned Neptune's Spear, had expected to read a lot about his unit—some of it even true—and had participated in conversations with colleagues about the future of the cover narrative given to JSOC. Maybe it was time to loosen things up a bit. A big mission such as this would inevitably degrade JSOC's capacity to some nontrivial degree, as the efficacy of special operations forces is often inversely proportional to the publicity given to the mission.

Brian is no longer a DEVGRU commander, but as with all JSOC colonels and captains, his identity is considered a state secret, protected by the Defense Cover Program. (Brian is also not his real name; because Nicholas Schmidle referred to him by that name in his excellent August 8, 2011, *New Yorker* article "Getting bin Laden," we will too.)

As Brian worked with SEAL element planners and intelligence analysts in a warren of rooms at CIA headquarters in Langley during the first months of 2011, he was bemused to find that he was worried about success. He feared that in the operation's aftermath, reporters might harass the Command for more information about how it worked and what it did. This was, admittedly, a mild concern. There has always been some level of curiosity, and there always would be. A more paramount concern was that someone might leak details of the mission before it happened. The closer to the witching hour, the higher the risk of a compromise. Simply put, JSOC commanders didn't trust everyone at the White House who would have to be "read in" to the operation. Admiral McRaven did, however, trust Panetta and the director's decision to brief certain lawmakers on the House and Senate select committees on intelligence. (Though no lawmakers received operational briefings about the mission until Osama bin Laden was introduced to the Arabian Sea, the chair and ranking committee members were given cryptic notifications by Panetta that the operation would happen about six hours before it did.)

Thankfully, Brian's initial fears proved unfounded. Yet what he did not expect were the throngs of tourists flocking to Dam Neck, Virginia, hoping to spot members of the team at known SEAL bars and haunts. Or the two motion pictures put almost immediately into production, with filmmakers contacting members of the squadron. Or the History Channel and the Discovery Channel specials, with commentators either knowing nothing at all or revealing too much. Even President Barack Obama participated in one of them. If, as it seemed, JSOC was no longer secret, what would it be? How could it be effective when its existence was all but officially acknowledged and its activities openly reported? Brian, in fact, turned out to be the country's best secret keeper for a while. Because Neptune's Spear was his operation, he designed its security protocols. What that meant, in practice, was that almost nothing was committed to paper. There were no "read-aheads" distributed to aides in advance of meetings. No one took notes. "We did what the enemy did," he said. "We went off the grid." He kept a lot of the operational details inside his brain.

"It increasingly became a concern for us that it was going to leak," he said. "We had a few operational constraints, one of which was that we needed to go in on an illumination cycle in Pakistan. That was at the beginning of the month, when the moon was bright. I was concerned that if we waited for June, four long weeks—the chances would have risen exponentially that something would leak."

When Brian says "leak," he doesn't mean a front-page story in the *Washington Post*. "Even if there had been some chatter about it, if any of that had gotten back to the Pakistani government, it would have been over."

When he assumed command of SOCOM, Admiral McRaven sent word to JSOC: the story of U.S. special operations forces is a good one, and he wanted to talk forthrightly with the American people about it. Americans could, and should, be proud of their special operations forces. There would by necessity be exceptions: he would protect the identities of those involved in missions, and he would never talk about missions themselves. In keeping with this promise, he declined to talk about Neptune's Spear or any other mission for this book.

By some estimates, 80 percent of JSOC missions launched before 2000 remain classified. Some of these are likely secrets they hope will never get out. Operators from Delta Force and SEAL Team Six infiltrated China with the CIA and mapped the locations of Chinese satellite transmission facilities in the event that the United States ever needed to disable them. On more than one occasion, they've engaged Iranian troops on Iranian soil. They've fought in Lebanon, in Peru, in the Palestinian territories, and in Syria. They also spent a lot of time shooting up abandoned buildings in U.S. cities, rehearsing hostage rescue situations of every kind. The Command hoards contingency planners. When the president travels overseas, a JSOC team usually shadows him. Its members are trained to take charge should the mammoth security structure of the U.S. Secret Service break down.

Although the bin Laden mission may have been less complicated than other, less well-known operations, it was in many ways the culmination of decades of work. Since the terrorist attacks of September 11, 2001, no single entity—not even the CIA—has done more to degrade and isolate al-Qaeda, to prevent Hezbollah from funneling drug money to terrorists, or to check Iranian influence. Pick a threat, and there's a good chance the Command is there "mowing the lawn." (This metaphor is a favorite of JSOC flag and general officers.) The cost of doing so much—indeed, the necessary cost of success—is that the secret force is no longer impenetrably black. Its operators are tired. The casualty rate has been high. And a perennial, hush-hush debate inside the Pentagon has grown vociferous.

During the last decade, the United States has created the most impressive rapid military response machine in the history of the world. Simply stated, JSOC can kill more efficiently and effectively than any other force on earth. How then can we safely, legally, and responsibly employ it?

The law is murky. The CIA is permitted to engage in something called "covert action," and can use JSOC to do so. By law, a covert action is "an activity or activities of the United States Government to influence political, economic, or military conditions abroad, where it's intended that the role of the United States Government will not be apparent or acknowledged publicly."[2] As we have discussed, the president must formally "find" that such an activity is warranted and must inform select members of Congress in advance.

The legal definition of "covert action" does not cover intelligence collection; it does not cover "traditional diplomatic or military activities, or their routine support" or support to law enforcement or other government agencies. In practice, if another agency is engaged in something approximating a covert action, the CIA can stand in support of that agency and not be subject to the statutory requirements imposed by Congress. In theory, it is tempting for a president who wants to do something secret to charter it under something like "traditional military activities," which is a phrase that is sufficiently balloonlike to purchase just about everything that JSOC does.

Since its founding, the CIA has been a bit of a free body in the orbit of secret activities. Its regulation by Congress has a lot to do with the tendency of its leaders to push the boundaries of policy and not be held accountable for it. The Department of Defense, however, is a very hierarchical organization, and accountability is not left to a separate branch of government. It is embedded within the organizational structure and culture of the American defense establishment, more so after the Goldwater-Nichols reforms of the 1980s. JSOC reports to the civilian secretary of defense, who reports to the civilian National Security Council and then directly to the president. Internally, JSOC components are constrained by the services (the U.S. Army and the U.S. Navy) that fund them, and their leaders are held to account by the oaths they've sworn, the combatant commands they work under, the umbrella command they work for, and by the Joint Chiefs of Staff, to say nothing of the civilian under secretary who oversees special operations. Many more people know about JSOC operations than might be read in to a CIA "compartmented" for a covert action. Congress, however, isn't necessarily in that number, which is one reason many observers of secret wars tend to worry about JSOC and accountability. But it *is* accountable—just not to Congress.

Practically speaking, Congress cannot by its nature and expertise or the Constitution tell the commander in chief how to conduct a war. And if Congress has deemed the inchoate battle against terrorism to be such a war, there is very little it can do, in retrospect, to regather or reclassify certain types of operations as distinct from that war. The big battles of tomorrow—countercyber, counternarcotics, and counterterrorism, are American defense priorities. The Defense Department has all the authority it needs to resource and execute its mission. Special operations forces will fight many of these "small wars," and they are legally permitted to operate without oversight in ways that the CIA legally cannot. If Congress finds this untenable, it can change the law. That it has not suggests that it is comfortable with the arrangement; its silence provides the consent that the president seeks for the employment of his secret army.

It's safe to assume that most Americans are just fine with secret counternarcotics missions in Venezuela. But what about when the nexus of "traditional military activities" includes the possibility that a U.S. citizen will be killed? Indeed, can a "traditional military activity" be directly targeted at an American overseas? In the system of secrets, would it be more palatable for any such action to be classified as a "covert action" and thus more accountable to Congress? Here the executive branch is on shaky ground. In 2012, news leaked that President Obama was consolidating the various permission structures across government that allowed drone-based missile strikes outside of declared war zones. This was greeted with some dismay but was arguably a necessary development. When the ultimate executive power is used, it ought to be the executive himself who is held accountable to the public—not some midlevel functionary at the CIA's counterterrorist center. At least now we know exactly who's to blame when civilians or noncombatants are slain in America's secret wars.

In no way are the moral objections to drone warfare answered by such post facto accountability, and there is no moral doctrine that justifies the accidental killing of an American juvenile. On October 14, 2011—a few weeks after his father, Anwar al-Awlaki, was killed in the Yemeni desert—sixteen-year-old Abdulrahman al-Awlaki was blown to bits by an American strike while he was eating lunch along with (we are told) some of his father's friends. The younger al-Awlaki did not choose a life of terrorism; he was born into it. He did not renounce his American citizenship. He did not encourage, as his father had, terrorism against the United States. He was simply *there*. The Obama administration will not acknowledge his death formally, even though his blood is on their hands. The administration believes they are constrained by the secrecy of the drone program, but they also know that they cannot justify or even explain al-Awlaki's death without referring to the fog of small wars. Attorney General Eric Holder has insinuated that the elder al-Awlaki got his constitutional due process because the executive branch had internal deliberations before deciding to kill him. Because Congress has authorized the executive to kill terrorists generally, that would suffice.

And as thin as it seems, that may be the best legal argument for a national security program that many Americans defend as legitimate. Still, while obscuring the technical details of a program, secrecy also stifles robust debate about its fundamental morality. It would seem that most Americans do not object to the drone war, but it's unlikely that a majority know about Abdulrahman's inglorious death either.

# CHAPTER 10

# Necessary Secrets

Most Americans, though they might disagree with the morality of nuclear weapons, would agree that the United States is within its rights to use secrecy to preserve the security and integrity of the nuclear arsenal. The U.S. Air Force protects three resources in the continental United States with no-notice, lethal force at all times. These assets, designated Protection Level One, include Air Force One; one-of-a-kind aircraft (the stealth helicopters used in the Osama bin Laden raid, for example); and nuclear weapons. In 2006, an Internet video portraying Air Force One being vandalized by a graffiti artist went viral. Those in the know immediately recognized it as a hoax. It had to be: security around the president's aircraft is as hardened as the White House itself. A staff of armed personnel known as Ravens stand watch 24/7, backed up by heavier assets nearby. Unauthorized personnel who get too close to Air Force One will not be handcuffed. They will be shot.*

---

*Military and civilian employees who get unfettered access to the president (or to the National Command Authority) must undergo a rigorous background check conducted by the Defense Security Service or the FBI. Once they pass, they are read in to a special access program called "Yankee White," which grants them unfettered access to presidential workspaces that might contain classified information at any level. Military personnel—Air Force pilots, Navy stewards, Marine engineers, say—are rated according to a system that either permits or denies them access to a loaded weapon when the president is around.

The Posse Comitatus Act ostensibly prevents military forces from engaging in law enforcement operations on U.S. soil. Yet Congress may expressly permit the military to conduct activities deemed necessary. Conspiracy theorists have long argued that there is a body of secret exemptions to the act that give the military license to detain and even kill Americans during national emergencies. This is false, though commanders can use lethal force to secure critical infrastructure and property and save the lives of others if they arrive at the scene of a disaster before civilian law enforcement. Indeed, Posse Comitatus does not address a wide range of military activities on American soil, from commando training missions in the middle of busy cities to operating military-grade equipment at the request of the FBI. During some National Special Security Events, for example, the Predator drone that hovers above the event site is not piloted by civilians, although civilians process whatever intelligence it gathers. These powers are not claimed in secret, though they certainly exist in secrecy's penumbra, and the deep penetration of military power remains a very sensitive subject for the civilian politicians elected to run the government.

Wherever a nuclear weapon is transported on the ground, convoy commanders have exclusive jurisdiction over its defense. In a nuclear National Defense Area, as its legal umbrella is called, the use of force is not only authorized, it is de facto. One JAG (Judge Advocate General) officer told us, "Nothing impedes the transport of a Protection Level One resource." When a nuke is rolling, anything and anyone in its path can and will be fired upon. If a nuclear weapons convoy is ambushed, the National Defense Area can expand or contract, and the full might of the American military is then brought to bear. Stand in front of a nuclear weapons convoy, and one is unlikely to live to tell the story.*

It should be self-evident that details of a nuclear weapon in the wild are a necessary secret. Other such necessary secrets include things like: our global contingency plans (such as one to try and seize control

---

*Aside from physical security, nuclear war plans themselves are still among the secrets that are given the highest degree of physical protection. The most secret of these plans is the list of Desired Ground Zeroes, or DGZ, that combatant commands and the U.S. Strategic Command regularly collaborate on and revise.

of Pakistan in the event of a coup, a protective measure to defend its nuclear arsenal from extremists); the location of fiber optic lines carrying high-grade government traffic inside the United States; the logistical details of missions by the Department of Energy to reclaim highly enriched uranium; and all information related to the protection of the president of the United States. (Indeed, for years the Secret Service refused to tell Congress how many agents accompanied the president on foreign visits, claiming that the information was too sensitive to trust with oversight committees. The April 2012 prostitution scandal in Cartagena, Colombia, put an end to that tradition of silence. In order to convince Congress that the agency was able to hold itself accountable, the Service revealed that 175 special agents made the trip. Nine of those agents violated agency regulations. Now that the secret is out, could a would-be assassin benefit from such information? Maybe. But complacency is the enemy of security. The number of agents traveling with the president will probably change as a result.)

Frivolous secrets, meanwhile, are often generated as a result of being "caught in the wash" of the necessary. A document's overall classification level is dictated by the highest classification level of any of its components.[1] That is to say, a fifty-page record with a discreet state secret in a single sentence on a single page is so classified in its entirety, with the tops and bottoms of each page conspicuously marked Secret. When Ralph Waldo Emerson wrote, "The creation of a thousand forests is in one acorn," he might as well have been describing classification policy. Regulations dictate that unclassified sections of the document are to be marked as such, and Executive Order 13526 states that agencies should "use a classified addendum whenever classified information constitutes a small portion of an otherwise unclassified document."[2] Because of the sheer amount of paperwork produced by the bureaucracy, however, this rule is not universally followed, and once a document passes through the secrecy membrane it takes a very long time for the mundane to emerge.

There is also a less generous explanation for frivolous secrets. They have become negotiable currency printed by an exclusive mint, or what Daniel Patrick Moynihan called a market. As he writes in his book *Secrecy*:

Departments and agencies hoard information, and the government becomes a kind of market. Secrets become organizational assets, never to be shared save in exchange for another organization's assets. Sometimes the exchange is in kind: I exchange my secret for your secret. Sometimes the exchange resembles a barter: I trade my willingness to share certain secrets for your help in accomplishing my purposes.[3]

More coarsely, one current senior director on the National Security Staff likened a staff meeting about some piece of secret information to "a contest where everyone, when they come in, unzips their pants and lays their dicks on the table."

Covert programs often measure their import by the degree to which their existence and operations are kept under wraps. This helps ensure future contracts and funding. Reams of unnecessarily classified material are the by-products of this mentality, with increased budgets and decreased oversight as the result.

But beyond the president, the bomb, and the troops, where does one draw the line of absolute necessary secrecy when the implications of sunlight aren't self-evident? And at what point does a leak become treason? This is perhaps the essential question in any discussion of national security, state diplomacy, the press, or the sprawling secrecy apparatus.

Secrets exist because we live in a world where not everyone gets along, and on certain occasions the United States is forced to take aggressive actions against other countries as a means of maintaining its own interests. There is, therefore, a direct correlation between secrecy and geopolitical power. Valid secrets in practice are an aggressive action undertaken on behalf of the president of the United States or the National Command Authority (that is, the lawful source of military orders) in the name of furthering American security interests, using tactics most reasonable Americans would consider acceptable when they eventually come to light. With regard to military operational matters, Mark Bowden most effectively described the tip of this spear in *Black Hawk Down*, writing about Delta Force, a known but unacknowledged U.S. Army unit:

> Secrecy, or at least the show of it, was essential to their purpose. It allowed the dreamers and the politicians to have it both ways. They could stay on the high road while the dirty work happened offstage. If some Third World terrorist or

Colombian drug lord needed to die, and then suddenly just turned up dead, why, what a happy coincidence! The dark soldiers would melt back into the shadow. If you asked them about how they made it happen, they wouldn't tell. They didn't even exist, see?[4]

Since the execution of Operation Neptune's Spear, special operations forces no longer operate exclusively in the shadows. That is a meal uneasily digested by longtime Joint Special Operations Command (JSOC) team members; once the curtains have been opened, it is hard to draw them back shut. In fact, since being promoted to commander of U.S. Special Operations Command in 2008, Admiral William McRaven has spoken openly about the increased need for transparency regarding the nation's counterterrorism forces. McRaven, according to people who have spoken with him, would rather JSOC spend less time creating layers of myth around itself and more time thinking about how to protect its core assets at a time when, as one senior administration official who works with McRaven said, "every time there is an explosion in the world, everyone knows about it within minutes."

Shortly after the killing of Osama bin Laden, and detailed information about the tactics, techniques, and procedures used by DEVGRU shooters showed up in the mainstream media, retired colonel Roland Guidry, one of JSOC's founding members, took the rare step of contacting journalists to complain about the sunlight bathing the SEALs. "The pre-mission Operational Security was superb, but the postmission OPSEC stinks," he said. "When all the hullabaloo settles down, JSOC and [the SEALs] will have to get back to business as usual, keeping the troops operationally ready and getting set for the next mission; the visibility the administration has allowed to be focused on JSOC and [the SEALs] will make their job now more difficult."[5]

Guidry said that the "administration's bragging" about details such as the existence of the bin Laden courier network and efforts to eavesdrop on cell phones would encourage the enemy to adapt by changing their cell phones, email addresses, websites, safe houses, and couriers. He also thinks the administration should not have disclosed precisely what types of equipment it found in bin Laden's compound, such as the terrorist's use of thumb drives to communicate. "Why did the administration not respond like we were trained to do thirty years ago in early JSOC by uttering two simple words: 'no comment'?" he asked.

He wasn't alone in his criticism. Retired lieutenant general James Vaught, a former Delta Force commander, confronted Admiral McRaven directly:

> Since the time when your wonderful team went and drug bin Laden out and got rid of him, and more recently when you went down and rescued the group in Somalia, or wherever the hell they were, they've been splashing all of this all over the media. Now back when my [Delta] special operators extracted Saddam [Hussein] from the hole, we didn't say one damn word about it. We turned him over to the local commander and told him to claim that his forces drug him out of the hole, and he did so. And we just faded away and kept our mouth shut.
>
> Now I'm going to tell you, one of these days, if you keep publishing how you do this, the other guy's going to be there ready for you, and you're going to fly in and he's going to shoot down every damn helicopter and kill every one of your SEALs. Now, watch it happen. Mark my words. Get the hell out of the media.[6]

To be sure, the administration—construed broadly—did not intend for too many specifics to get out. The National Security Council (NSC) wrestled with the dilemma early on, knowing as soon as bin Laden was engaged that the demand for information would be intense. Though no strategic communications expert had been read in to the op before it was executed, the White House and the Pentagon hastily prepared a strategy. Mike Vickers and deputy CIA director Mike Morrell would brief reporters on a conference call the night of the capture, after President Barack Obama finished speaking. The White House would issue some details about the time line by having John Brennan, the respected deputy national security adviser for counterterrorism, brief the press corps. And then everyone would shut up.

Because the SEALs themselves were not debriefed until after the White House had released its initial timeline, bad information got out. Bin Laden had pointed a gun at the SEALs, reporters were told, and used his wife as a human shield. Neither was true—but both were conveyed in good faith. Reporters, sensitive to the way the administration would try to use the bin Laden capture to boost the president's image, were relentless in their efforts to pinpoint precise details. Intelligence agencies, seeking their share of credit, offered unsolicited interviews with analysts who had participated in the hunt. Maybe it was simply the pent-up tension caused by keeping the secret so long, but in the days after the raid, "the national security establishment barfed," is how Denis McDonough, another deputy national security adviser, put it to a colleague.[7]

James Clapper, the director of national intelligence, had four secrets he did not want published at all. One was the stealth technology used on the Black Hawk, but there was nothing he could do once it crashed. Another was the presence on the ground of CIA operatives—it took less than a week for a detailed story to be published in the *Washington Post* about the CIA renting a house near Osama bin Laden's compound. (It later emerged that the CIA had had a station in Abbottabad for quite a while and had enlisted an unwitting local doctor to run a vaccination campaign to try to get blood samples from the bin Laden compound. The doctor and others suspected of helping the CIA were taken into custody by the Pakistani intelligence service and would later be released only after much begging on the CIA's behalf.)

Secret three was the type of drones that hovered above the raid: RQ-170 Sentinels, which operated out of Tonopah Test Range near Area 51 in Nevada, capable of jamming Pakistani radar with one pod and transmitting real-time video to commanders with another. A message posted to Twitter by one of the authors on the night of the raid and a subsequent comprehensive *Washington Post* story broke that secret. (In early December 2011, an RQ-170 gathering intelligence on possible insurgent training camps inside Iran lost contact with ground controllers and subsequently floated down deep inside the country. Briefly, a JSOC recovery operation was considered, but that was before the Iranians discovered it. At that point, a mission would be tantamount to war. The United States had to adapt to the possible compromise of Top Secret cryptographic devices and stealth material.)

Secret four was the identity of the SEAL unit that had taken the mission and, in particular, the identities of the operatives. The unit name was revealed the night of the raid, but the intelligence community and Special Operations Command (SOCOM) were horrified a month later when several reporters asked them to verify a list of names and ranks that had been distributed to them by sources unknown. Someone had leaked the names of some of the SEALs on the helicopters.

Military officials begged the reporters not to publish the names or even reveal that the list existed. The reporters acquiesced. A Department of Defense agency—most likely, the Air Force Office of Special Investigations—began to work quietly with the FBI to see who might have possibly leaked such protected information. Inside SOCOM, suspicions were directed at the White House, which, some believed, was availing itself of every opportunity to highlight Obama's decision to approve the raid. (White House officials insist that no one there would be so stupid as to leak the names of Tier One operatives to reporters, and SOCOM's Ken McGraw said he was not aware of the incident.)

Inside JSOC, the Delta guys blamed the larger SEAL community for inviting the attention. Whoever leaked the names might have taken a lesson from the SEALs themselves: when Obama met with them several days after the raid, he was told not to ask the men who actually killed bin Laden because they wouldn't tell even the commander in chief. Bill Daley, Obama's chief of staff, asked anyway and was told by the squadron leader, "Sir, we all did."

Operationally, the most important element of transparency for JSOC is not what those on the outside can see, but what those on the inside can see of each other. In fact, that's why the Command was founded in the first place. The 1st Special Forces Operational Detachment-Delta—better known as Delta Force—had their first major hostage rescue, in Iran, end in disaster. Operation Eagle Claw was a joint mission of U.S. Army Rangers and Delta Force operators transported by U.S. Air Force MC-130 cargo planes to a secret staging area designated as Desert One, in Iran. CIA paramilitaries and Air Force combat air controllers had scouted the area. Marine helicopters from a Navy aircraft carrier were set to rendezvous at the base, but when harsh weather and mechanical failures beset the incoming helos, the mission was delayed and ultimately aborted.

The delay, however, created another problem: the idling aircraft at Desert One now required refueling. A miscommunication between an Air Force combat controller and a Marine pilot caused a helicopter to collide with a transport plane. A total of eight airmen and Marines died in the explosion. The survivors departed by MC-130 in an emergency evacuation. In addition to the loss of life, the United States suffered a crushing humiliation on the world stage, U.S. special operations forces (already generally held in poor regard by conventional military leadership) appeared second-rate at best, and the Iranians gained abandoned helicopters and the intelligence within.

Following the disaster, Colonel Charlie Beckwith would immediately press for the formation of a new kind of "joint" command that he'd long proposed, which could train for and execute special operations requiring the best of each branch of the U.S. military. The muddled chains of command, branch rivalries, varied operating procedures, and ad hoc arrangement that doomed Eagle Claw would be cleared away and reorganized into a unified force—a military within the military.[8] By the end of 1980, the organization would essentially absorb the U.S. Army Delta Force and a new U.S. Navy unit called SEAL Team Six (a number inflated by its founder, SEAL Team Two commander Dick Marcinko, to alarm foreign intelligence services) and train alongside the newly minted 160th Special Operations Aviation Regiment (Airborne), or SOAR, an elite collection of the most highly trained rotary-wing aircraft pilots in the U.S. Army.

In 1987, the organization was subordinated to a new U.S. Special Operations Command, though JSOC reported directly to the National Command Authority, meaning that its units could be tasked directly by the president and the secretary of defense. The Command existed on the fringes of military operations. If it worked in the shadows before, secretly deploying hunter-killer teams around the world to do the necessary dirty work of the White House, it would now vanish completely, but for occasional glimpses in such places as Bosnia, where it hunted war criminals, or in Panama, where it allegedly pursued Pablo Escobar.

The crucial role of JSOC units in the early phase of the campaign against terrorism (when al-Qaeda was largely concentrated in the Punjab) has been chronicled. Sean Naylor's *Not a Good Day to Die: The Untold Story of Operation Anaconda* tells it best—so rich in detail, in fact, that Naylor was declared persona non grata by some JSOC commanders for revealing too much about their operations. In brief: Delta sent half of its force to Afghanistan. Major General Dell Dailey, then commander of JSOC, ordered a second task force of the less experienced DEVGRU SEALs to the region, setting off some territorial friction. Delta operated autonomously, while the SEALs operated with experienced and chagrined U.S. Army Rangers. Despite any simmering tensions, the various teams set about pursuing high-value targets without the benefit of solid intelligence and almost no technical intelligence surveillance assets. Yet many operators on the ground had spent the 1990s on the hunt in Bosnia and Kosovo and leveraged their capabilities to the fullest. In March 2002, the men killed as many as five hundred Taliban and al-Qaeda fighters in the Shahi Kot Valley in Afghanistan's Paktia province, working alongside Green Berets and U.S. Army infantrymen from the 101st Airborne Division. Early failures (such as losing Osama bin Laden at Tora Bora) were matched with successes (for example, the Delta Force capturing Saddam Hussein).

Details of later successes, such as the direct action mission that killed Abu Musab al-Zarqawi, the leader of al-Qaeda in Iraq, are still coming to light. In this baptism of fire, it is easy to imagine the remnants of problems that beset Somalia falling away—no more reliance on nonmilitary operators, no more weak intelligence, no more rivalries. JSOC's missions in the global war on terror were taxing, but they *were* normal JSOC missions—reactive, shrouded in secrecy, and peripheral to the larger war effort. In Iraq, several small JSOC teams covertly infiltrated the country before the war officially began. Their goal: find and, if needed, secure chemical and biological weapons Saddam was sure to use against the allied forces. General Stanley McChrystal, the incoming commander of JSOC, would change all of that. He would set the Command on the decisive course that put a controlled pair in Osama bin Laden.

•  •  •

General Michael Flynn first worked with McChrystal in the Afghanistan campaign, when the former was the intelligence officer for the Army's XVIII Airborne Corps and the latter assumed command of Task Force 180. At the start of the Iraq campaign, Flynn became a senior special operations forces intelligence officer, and McChrystal was called to Washington for Joint Staff duty. Secretary Donald Rumsfeld soon appointed McChrystal to head JSOC, and a year later McChrystal asked Flynn to be his top intelligence officer.

To the extent that a man such as Flynn has martial fantasies, one has always been to integrate intelligence and fight a war in real time. In Afghanistan, early efforts at fusion teams (called Cross Functional Teams) were modestly successful but "depended on voluntary participation and their authorities were limited," according to an influential study by National Defense University academics Christopher Lamb and Evan Munsing.[9] At Bagram Airfield, the first formal Joint Interagency Counter-Terrorism Task Force helped several task forces in the early phase of the al-Qaeda conflict. Yet intelligence analysts did not sit in the same meetings as operators. Real-time access to databases was limited. Everyone understood the concept—battlefield forces needed intel—but no one really knew how to execute it. And everyone was obsessed with keeping JSOC's secrets a secret, even at the cost of collecting and sharing actionable intelligence.

As his intelligence officer (or J-2, or "two"), Flynn operated with General McChrystal's full authority. He leveraged his friendships with senior members of U.S. intelligence to send more analysts into the field. By force of personality, and during the course of several years, Flynn convinced officials everywhere from the State Department to the Internal Revenue Service to staff the experimental new interagency fusion teams he was developing. He crossed Iraq, trying to better integrate JSOC's mission (which mostly involved hunting high-value targets) with other special operation forces and conventional units. (Before Flynn's efforts began, when JSOC conducted a combat mission, the battlespace would be cleared of conventional forces lest anyone disturb the secrecy of a black operation.) Flynn discovered that most intelligence and interrogation reports collected by JSOC units were stamped ORCON, meaning, "originator controlled," which effectively precluded anyone else—even the CIA—from seeing them. He wondered how often conventional forces missed an opportunity to capture or kill a bad guy because they couldn't gain access to JSOC task force intelligence. Flynn issued an order that JSOC information should be classified only at the Secret level, bringing tens of thousands of intelligence analysts around the world into the fold.

McChrystal and Flynn slowly coaxed the FBI and the Defense Intelligence Agency back into JSOC interrogations and insisted to the agencies that he would deal with abuse complaints directly. McChrystal even charmed the CIA, bringing its main special operations liaison into his secure video conference calls (but he instructed the man to never, *ever* tell his superiors at Langley untruths about what JSOC was up to). McChrystal was famously enthusiastic for videoconferencing, using the technology to "gather" officers, operators, ambassadors, politicians, and members of the intelligence community around the world in the same room to resolve issues and design strategy. In fact, his unit spent more than $100,000 on video teleconferencing bandwidth during the early stages of the counterinsurgency operation in Iraq. (As his counterterrorism efforts in the Horn of Africa increased, he likewise coordinated regular videoconferences between CIA station chiefs, U.S. ambassadors, and policymakers in Washington.)[10]

If it surprises you that it took years for the CIA—which is tasked with gathering intelligence on terrorists—to establish a regular, senior-level presence in daily conference calls with the military units tasked with killing terrorists, you can begin to sense the frustration that fed Flynn's and McChrystal's determination to set things right.

Changing the culture of a mysterious organization such as JSOC is hard, and it took more than three years before Flynn and McChrystal could create the real-time, flattened battlefield that allowed coalition troops to significantly reduce violence in Iraq. General Doug Brown of Special Operations Command eventually pulled in more than a hundred liaison officers from agencies and entities across the government, telling them that they were expected to be part of the team, not just note takers at briefings.

McChrystal and Flynn came to realize around the same time that JSOC's operational tempo could be rapidly stepped up by introducing radical decentralization and radical transparency into an organization that had always been centralized and extraordinarily discreet. Flynn once told one of McChrystal's deputies that his "A-ha" moment came when he saw that the key to actually doing tactical military intelligence right was as simple as making sure that everyone had access to everything.[11]

At another moment in history, with any other unit, these insights might not have produced even a ripple of change, much less a wave. Yet JSOC was special and feared, and the bureaucracy paid extra attention to it. McChrystal was uniquely suited for the challenge—humble and exacting, capable of incorporating into his inner circle personalities (such as Flynn's) that were the opposite of his own.

And there was urgency. Nothing but JSOC's networked warfare was working—not the CIA's operations, not whatever the National Counterterrorism Center thought it was, not outsourcing intelligence to liaison organizations. JSOC's success begat success. Iraq was a horrible place to be as JSOC's operational strategy gelled. Sometimes, Iraqi police would have to cart fifty dead bodies a day to the morgue in Baghdad alone. Lieutenant General David Petraeus, the commanding general of the Multi-National Force in Iraq at the beginning of the McChrystal era and then, in his second tour, as the usher of President George W. Bush's surge, had a slightly more measured view of JSOC's success; he knew how much his conventional forces were contributing to missions that JSOC was supplementing, and he was not above pulling rank to refuse to authorize a JSOC mission when he felt it would compromise another strategic goal. Yet he deeply respected McChrystal for his strategic vision. Likewise, McChrystal saw in Petraeus the model of a warrior-intellectual that he aspired to be. The two men got along well; had their relationship not developed, it would have been disastrous to the mission.[12] During his brief tenure as director of the CIA, Petraus was on better terms with special missions unit commanders than any of his predecessors ever were, because they served under him just before his appointment.

McRaven was equally instrumental in the changes afoot at JSOC. The former SEAL Team Six member and SEAL Team Four commander had just spent eighteen months as a director on the NSC. He'd been itching to get back to the combat zone during his tenure at the NSC, but his time at the top of the chain proved useful. He now knew the bureaucracy in ways that McChrystal and Flynn did not, and he knew its trigger points. McRaven was given command of the Combined Joint Special Operations Task Force–Arabian Peninsula, which oversaw all JSOC operations in Iraq. He had a direct line to the White House through his former boss, Michele Malvesti, the senior NSC director for combating terrorism. (They shared adjoining desks in the Eisenhower Executive Office Building.)

After mending old wounds and reorganizing the bureaucracy, the three men turned their guns to the doctrine itself. Flynn and McChrystal wanted to operationalize what Flynn calls "network-centered warfare," a PowerPoint term that conceals as much as it reveals. With Malvesti's help, they developed a new model of using intelligence to aid combat against terrorists and insurgents. Technology now allowed (at least, in theory) for the reduction of blinks between collecting and exploiting a piece of intelligence. The model went by the initials FFFEAD, or F3EAD—find, fix, finish (that is, the getting of the bad guys), exploit, analyze, and disseminate (that is, using the first get to get other bad guys). The "finish" of F3EAD—the kill—is certainly the most dangerous part of any operation. "But exploitation is where you truly made your money and enabled you to go after a network, [as opposed to] a single target, once we all embraced F3EAD, which was relatively quickly," said a U.S. Army Ranger who served in Iraq. "This was the strength of McChrystal and Flynn. They believed in the process and then set out to resource it."

As simple and intuitive as it sounds, F3EAD was terrifically difficult to actually do. Most soldiers—even the elite special operations forces—were trained on a much less elegant model that privileged firepower and hardware over thinking and strategizing. For Flynn, the key word in the model is "disseminate." Information, he told one colleague, "was fucking less than worthless" if it couldn't be widely distributed. This meant that JSOC's culture had to change. It had more fully embraced bleeding-edge battlefield computing technologies than any command in military history. The next round of successes would require using those tools, and tools not yet invented, to show the Army and the world what war in the twenty-first century looked like.

CHAPTER 11

# The Tools for the Job

On November 3, 2002, the CIA and the U.S. Air Force launched a Hellfire missile from a Predator drone that had been following Qaed Salim Sinan al-Harethi, a coplanner of the plot to bomb the USS *Cole* in Yemen in 1998. On the ground, tracking the convoy from a distance using lasers and other technology, were U.S. military personnel who had been given civilian cover by the State Department. This was to be what the CIA would later call a noncovert but deniable mission. The United States would kill al-Harethi, the Yemeni government would duly protest, the United States would deny involvement, and both countries' objectives would be satisfied.

The drone strike was successful. Paul Wolfowitz, deputy secretary of defense, subsequently confirmed that the United States had indeed developed an assassination-by-drone capability—and a "very successful" one at that.[1] (He elided mention of an internal debate within the National Security Council about whether al-Harethi should be snatched up by a U.S. Joint Special Operations Command [JSOC] team for interrogation.) Not only did Wolfowitz's braggadocio resonate poorly around the world (the strike was condemned at the United Nations), but it also soured the fragile relationship between the United States and Yemen—precisely the type of relationship that allowed the United States to conduct a secret counterterrorism campaign inside the country in the first place. A Yemeni general later complained that Americans have no regard for "the internal circum-stances in Yemen."[2]

Then Yemen retaliated. Though its president and a few members of his security cabinet had known of the strike in advance, the working layers of Yemen's intelligence apparatus, which had functional ties in some instances to militants, retaliated. They explained to the press precisely how the operation had been coordinated and how it had worked. Edmund Hull, the U.S. ambassador to Yemen, had acted as an intelligence scout, sneaking away from Sana'a to meet with tribesmen who had clues to al-Harethi's whereabouts.[3] Hull got a tip, and the NSA found the cell phone pings from a number belonging to one of al-Harethi's associates.[4] Deniability was no longer an option for Yemen, which in subsequent years would struggle under the weight of an al-Qaeda invasion and renaissance and would simultaneously try to find ways to demonstrate its independence from the United States. Yemen made it clear that they would allow no U.S. troops on the ground, except for special operations forces trainers whom they could keep tabs on. The United States did not abide by the agreement. Teams of CIA and JSOC intelligence operatives rotated in and out of the country, often being airdropped into the desert at night or using the cover of a SIGINT mission, of which there were many. The Pentagon quietly established a military liaison element—an MLE—that would ostensibly be used as a cover for direct action missions.

But Hull forbade them from engaging suspected terrorists directly; instead, they gathered human intelligence and helped aviation assets, both manned and unmanned, to find their targets.* Though the number of U.S. personnel on the ground at any one time was small, the pace of operations was intense. Even Marine helicopters were used to drop ordnance.[5]

When the United States negotiated secret agreements with Pakistan to allow drone strikes in restricted areas, it showed sensitivity to Pakistan's internal politics. Pakistan would be seen as

---

*Ambassador Hull insisted on a signed declaration from General Doug Brown, commanding general of U.S. Special Operations Command, preventing any "kinetic missions from taking place, aside from limited intelligence gathering and civil affairs operations."

providing intelligence for the strikes; the United States would play a supplemental role. Indeed, when the first Hellfire struck a Pakistani target in June 2004, the Pakistani army claimed responsibility.[6] But then the missiles began to go astray, and invariably innocents were killed. The indignation of the average Pakistani was roused. Political factions in Pakistan fanned the flames of protest. In order to rebut the notion that the strikes were causing too many civilian casualties, the U.S. government began to speak about the program to some journalists, on background. Other journalists developed sources within Pakistan's government, which was quite willing to confirm the details of every subsequent strike, including their intended targets. By the time President Obama joked about the program at the White House Correspondents' Dinner in Washington in 2009, the "cover" for the program had evaporated. The CIA would swear by the program (operated in conjunction with JSOC), pointing to the number of high-ranking al-Qaeda officials who had been killed.

Obama's first director of national intelligence, Dennis Blair, wanted the CIA to use its capability more strategically. His reading of intelligence suggested that the collateral harm of the operation—the anger that the strikes caused among Pakistanis, even though the targeting was precise—was damaging to U.S. security interests. The CIA, in a deft bureaucratic move, simply stopped providing Blair's office with advance notice of strikes.[7] The dispute went all the way to the Office of the Vice President, which sided with the CIA, although Blair "won" the ability to have a director of national intelligence representative at CIA covert action briefings at the White House.

Here again, we see the difference between a "good secret"— the technology platforms themselves, such as unmanned aerial vehicles—and the ambiguity resulting from such secrets, in this case essentially invisible, clinical robotic warfare, where missiles appear from nowhere and annihilate villagers with few fingerprints.

Nobody feels bad for dead terrorists. But when a U.S. F-16 fighter pilot makes a mistake and civilian deaths result, there's a moral element that doesn't exist when a literally heartless drone does the same thing. Like all creatures of biology, humans evolved to understand the intimacy of killing. Drones change the equation, and its unclear how our mammalian brains cope. But the reality is that no matter who is behind the strike—the United States or the local government—those on the ground predisposed to hating the United States will always blame us. And this technology allows mission creep in a way never before seen. Spying on Pakistan is nothing; to a certain extent, the United States can now spy on or bomb any country in the world at any time. While Spain probably doesn't have to worry, the Third World does. And terrorists in such failing or failed states depend on the United States to employ boneheaded uses of military force. Covert applications of military force are the most tempting actions of all. Good secrets can very easily go bad.

For this reason, it is hard to stay technologically neutral about drones. They are a ubiquitous presence in global airspace. More than a dozen major police agencies in the United States are testing them. The U.S. military owns about 6,500 of them; the intelligence community probably controls about 500. A small percentage is equipped with missiles; most are used for surveillance, signals intelligence collection, and clandestine tracking.

When McChrystal assumed command of JSOC, it didn't have a single drone to its name. To schedule orbits, JSOC reconnaissance planners had to ask the Joint Chiefs of Staff, the Air Force, or even the CIA. There were in fact very few intelligence, surveillance, and reconnaissance resources. General Michael Flynn, JSOC's intelligence chief, had to beg for time on specialized collection platforms such as Medium Altitude Reconnaissance System airplanes, with which he could track insurgents on the ground, and RC-12 Guardrails, innocuous jets that contain highly sensitive signals intelligence collection equipment. With the National Security Council's assent, Flynn expanded a unit called the Technical Development Activity, which secretly developed manned reconnaissance and surveillance aircraft. He chained it to JSOC for use in Iraq, Pakistan, and, later, Yemen. In Iraq, Flynn and his counterparts established a Joint Reconnaissance Task Force (JTRF) to manage all theater-based requests for special operations force drone orbits. The JRTF was classified; it has now become a JSOC headquarters element and is commanded by one of the Navy's top special operations officers. In conventional battlespaces, drones are assigned to Combined

Air Operations Centers that schedule their orbits, and to several U.S.- and Europe-based reconnaissance fleets, which operate them remotely. The Air Force Distributed Common Ground System links all tasking orders together. More than sixty military installations in the United States house the machines, mostly for testing purposes.[8] A dozen unclassified UAV variants are operational, along with a half dozen, which remain classified.

As JSOC ramped up its task force operations in Iraq, the CIA was initially reluctant to provide institutional resources. The National Security Agency, however, under the directorship of General Keith Alexander, was quick to see the benefits of giving Flynn the best personnel and manpower. Several joint CIA/NSA Special Collection Service teams rotated through Balad, Iraq. Alexander personally participated in a secure teleconference with General McChrystal at least once a week. He sent dozens of engineers directly to Flynn's headquarters in Balad and to other forward-deployed sites, where they implemented a TiVo-like system for signals intelligence that allowed analysts to rapidly process the take from the NSA's near-total tapping of the telecom networks of several Iraqi cities. SOCOM Technical Surveillance Elements set up cameras and RFID (radio frequency identification) chip tracking sensors. A quiet Pentagon procurement office, the Rapid Response Technology Office, and a classified department called the Special Capabilities Office provided more than three hundred technological assets to assist intelligence and special military operations in the CENTCOM (U.S. Central Command) theater.[9] About 60 percent of them went operational.[10] The Army's Technical Operations Support Activity figured out how to merge sensor data collected on the ground with experimental drones in the air, providing what commanders call "persistent" surveillance. Commanders could now track the bad guys and see their activities 24/7 and could analyze patterns with incredible efficiency. (One promising project involves sensors attached to balloons—the Persistent Threat Detection System.) Tactical satellites were fielded, and by 2009 units could task them to view multiple targets and track as many as ten thousand objects per pass. (The unclassified Pentagon office that works on these projects is called the Operationally Responsive Space Office and is run directly out of the Office of the Secretary of Defense.)

One operational technology that was first attached to drones and later to Artemis geostationary satellites helped JSOC (and later Task Force ODIN in Iraq) figure out where IEDs (improvised explosive devices) might be placed by analyzing how recently the soil had been disturbed. A joint National Geospatial-Intelligence Agency (NGA)– U.S. Strategic Command project called NGA SKOPE allowed JSOC units to merge data collected from virtually any intelligence source and predict, based on patterns of movement, where insurgents were likely to be and what they were likely to do. (To understand how this works, imagine sensors surreptitiously placed on cars belonging to suspected IED planters. Based on the cars' locations and orientations during an IED attack, the SKOPE cell could predict future attacks based on similar movements.)

Three technologies developed by the NSA during this short burst of time proved pivotal. One, which the government has asked us not to describe in detail, involves the ability to pinpoint cell phone signals to within inches of their origin. (In their book *Top Secret America*, Dana Priest and Bill Arkin refer to an "electronic divining rod" that allowed operators to hone in on cell phone–using bad guys as though the operators were using metal detectors at a beach.)[11] Another involves the use of RFID chips in what can only be described as an ingenious way. (Again, details are withheld because the technique is highly classified and still in use.) One technique that SOCOM has shared with researchers, originally code-named BLUE GRASS, involves attaching tiny RFID emitters to vehicles and tracking them through a variety of different platforms.[12] In 2005, Project SONOMA helped analyze where cells of insurgents planning IED attacks were clustered. And JSOC was using dyes and perfluorocarbons to track insurgents before the rest of the military was aware that this capability existed.

It also helped when NSA scientists figured out a way to "unwipe" supposedly cleared cell phones and extract every number ever called by that phone. When a cell phone is captured at a site, the NSA techs download its data using the new technique and feed it to other analysts who are monitoring the data pulled from cell towers across Iraq. If two numbers match, a team is sent to the area to investigate. The NSA, with help from British intelligence, has created a massive database of computer hard drive and thumb drive identification numbers, allowing analysts to trace connections among militants through the technological litter left at sites.

JSOC fusion teams and their augments also benefit from the completion of a comprehensive biometrics database that allows for quick identification of insurgents, as well as a quiet revolution in DOCEX (document exploitation) techniques. Using technology relying on sophisticated algorithms that assign values to data based on the probability that a faint "I" might indeed have been an "I," DOCEX specialists can reconstruct documents that have been burned. Meanwhile, the Defense Intelligence Agency (DIA) consolidated its media exploitation center and figured out a way to speed up its analysis.[13] As late as 2003, lumbering military transport planes had to fly into Andrews Air Force Base in Maryland to drop off unsorted pocket litter by the crate, leaving the DIA's teams with reams of paper and little context.

To the credit of the Department of Defense and SOCOM, most of these technologies were classified only until they were fielded and then were quickly downgraded to allow the people fighting the wars to gain access to them and push their limits. Had the intelligence agencies been stingy—if they'd been unwilling to relax security controls or had set up shielding special access programs—the fusion cells that eventually beat back the insurgency in Iraq and have been used by U.S. forces ever since would simply not have existed. NGA's SKOPE cell, for example, was highly classified for about two months. Now it is ubiquitous, and its main architect is permitted to acknowledge its existence in the press.[14] "A lot of organizations like this—the Rapid Equipping Force, the Robotics Systems Joint Program Office, the Joint IED Defeat Organization, the Biometrics task force, and probably down at JSOC—were essentially start-ups deploying technologies that were unique to the threats of counterinsurgency," said Brian Smith, an Air Force captain who worked on energy projects for the Rapid Equipping Force during the early years of the Iraq War.


In October 2011, Flynn, the former JSOC J-2, was promoted to lieutenant general and appointed a deputy director of national intelligence. He has been outspoken about the need for reform within the military intelligence community. Many of his fellow flag and general officers in the intelligence community consider him to be *too* out-spoken. His nomination took more than eight months to gestate, as forces within the Pentagon—inside the Army in particular—pushed back, whispering into the ears of senators that Flynn's tactics did not work when he followed McChrystal to Afghanistan in 2009. (Flynn had the last laugh. Today he is the director of the DIA and commander of all intelligence forces in the Department of Defense.) Some Democratic senators on the Armed Services Committee believe that Flynn's championing of bulk data analysis provided a brutally efficient way to kill too many innocent Afghans and may not have been as effective as the military suggests. By this, they mean that instead of targeting people, infantry and special operations forces targeted telephone numbers—they would target gatherings of people who had been surreptitiously tagged with chemicals or RFID chips, even if they didn't precisely know who these targets were.

Officially, the DIA's Joint Interagency Task Force–Counter Terrorism vetted the targets, with input from the NSC. In reality, the Joint Prioritized Effects List—the target board—had a lot of phone numbers that a computer had associated with the broad periphery of the insurgency, rather than names of specific terrorists.[15] Flynn's response to this is simple: for one thing, raids weren't ordered because some Afghan villager happened to call a Taliban commander; there needed to be a better reason to send Americans into harm's way than that. One of the hardest tasks that Flynn's intelligence team faced was figuring out whether contacts between innocent Afghans and those associated with the Taliban were innocent or nefarious. Doing that required a significant amount of collection and analytical time. It required a granular level of knowledge about each village. Plenty of people were collecting all sorts of information— Provisional Reconstruction Teams, Human Terrain Teams, Civil Affairs officers, and intelligence gatherers—but it wasn't being fused or analyzed or appropriately disseminated.

Flynn wanted to create a middle level of what he termed "information brokers," who could analyze everything and determine patterns that would allow all parts of the Afghanistan effort—especially the mission to rebuild civil society—to succeed. As he described it, "This vast and underappreciated body of information, almost all of which is unclassified, admittedly offers few clues about where to find insurgents, but it does provide elements of even greater importance—a map for leveraging support and for marginalizing the insurgency itself." He attempted to divine, in villages and provinces, who was good and who was bad and attempted to flesh out (as much as possible) which members of the Taliban were secretly cooperating with the State Department or the CIA and which members were susceptible to U.S. influence. But Washington saw American body counts and ordered General McChrystal, as the commanding general of the International Security Assistance Force, to force Flynn to reprioritize his resources. He had to stop the flow of money and trainers from Iran who were arming insurgents. He had to counter growing Pakistani influence in the region and deal with the nettle of cross-border political complexities. And he had promised to provide conventional forces in Afghanistan with the same high-grade, high-velocity intelligence that special operations forces received.[16]

On a fresh patch of land in the northwestern corner of Fort Bragg, specially cleared construction workers are completing a massive 110,000-square-foot building that will serve as the crown jewel in JSOC's empire. The building will headquarter the JSOC Intelligence Brigade (JIB), which analyzes raw and finished intelligence for the Command's special missions units. The JIB has quietly existed for more than three years, escaping the notice of congressional intelligence overseers. Under a program started by Generals McChrystal and Flynn, JSOC borrowed hundreds of intelligence analysts from the sixteen U.S. intelligence agencies, many of them rotating through quick frontline deployments. These augmentees greatly helped JSOC conduct its operations, but the Command was not able to develop a cadre of analysts who were JSOC's own, with institutional muscle memory that would make the fusion of intelligence and operations more efficient in the future. The JIB, in essence, sets in stone JSOC's new way of doing business.

In 2010, Admiral William McRaven attended the quiet ribbon cutting of his newest jewel: the Intelligence Crisis Action Center (ICAC) in Rosslyn, Virginia, funded through a classified line item in the Pentagon's budget. Until just recently, it operated on two floors of a nondescript office building that also housed a language learning center and a dry cleaner. At the time when McRaven christened the center, its existence was a secret to many U.S. intelligence officials, who learned about it by way of an Associated Press newsbreak in early 2011. According to a senior military official, it has about fifty employees and reports directly to the JSOC Directorate of Intelligence and Security.[17] Its primary function is to serve as a command post for JSOC operations around the world. It is informally known as the Targeting Center, and because of operational security concerns it has changed its name twice.

These entities are sensitive subjects at the highest levels of the U.S. counterterrorism community, because each represents the extraordinary achievements of the JSOC units and also reveals by its own existence the inadequacy of the other intelligence fusion centers set up by the government to do mostly the same thing. JSOC's successes have brought with it blowback and envy and more than a bit of criticism from military officials who think that conventional forces and regular special operations forces units were just as important as the smaller, secretive standing task forces in degrading al-Qaeda's infrastructure.

Though the addition of an intelligence brigade to JSOC is a natural consequence of its success and growth, when the Associated Press disclosed the existence of the ICAC to the general public, a spokesman for SOCOM made a point of telling reporters that its functions would not duplicate those of the National Counterterrorism Center (NCTC). Mike Leiter, the director of the NCTC, worked closely with McRaven to make sure the two centers didn't overlap. "I spent hours with Admiral McRaven on this," he said. "We saw this as a natural evolution in what they were doing. We sent some of our guys over there, and they sent some of their guys over here."

Managers at the CIA and the DIA regarded JSOC's growing footprint with alarm. Some whispered to journalists that JSOC was building a secret intelligence empire without oversight or scrutiny. More prosaically, they feared that the Command's activities, in both the collection and the analysis of intelligence, would duplicate their own.

Sensing friction, Michael Morrell, then acting director of the CIA; Michael Vickers, the civilian intelligence chief at the Pentagon;

and General James Cartwright, the former vice chairman of the Joint Chiefs of Staff, tried to reduce tension and conflict arising from JSOC's expansion. In the field, JSOC units and their counterparts at the CIA and the DIA work well together. In Yemen, after some early conflicts, the integration is almost seamless, with JSOC and the CIA alternating Predator missions and borrowing each other's resources, such as satellite bandwidth. Often, JSOC element commanders will appear on videoconference calls alongside CIA station chiefs—all but unheard of until very recently. Yet some midlevel managers at the intelligence agencies remain resistant to the type of integration envisioned by the National Security Council.

McRaven, much like JSOC itself, is at cross-purposes. He knows that his intelligence assets will not survive budget purges unless they fit well within the rest of the community. Yet he also wants to preserve the razor-sharp edge of the special missions units at a time when, due to publicity and overtasking, it risks being dulled.

CHAPTER 12

# The Known Unknowns

"Chris C." joined the Army after reading about the heroics of Americans in Fallujah. A few months out of West Point, he was deployed on a fifteen-month tour of Iraq as a battalion-level intelligence officer. In order to find insurgents, his soldiers worked from scraps of human intelligence—a rumor here, an overheard conversation there. It's easy to forget, in an armchair discussion of government secrecy, that the point of intelligence is to learn our enemy's secrets. In a war zone, no one forgets this. Based in Salahuddin province north of Baghdad, Chris and his team had to share access to a single drone for overhead surveillance. There was no National Security Agency presence and thus no real signals intelligence. Sometimes, a JSOC task force would inform Chris's commander that they were about to raid a part of the city. "We were told: the Task Force is going into our area, and here is the grid they're going to hit. I would look at the grid and say, 'Oh, I know who they're going to hit, because we'd just been there looking for the same person.'"

In Balad, General Michael Flynn had come to appreciate the wealth of information that intelligence collectors with conventional forces could provide. He recognized that such intel could benefit the regular troops as well as the JSOC task forces. While JSOC soldiers went home every three months, conventional forces were on twelve- to fifteen-month rotations.

General Stanley McChrystal and Flynn knew that JSOC needed to better understand the populations their task forces worked among—an intelligence capability that only units such as Chris's could provide. Knowing the sinews of a local community could help the U.S. military establish degrees of trust with tribal and authority figures. General David Petraeus, for example, would use early successes by conventional commanders such as General H. R. McMaster, the commander of the 3rd Armored Cavalry Regiment in Iraq, to develop his counterinsurgency doctrine. "JSOC, earlier than any other element in the U.S. government, understood the importance of messaging and how actions can influence populations," said Mike Leiter, the former director of the National Counterterrorism Center.[1]

Officers such as Chris C. had an institutional knowledge of tribes, geography, and environment that had eluded JSOC. Flynn was determined to merge the two systems. "Ninety percent of the intelligence we needed was not in JSOC," he told one observer in 2010.[2]

Indeed, Chris's unit provided the tip that led the JSOC task force to Abu Abdul-Rahman al-Iraqi, the spiritual adviser to al-Zarqawi. Chris's officers had long watched an internecine tribal conflict north of the Tigris River. Just after a firefight, Chris got word that Haj al-Bazari, a high-ranking al-Qaeda operative in Iraq, had been injured and taken to a cousin's home in the area. A database cross-check revealed that one of al-Bazari's cousins had a wife who was an ob-gyn. Chris's team searched her house and found bloody gauze and a truculent doctor refusing to tell anyone what had happened. She was detained. When her husband arrived at the American detention center, he pleaded for her release. He had little money but was a member of a major facilitation network that included former Baathist elements funded by Syria. He offered the Americans information instead.

Chris's commander contacted a JSOC task force. They flew in and grabbed the husband and interrogated him. That was the last time Chris heard about the guy until, out of the blue, a JSOC shooter team came by to thank him. (This was another early McChrystal-Flynn innovation: allow units that operate in the shadows to work with units that operate in the sunlight.) "They told me that the guy was a high-level financier and that he had led them to Sheik Abdul Rahman," he said.

By December 2007, when Chris's second tour of duty in Iraq began, JSOC task forces were fully integrated with the rest of the effort. Chris's battalion was assigned to the eastern half of Mosul and was constantly fighting to keep the province from collapsing under the weight of foreign fighters, many from Saudi Arabia. Communicating with the JSOC team in the area, Task Force 9-14 (also known as Task Force North), was much easier than before.

Chris had access to their interrogation reports and worked with a TF 9-14 intelligence officer to devise a strategy for his area of operation: they would target specific midlevel operatives who might lead to the bigger gets. His team produced a steady stream of intelligence reports about local politics and conditions on the ground. Not once was he denied access to JSOC products, and TF 9-14 was literally a phone call away. "Once this started happening, it was just awesome in terms of what we were able to do," he said.

Here is how a colleague of General Flynn's described the change in procedures on the ground:

What would normally happen is: the shooters would kick down a door and snatch everyone and drag them to the front room, and then take everything with them, and put it in a trash bag. The bad guys would be taken to a detention facility and the pocket litter would come back to [the intelligence analysts]. Flynn thought this was stupid. Instead, he gave the shooters—think of this—the Delta guys, mini cameras, and schooled them in some basic detective techniques. When you capture someone, take a picture of them exactly where you captured them. Take detailed notes of who was doing what with what. Don't merge all the pocket litter.

Then, the shooters were supposed to e-mail back an image of the person they captured to Balad [JSOC's intelligence headquarters], where analysts would run it through every facial recognition database we have, or fingerprints or names, or what have you. We'd get hits immediately. And so our intel guys would radio back to the team in the field, "Hey, you've got Abu-so-and-so, or someone who looks like them. See if he knows where Abu–other-person is."

And that's what the shooters would do. They'd tell their captured insurgents that for a price, they could help them. A senior JSOC intelligence commander said, "They'd say, I know you, you're so-and-so. And if you want us to help you, you need to tell us where this other person is. And it would work. And then, when we got a new address, sometimes within twenty minutes of the first boot on the door, we'd have another team of shooters going to another location." Follow-up interrogations were plotted out like dense crime dramas, with dozens of participants, including some by video teleconference.

Instead of three operations every two weeks, JSOC was able to increase its operations tempo (or "optempo") significantly, sometimes raiding five or six places a night. This completely bewildered insurgents and al-Qaeda sympathizers, who had no idea what was going on. In April 2004, according to classified unit histories, JSOC participated in fewer than a dozen operations in Iraq.* By July 2006, its teams were exceeding 250 a month. McChrystal's operations center was open for fifteen hours a day, regardless of where he was. There is a strong correlation between the pace of JSOC operations, the death rate of Iraqi insurgents and terrorists, and the overall decline in violence that lasted long enough for U.S. troops to surge into the country and "hold" areas that used to be incredibly dangerous.

In Christopher Lamb and Evan Munsing's thesis-length assessment of intelligence in Iraq, Secret Weapon, Flynn's "pivotal" efforts at fusing intelligence and operations, developing real-time reach back to analysts, and the flattening of authority are lauded as "the secret weapon" behind the surge—not some special weapon, as Bob Woodward has hinted. Notably, Flynn is rendered in the piece as "General Brown," and the authors were not permitted to mention that his team was actually JSOC.[3] Such is the nature of the Defense Cover Program—Flynn himself was a target for terrorists and many nation-states.

The problem with being a secret organization is that when a harsh light is cast on questionable activities—even activities performed

*This figure was confirmed by a senior military official who asked to remain anonymous.

with patriotic intent or, at least, performed when no better options seemed available at the time—there's no opportunity for a rebuttal. "We are in a difficult position, in that there's not much we can do to make the case for ourselves," William McRaven said in 2010. "There are some things we can try and do to respond to things like Seymour Hersh articles," referring to the journalist's allegations that JSOC fostered a culture that resulted in torture and later served as Dick Cheney's personal assassination force, "but we are constrained."*

For all of McChrystal's advances and achievements, McRaven still inherited a work in progress. Even with all of the attention paid to ISR (Intelligence, Surveillance, and Reconnaissance) assets, JSOC had only thirty-three planes to its name, and its drones were making only five orbits per day over Iraq. Fusion cells that worked well in some areas didn't necessarily work in others. With a new U.S. president, the rules of engagement in Iraq were about to change, and attention would soon shift back to Afghanistan and more decisively toward Africa. The spigots were still open, but JSOC's bureaucracy was growing overburdened.

One of the earliest problems McRaven had to deal with was the Status of Forces Agreement (SOFA), signed with Iraq and which forbade the United States from conducting most counterterrorism raids without warrants. Warrants? JSOC doesn't do warrants—that's a law enforcement thing. Many in the Command wanted to ignore the SOFA entirely. McRaven, however, insisted that his team figure out a way to fulfill the agreement. To do this, he directed JSOC funds to build mini-courthouses, first in Baghdad and then elsewhere in the country. JSOC flew in JAG (Judge Advocate General) officers from the United States, and McRaven personally briefed the Iraqi leadership, describing the constraints under which JSOC often operated. He asked for their help.

As a result, Iraqi judges were empowered by the U.S. military and began issuing warrants based on the testimony of JSOC intelligence analysts, SEALs, or Delta guys themselves. Occasionally, operatives appeared in the courtroom, though always shielded. More regularly, Iraqis used information collected by JSOC in lieu of an operator

---

*We were given the JSOC commander's direct office phone number by a source. McRaven picked up on the first ring.

being present. McRaven at first faced internal resistance for bringing in the Iraqis—JSOC was supposed to be a secret organization. Yet as operators saw how well the courthouse system worked, they soon dropped their objections and quickly adapted.

Likewise, they adapted to McRaven's establishment of an Afghan partner unit within JSOC. It consisted mostly of civilians, many without a shred of military experience, and began to accompany JSOC units on raids. This was a particularly important outreach following a JSOC disaster in April 2010, when a Ranger unit killed five Afghan civilians in Khataba, the result of a bad tip from an unreliable source. McRaven took the extraordinary step of personally apologizing to the family and admitting that the men under his command had made a "terrible terrible mistake." As reported, McRaven, near tears, told an elder, "You are a family man with many children and many friends. I am a soldier. I have spent most of my career overseas, away from my family. But I have children as well. And my heart grieves for you."[4] McRaven figured that the Afghan partner units could prevent these kinds of mistakes—the kind that made the job harder for every soldier, conventional or special operations, who was fighting in Afghanistan. McRaven further reached out to conventional units, asking commanders how his units could better assist their missions.

As of yet, JSOC does not seem to have found the kind of successes in Afghanistan that it did in Iraq. The enemy is different, more embedded in the population. The geography makes intelligence gathering more difficult. And the strategy from the White House is different. Yet as a force multiplier and as a hub of best practices, the Command may have prevented a decisively unwinnable situation from descending into disaster.

When JSOC eventually finds itself in the news for a high-profile failure instead of yet another astounding success, it will not likely be for what it did in Iraq or Afghanistan. Instead, it will be for its operations in countries we are not officially at war with (inasmuch as we "officially" go to war). Covert but deniable operations in non–combat zones often start as "forever" secrets; the whole point is to slip in, kidnap or kill or retrieve or steal, and exfiltrate without leaving fingerprints.

That's why the most sensitive special missions unit listed on the base directory of Fort Belvoir in northern Virginia is the Mission Support Activity (MSA). It is JSOC's clandestine intelligence-gathering organization and is formally considered a Tier Two special missions unit, performing Tier One functions.* Until 2009, its code name was INTREPID SPEAR, and its cover changes every two years. In 2010, it was known as the U.S. Army Studies and Analysis Activity. Inside JSOC, it's known as the Activity, or Task Force Orange. Doctrinally, it is responsible for "operational preparation of the environment." The MSA has several fixed operating locations around the world, including at least five secret bases inside the United States. (A source says the Activity is now funded under the name "Joint Support Activity.")

Close readers of Bob Woodward's books about the Bush administration may recognize the MSA's code name during the first months of the war in Afghanistan: GREY FOX. GREY FOX operators were on the ground with CIA paramilitaries and special operations forces shooters within days of September 11, 2001. They were instrumental in the capture of Saddam Hussein. (In the famous photograph of Saddam crawling out of his spider hole, you can see the boot of an MSA operator.) Included in the MSA's numbers are elite signals intelligence collectors (their procurement history includes a lot of commercial radio scanners), pilots, and, to a lesser extent, case officers, interrogators, and shooters. They gather intelligence for counterterrorism operations, but some are cross-trained to kill.

In 2001, the MSA, then known, confusingly enough, as the Intelligence Support Activity (ISA), was the bastard child of the U.S. Army. It had survived years of controversy and scrutiny, including several congressional attempts to shut it down, scandals involving extralegal activities, and financial improprieties. It was underutilized and poorly integrated with the rest of the force's intelligence services. In 2003, over the strenuous objection of army leadership, Marshall Billingslea transferred the ISA to JSOC. Its new command quickly changed the ISA's designation and cover name and put it to work. (The unit's last known cover name was changed after a reporter

---

*A former Navy SEAL, Jack Murphy, has called MSA a Tier One unit, alongside Delta and DEVGRU, but U.S. Special Operations Command does not classify it as such.

used the phrase in an email to a Pentagon official. This constituted an operational breach sufficient to warrant the termination of a dozen security contractors.) Billingslea did not intend for the MSA to engage in direct action missions. Rather, he believed that the Tier One teams could benefit from the battlefield intelligence-gathering skills that the MSA could bring to bear.

After Billingslea left the Pentagon, however, the incessant demands on JSOC would turn the MSA into something resembling a Tier One unit, with members tasked with missions that involved the direct collection of intelligence for the sake of intelligence — something that American law has a problem with, or, at least, the laws that civilians are allowed to see. The MSA was never designed to be a tactical unit per se, but intelligence and military officials confirm that after 9/11 they executed direct action missions in Somalia, Pakistan, and several other countries. Congress was largely kept in the dark, and to some extent it still is. In 1982, after the ISA/MSA's creation, Defense Secretary Frank Carlucci, not shy about flexing the Pentagon's muscles, worried that "we seem to have created our own CIA, but like Topsy, uncoordinated and uncontrolled." An organization with such a secret mandate had to have accountability as its essence, Carlucci wrote in a memo, but "we have created an organization that is uncontrolled."[5]

As the Mission Support Activity expanded under JSOC's purview, it began to execute missions independently and outside of declared war zones. In countries such as Yemen, Kenya, Somalia, and Ethiopia, Task Force Orange gathered intelligence directly, technically reporting to the CIA, whose operations were ostensibly based on covert action findings but in reality adhered to the Al Qaeda Network Exord, an executive order signed by President George W. Bush after the terrorist attacks on September 11, 2001. Members of the MSA staffed new military liaison elements (MLEs) installed by SOCOM in U.S. embassies around the world, much to the consternation of the State Department. (The use of MLEs was significantly curtailed when Robert Gates replaced Donald Rumsfeld as defense secretary, although a 2010 SOCOM budget document includes a line item for their funding in Africa.)

The MSA, with a budget of $80 million, trains its personnel to be essentially dropped into denied areas and to operate more or less on their own. Some MSA elements operate highly specialized surveillance and reconnaissance planes, such as a heavily modified RC-12 Guardrail (code name: LIBERTY BLUE), used for years to track al-Qaeda operatives as they meander through the deserts of North Africa. Others zip around terrorist training camps in MH-6 Little Birds, small helicopters used extensively by the U.S. Army.

In two countries with which the United States is not at war, according to three former U.S. officials with knowledge of its operations, MSA elements were tasked with tracking and killing specific terrorist targets. Technically, only the CIA can do that—which was why SEAL Team Six was very publicly placed under the titular authority of CIA director Leon Panetta when it conducted the bin Laden raid, even though Admiral McRaven and a Navy captain managed the operation. Under U.S. law, the military's intelligence activities outside war zones are restricted to Title 10 of the U.S. Code. The CIA, meanwhile, operates under Title 50, which permits covert action, including targeted assassinations of terrorists, so long as a covert action finding has been transmitted to Congress.

Given the secrecy associated with the MSA missions, it is not clear whether the CIA had full cognizance of what the Defense Department was doing, particularly in the early years of the global campaign against transnational terrorism. In places such as Africa, "the authorities were fucked up and no one knew who was in charge," a still-serving JSOC officer said in an interview. This would change around 2004, as JSOC and CIA objectives diverged. Seizing the initiative, General McChrystal increased the Command's footprint in Nairobi, Kenya; Camp Lemonnier, Djibouti; and Addis Ababa, Ethiopia. JSOC focused its efforts on "intelligence collection and target development."[6] In 2006, JSOC went kinetic in Somalia, actively hunting for al-Qaeda leader Saleh Ali Saleh Nabhan. He was killed in 2009.

Shortly after 9/11, one MSA case officer was nearly killed while following a target (much as a CIA case officer might) in Beirut, when he was kidnapped outside his hotel. He escaped, shot his attackers, and wound up receiving—secretly—a medal for his valor. The number of case officer types hired by the MSA ramped up after 9/11 and is slowly spinning back down. Yet JSOC's human intelligence–gathering activities continue to expand—and this is not a secret.

A recent official job solicitation reports that the Command is recruiting "[a] Human Intelligence Operations Officer, responsible for planning and executing highly specialized, mission critical HUMINT requirements for JCS Directed Operations and contingency plans. Coordinates the de-confliction, registration and management of Title 10 and Title 50 recruited HUMINT sources."

The hiring unit is JSOC's Directorate of Operation, Security, and Intelligence Support Division at Fort Bragg, which includes all of JSOC's intelligence assets, with the exception of the MSA. The effectiveness of the MSA operations is difficult to determine, but their legality is an easier question to answer. In Afghanistan and Iraq, the Defense Department ran the show, using traditional authorities granted to it under Title 10 of the U.S. Code. Outside the war zones, the CIA had primacy. United States law is fairly explicit about this: covert action to collect intelligence cannot be led by the military, in part because the oversight mechanisms aren't set up to monitor them.

Under the large umbrella of "preparing the battlefield," which later became "preparing the environment" (an environment being a bigger thing than a battlefield), and based on their successes elsewhere, there was reluctance in the Bush administration to de-conflict cases where the CIA and JSOC had different ideas about what they wanted to do in a country where the president had signed a finding. For example, the CIA objected to a JSOC Somalia mission at the last moment in 2003; the National Security Council sided with SOCOM. The CIA had legal authority, but SOCOM had, by presidential fiat, the lead in terms of counterterrorism. When the twain diverged in thinking, significant interagency conflicts resulted.

When it came to unleashing JSOC in countries with which the United States was not at war, the NSC was cautious. Terrorists on the target lists were fair game pretty much anywhere in the world, and the sovereignty of several countries was quietly disregarded as tiny hunter-killer teams invaded. Large-scale military involvement, however, was iffier, and although the White House had embraced the kinetic success of JSOC in Iraq, it would not endorse the same type of resource surge into places such as East Africa, to which terrorists were fleeing. This was maddening for JSOC commanders: they were "lawnmowers," chopping the heads off of al-Qaeda. They had successfully disrupted Iranian attempts to use Hezbollah to destabilize any number of operations—and *now* Washington was suddenly very cautious? There was a resource crunch too. General Doug Brown of SOCOM didn't have the resources he needed for foreign internal defense operations in Africa, "and that vacuum could be, and was, in some cases, filled by Al Qaeda," he told a historian.[7]

JSOC's role in some of the more legally marginal elements of the war on terrorism had brought unwanted attention and significant friction with the State Department. Secretary of State Condoleezza Rice encouraged ambassadors in countries where JSOC operated with impunity to speak up. One was Peru, where a DEVGRU operator with red hair (his nickname was "Flamer") got into a physical dispute with some locals. JSOC wanted the CIA to help exfiltrate him from the country. The CIA refused, and JSOC had to scramble its own assets to collect its sailor. Why was JSOC in Peru? It's not clear. The NSC, not wanting to unleash JSOC's capacity in areas outside the war zone and cognizant of the publicity that the units were getting, began to pull back on the reins.

The United States believes that in the summer of 2007, as many as three hundred al-Qaeda-trained fighters fled to the Horn of Africa. Though JSOC was on the ground, missions were highly restricted by an overly cautious Washington. "Flynn watched, literally, because they had these guys tracked, as hundreds of al-Qaeda fighters went to Somalia and into Yemen and elsewhere in the Horn and got better trained," a senior military official said. It would take a new president and a new classified presidential order to unleash JSOC's global strike capability again.

Lieutenant General Michael Flynn is the director of the Defense Intelligence Agency, the top intelligence officer for the Department of Defense. He has dominion over the newly established Defense Clandestine Service, a military counterpart to the CIA's National Clandestine Service. David Petraeus, now retired from the Army, served as the CIA's director. Admiral William McRaven is the commander of Special Operations Command. The men who sharpened the tip of America's spear now run the entirety of the arsenal.

As for the U.S. Joint Special Operations Command, there is virtually nowhere they cannot go, no one they cannot target, and nothing they cannot track. They serve at the pleasure of the president of the United States and operate with minimal oversight and public exposure only with the greatest of successes or the worst of tragedies. Congress keeps insisting on more insight into JSOC missions, and the Command is showing some leg. The United States has never had such a weapon, and the president has never had such power. The question is what happens next. Does every president from here on use his or her authority responsibly? Or does power breed overconfidence and, ultimately, carelessness? Misdirected force can redound with terrible consequence to national security, and the president hoisted with his own petard.

# CHAPTER 13

# The Structure
# of Secrecy

A rea 51 isn't the only place where the bodies are buried, the aliens are imprisoned, and flying saucers are kept. Some secrets are kept near Ruth's Chris Steak House in Crystal City, Virginia. The restaurant and the secret share the eleventh floor of a federal office building easily accessed by anyone. Its neighbors include the Special Inspector General for Reconstruction in Afghanistan, the National Security Division of the FBI, and what used to be the Counter-Intelligence Field Activity of the Defense Intelligence Agency. Each of those offices, however, advertises itself when you get close. Armed guards with loaded rifles, motion sensors, and barriers serve as a neon warning sign that visitors are not welcome.

But not this secret. Near the elevator and through the glass windows is what appears to be a dentist's office. It's not. A careful observer might notice a single distinguishing feature: a copy of *The Starfish and the Spider,* a book about organizational theory that successful contemporary military and intelligence officers have come to see as a bible. (The theory is that an organization is best structured like a starfish, which can regrow a function if it is injured or sliced off, as opposed to a spider, which operates from a centralized brain.)

After the attacks of September 11, 2001, as the Department of Defense and the U.S. intelligence community struggled to adapt to their new counterterrorism mission, a group of forward-thinking U.S. Air Force intelligence and technology types—some of them military, some civilian—approached a few trusted members of the defense appropriations committee in Congress. They identified a problem: the military and intelligence community's technology and acquisition infrastructure was far too cumbersome to equip war fighters and intelligence officers. The enemy would always have a tactical advantage simply because of the checks and balances, and byways and folkways, that were built into the system.

They had a solution: a new research, development, and testing office, reporting directly to a few policymakers and military officers. The office would have a single mission: solve technological problems quickly, without the vagaries of the bureaucracy getting in the way. The organization would be secret. It would not accept ownership of its products, and it would have no pride of authorship. It would not be established as a program office, or even as a special access program, because in both cases it would be swept under the umbrella of either Title 50 of the U.S. Code (the laws of the military) or Title 10 (the laws of the intelligence community). As a free agent, it could serve both communities without restraint. Funding that was the easy part. So many Air Force programs exist in two different universes: the budget line item and the real-life entity. The Defense Department has enough discretion to move money around, particularly if it is directed toward an entity that was created to elude by federal acquisition laws, as this organization was.

Now seven years into its existence, this organization has been the germ laboratory for several transformational counterterrorism technologies. It stood up NIGHT FIST, the joint Air Force–CIA cell that allowed for real-time monitoring of dangerous targets, even through dense fog or clouds. It perfected the RFID tracking and tagging materiel used to kill more than ten thousand terrorist suspects and their enablers. It invented, with the help of a contractor, a reconnaissance technology that can spot seemingly inert improvised explosive devices from high-flying drones. This organization has worked with the National Security Agency to perfect a method of extracting telephone numbers from cell phones previously considered destroyed.

One soldier attached to an intelligence brigade at the U.S. Joint Special Operations Command put it to us this way: "Suddenly, when we realized we needed it, we had tracking and tagging. And come to think of it, we really didn't know where it came from, or how we got it so fast."

The organization is accountable to virtually no one. Occasionally, a staffer will brief members of Congress about a particular program— but they will be identified as belonging to a different organization entirely.

"The big picture? I don't know if anyone in Congress really needs to have the big picture," was how someone who works for this organization told us. Had the entity been set up in a way that Congress could perform the type of oversight it wants to, "nothing would have gotten out to the field. Nothing." This person continued, "We exist because we have to exist."

We tried to protest, naming five other government entities that are supposed to do the same thing. One of them is even called the Rapid Equipping Force. "Too slow," was the response.

Indeed, as we tenderly verified the existence of this organization with people who would know—good people, law-abiding intelligence officials, generals, and admirals—not a single person disputed the premise.

The group is now called the Special Capabilities Office and is located in the Office of the Secretary of Defense (OSD/SCO). It is responsible for providing the technology that keeps soldiers safe and the al-Qaeda network from solidifying. The organization spends a fraction of one percent of the entire DOD budget. Its head is Brian Hibbeln, a physicist and former senior scientist at the National Reconnaissance Office.

The nature and rationale for the organization raises questions about the concentrated, unexamined exercise of executive power, and about the hapless bureaucracy so thoroughly dysfunctional and incapable of keeping pace with the needs of the intelligence community that the community's only recourse is an extralegal (though not illegal) structuring.* If the DOD, or a small group of people within the DOD, know—not just believe, but know, know for a fact—that they cannot perform their mission under the current regime of secrecy and oversight, and if the only way the country can be protected and soldiers lives saved is to create a secret entity: if all of those things are true, then solving the problem with secrecy is a hopeless endeavor. Organizations like the SCO exist in a way that raises questions about everything we think we know about government secrecy, and especially congressional oversight, which accordingly seems cosmetic and a simulacrum of a system that checks itself and balances competing principles.

Evolutionary biologists like to say that form follows function. In the national security world, the same thing happens. The structure of secrecy—its form—can tell a lot about its function. And the modifications made by agencies can reveal how an organization's culture of secrecy and classification has evolved to fit its institutional needs and external duties.

That's not to say that even the unclassified structure is easy to unravel. William Arkin, a persistent critic of secrecy whose research has contributed enormously to the public's understanding of the national security apparatus, published *Code Breakers* in 2006, a remarkable book containing thousands of program names, code words, identifiers, and secret locations—a telephone book, basically, of the deep state. Arkin's book received some attention at the time, but is now quite literally a reference book that special security officers are required to read in official (Top Secret) government classes. Several NSA offices have copies of Arkin's book lying around simply for them to be able to check out unfamiliar names they come across.

The modern system of classification came into being on September 26, 1951, when President Harry Truman signed an executive

---

*The OSD/SCO outed itself in 2010 at a classified military technology symposium whose agenda was made public. And it no longer operates from the office space described previously, so no operational details are being compromised in the retelling of the story. At the request of the Pentagon, the name of SCO's director is being withheld even though it is easily searchable.

order giving the CIA, a civilian agency, the power to decide what information ought to be classified in the interests of national security. National security was, as of that moment, no longer "merely a military consideration."[1]

The United States has three formal classification levels for collateral information: Confidential, Secret, and Top Secret, referring to progressively higher threats to security (from "reasonable" basis to conclude that national security will be harmed, to causing "exceptionally grave" damage to national security). These are terms of art, and very little effort has been made inside the government to drill down and distill across agencies what type of information will be Secret and what will be Top Secret. (Most classified information is Secret.) Accessing Secret information requires a fairly simple background check and a name check through various government databases. (An FBI or Office of Personnel Management or Defense Security Service agent will ask friends you list whether you've ever had a sudden surprise source of income or come into contact with foreign governments.)

A Top Secret clearance is extremely valuable: it adds tens of thousands of dollars per year to the average recipient's income, and it also costs the government several thousand dollars per person to grant, using a process called a Single Scope Background Investigation. Since the basic system was established, the prospect of a stringent background investigation has probably done more to deter would-be spies and unbalanced individuals from pursuing sensitive jobs than anything else.

Depending on the agency, applicants will be asked to take a polygraph, an instrument born out of the necessity to weed out communists and homosexuals from sensitive government service.[2] Only recently has the DOD admitted that the polygraph is not purely a scientific instrument; its measurements correlate slightly with physiological responses that liars give, but there are far too many false positives for the poly to be *the* conclusive test. (The CIA's polygraph examinations did not detect Aldrich Ames's deceptions; the FBI's did not detect Robert Hanssen's.)[3] In the words of the Intelligence Science Board, "there is no evidence supporting the assumption that autonomic and somatic responses reflect intentional deception."[4]

Yet there is no formal alternative to the polygraph, and there are other reasons it remains a ubiquitous tool. The polygraph's mystique is often used to simply scare people away or into confessing outright. (When the president travels overseas, the Secret Service will bring along a polygraph examiner in case they need to determine quickly whether someone acting suspiciously is intent on doing harm.) Top Secret clearance holders get repolygraphed every five years. And the questions asked are intrusive. If candidates already cleared require access to information denoting the sources and methods underlying intelligence collection—Sensitive Compartmented Information, or SCI—polygraph examinations will delve deeply into their intimate lives. (This is a "lifestyle" polygraph, as opposed to a "counterintelligence polygraph," which asks generic questions aimed at figuring out whether the person taking the test is a potential agent of a foreign government.)

The exact questions are not released because of the ease with which methods can be found to fool the examiners, but they tend to follow the times: one question regularly asked during lifestyle polygraphs is whether the person has ever sent a provocative picture of himself or herself to someone he or she did not know over the Internet. Lest you conclude that former representative Anthony Weiner would therefore be disqualified, the polygraph examiners and clearance adjudicators have latitude. If your sexual behavior is colorful and rich but is unlikely to mark you as a target for blackmail and doesn't interfere with your work, it won't matter as long as you admit to it. The same goes for mental illnesses such as depression. Depending on the agency and the task, sufferers from chronic depression can usually pass the background examination if they are honest about their condition and their personal psychiatrist concludes that they are not functionally impaired.

There is no standard across the government for putting people "on the box," as it's called. Soldiers are rarely subject to them, and Defense Department civilian employees obtain Top Secret/Sensitive Compartmented Information (Top Secret/SCI) clearances without them.

The three basic classification levels do not even begin to peel the onion. This is because—despite the expense of conducting background investigations, and under the guise of establishing the government's trust in an individual—the national security system does not in fact trust people with mere collateral clearances. The director of national intelligence (DNI) controls the SCI caveats that refer to (and in many cases limit access to) the sources and methods that produce intelligence.

As of 2012, there were four unclassified categories of SCI. They correspond to four classes of derivative intelligence. Special Intelligence (SI) refers to information derived from communications intelligence collection or signals intelligence. Talent-Keyhole (TK) refers to satellite imagery. Human Intelligence Control System (HCS) gives the bearer access to information that might implicate certain sensitive, specific human sources. This year, a new unclassified SCI compartment was added by the DNI. Geospatial intelligence requires clearance into Klondike, known by the trigraph KDK.

A few SCI terms are not officially acknowledged but provide a window into the organization of the deep state. Focal Point (FP) refers to military assistance to intelligence operations as well as civilian agencies that need DOD support. There are more than a dozen FP cells throughout the DOD, providing Defense assets to support CIA, NSA, and other classified activities. NC2-ESI is the new designation for information about nuclear targeting. (The main nuclear war plan is known as 8010-08 and is classified as Top Secret//NC2/ESI). A compartment known as Extremely Classified Information (ECI) refers to joint CIA/NSA programs. Technical Intelligence (TI) refers to product from drones. Especially sensitive satellite or reconnaissance technology is compartmented as RSV.[5] VRK is an NSA-specific compartment for intelligence derived from special sources. COIT is Compartments Intelligence, for especially sensitive DOD human intelligence and influence operations. Azure Blue, or AB, caveats come from an especially sensitive new reconnaissance platform. The compartment for information derived from measurement and signature systems intelligence (MASINT) is GG. Information from sensitive foreign sources is sometimes given the digraph CW. And so on.

In 1986, there were more than thirty SCI control systems, accounting for about five hundred different subcompartments.[6] Information that flows through one control system must be air-gapped (separated physically) from information that flows through another, unless they are handled jointly. This adds immeasurably to the confusion and expense of SCI. There are about two dozen SCI control systems today and about two hundred categories of SCI information. And there are still at least a half dozen other ways that the government protects its information. The CIA and the NSA use the unfortunately named BIGOT lists to specify access to named individuals, usually to protect their sources of information. (No, they're not calling people prejudiced. The term apparently derives from a notation that the British Secret Intelligence Service used to compartment information from their Gibraltar station. Information sent there: TO GIB. Information returned: BIGOT.) Nuclear code traffic is passed through a SPECAT—a special category channel protected from other extremely well-protected channels—through an air gap.

The DOD and some intelligence agencies create special access programs (SAPs) to circumscribe access to specific military and intelligence operations; treaty drafts; particularly sensitive new technical collection technologies; and procurement activities. (Most DOD SAPs concern procurement, acquisitions, and testing.) James Clapper, director of national intelligence, famously told Dana Priest that "only God" had cognizance of all of the SAPs in government. In truth, the creation of even the highest-level SAP—a "waived SAP" that only eight members of Congress get orally read in to—triggers a notification process that involves two hundred people inside the Pentagon and national security establishment, according to a senior government program manager who creates them. But those managing SAPs can create subcompartments within the SAPs that aren't (primarily for reasons of efficiency) subject to the same disclosure rules.

Where SCI is identified primarily by trigraph or digraph, SAPs are given unclassified nicknames (Neptune's Spear was the SAP within which the Osama bin Laden raid was planned) and a classified code word that formally controls their access (in this case, CRANK SHAFT). GREYSTONE (or GST)—the CIA SAP created to manage its rendition, interrogation, and counterterrorism programs—had more than a dozen subcompartments, each of them given numbers. For example, the pilots and contractors who flew rendition flights didn't need to know about the enhanced interrogation techniques that would take place at the CIA "black sites" in Europe and Asia. So they might be given access to GST-001; the interrogators might have been read in to GST-001 and GST-002, which would include the techniques and their use at the black sites, as well as the rendition portion of the program.

Even before entertaining questions of oversight, a balancing act occurs. It is prudent to keep sensitive sources and methods to a small group, simply because the chances of their being disclosed increases linearly with the number of people in the know. But the costs of compartmentalization can undermine the programs themselves. Consider the following example, which has been somewhat sanitized to protect the source and the technology. A certain very secret and highly valuable technical intelligence platform is run out of an Air Force base in the United States. There, operators control the platform and collect and disseminate intelligence. At a location overseas where this platform (call it BENJI) is based, there are ground operators. This program—think of it as a truck, an airplane, a drone, or a satellite, with a lot of special capabilities—is so sensitive that every tasking must be approved in advance by the National Security Council.

But the platform is so adaptable that it has a lot of customers. The DOD might want to use its abilities to monitor something in country X, whereas the CIA might want to use it to track nuclear fissile material movements in Pakistan. The problem is that the operators at PROJECT BENJI have to literally switch hard drives depending on which customer gets the product. For reasons that only the program manager himself or herself know, the Defense Department can't know what the CIA gets, and vice versa. Indeed, the DOD, sensitive to the implications of the platform's exposure, forces the ground operators to take a specific piece of equipment off of the platform before a DOD mission, lest anyone blame them. (Of course, if the platform is compromised, it's compromised; it doesn't matter a whit to Iran whether the DOD's Defense Threat Reduction Agency or the CIA is monitoring its nuclear program.)

Cries to reform this system and iron out its ironies—information classified Secret but marked with a caveat is given better protection than Top Secret information without one—have come from inside and outside government since the dawn of the Cold War. Robert Gates, former director of central intelligence and secretary of defense, once called the system the "greatest deterrent" to saving money in the national security arena.[7] Commissions on government secrecy tend to observe the same trends (more secrets, more people with classifying authority, bizarre examples of information that's been classified, and the toxicity of overclassification on the public's faith in government) and propose the same solutions: get rid of most of the caveats; strengthen automatic declassification rules; establish better auditing systems so that people are presumed to *have* access to information, rather than "no need to know."

The first major government report to call for reform of the process was convened by Congress during the presidency of Dwight Eisenhower. The sociologist Edward Shils noted that the secrecy system was set up to justify the "phantasies of apocalyptic visionaries," a phrase that would forever resonate with Daniel Patrick Moynihan.[8] Things were kept secret because no one could be trusted; because an existential threat existed in the form of nuclear weapons and communist intrusions; because the average American had to be protected by the government for the sake of the government's legitimacy. After the Cold War, this was manifestly no longer the case.

In 1993, the CIA and the DOD received a report from a commission chartered by Gates, suggesting that the state wipe away the twelve separate über-categories of classified information and replace them with two.[9] Classified information was classified, so there would be one collateral term—Secret—and certain very sensitive information would be compartmented with a code word, although the decision to compartment information would be taken very seriously.

The report was ignored. Three years later, a commission chaired by Moynihan took an even more caustic and sociological view of secrecy and recommended wholesale changes to the secrecy system. He coauthored legislation calling for a National Declassification Center, for the mandatory declassification of certain information, and for a wholesale overhaul of the classification apparatus.

David Schanzer, a top Pentagon lawyer at the time who was sympathetic to the Moynihan report, recalls how stakeholders fought back: "DOD had a strong revulsion to the bill on a cost basis. So program managers put together a cost case for all the requirements that Moynihan's bill would have had them do. Given the volume of material, it would wind up costing just the general counsel's office about $10 billion a year alone. We sent a letter to Moynihan, and as soon as he saw it, he got sick to his stomach because he knew that legislation wasn't going to be able to make it through that kind of opposition."

Because the classification apparatus is labyrinthine, those in power sometimes feel safe compounding the issue by making up new schemes. In 1984, Representative Dick Cheney, a young congressman from Wyoming, saw his assignment to the House Intelligence Committee "as an honor."[10] It was also his formal introduction to the deep world of secrecy. "The very nature of the committee's work requires absolute confidentiality and secrecy," he wrote in his memoir.[11] He visited the secret test site at Area 51 near Groom Lake, Nevada, to see an early version of the F-117 stealth fighter. He spent time at the then classified National Reconnaissance Office watching real-time satellite feeds. He was read in to the highly compartmentalized Continuity of Government procedures, a subject he would take a particular interest in. Under President George H. W. Bush, he would serve as secretary of defense.

Charged with vetting potential vice presidential candidates for Governor George W. Bush, Cheney managed a tight process with no leaks. Indeed, the first hint that he might be chosen came only a day before it was announced. After the inauguration in 2001, Vice President Cheney and his chief counselor, David Addington, former staff director of the Senate Intelligence Committee, created a layer of insulation around the Office of the Vice President. It was easy for Cheney to ignore any interest the press might have in him; he was not going to run for president and had no reason to develop a public persona. A former staff member who is close to Cheney today says that the original reason for walling himself off was that "he just didn't want to be bothered." After the attacks on September 11, 2001, Cheney may not have changed, but everything around him did.

The Secret Service assigned a full-time counterassault team to his detail. When terrorist threats spiked, he spent nights at Camp David, and when the threat was acute, at the Alternate National Military Command Center on the border of Maryland and Pennsylvania.

Early on, Cheney likely had a conversation with President Bush about managing the post-9/11 national security interagency process. No one knows for sure, because Cheney never discussed his conversations with the president. According to Steven Yates, deputy national security adviser to Vice President Cheney, "In eight years, not once did any of their private conversations leak." Even inside the "vault," as staffers called the vice president's office, "there was a one-way feedback mechanism. You give Cheney what he asks for and he told you what you needed to know," said Yates, adding, "When you walked out of that door, it closed behind you, courtesy of a lawyer named David Addington."

Did Cheney take it upon himself to task JSOC with specific missions, as Seymour Hersh has alleged? Yates said he doesn't know. "But there is nothing illegal about the vice president doing something the president gave him permission to do." (General Stanley McChrystal, the commander of JSOC from 2003 to 2007, does not recall having spoken to Cheney during the period.) According to Yates, no one ever discussed whether Bush and Cheney had a conversation in which power was formally delegated. But Cheney, perhaps more than anyone in the White House, knew about how sclerotic the national security bureaucracy could be and had little patience for the lawyerly way in which the National Security Council adjudicated policy. "Cheney had a habit of reaching, three, four rings down into the bureaucracy, asking people on the ground what was really happening. And that frosted people on the NSC."

Said Yates, "People in government like Dick Cheney and Don Rumsfeld know more about the different elements of the government, the intelligence community, its assets, what the military can and cannot do. They, as much as anyone else, know where to look for those black boxes that no one likes to touch."

Still, Cheney's office took secrecy to excessive lengths, as Bill Leonard, the head of the Information Security Oversight Office (ISOO) at the National Archives, would find. Leonard's job was to oversee the way the government classifies national security information. From the start, he noticed weird things coming from the administration. For one thing, the White House counsel always deferred to the Office of the Vice President whenever anything related to Cheney landed on Leonard's desk. Things as mundane as the vice president's talking points were labeled *Treated as Top Secret/ SCI*, or *Treated as Top Secret Codeword*.

What is the significance of such markings? In 2003, Cheney and his staff discussed how to handle the public relations aspect of an editorial in the *New York Times* written by Joseph Wilson, a former U.S. diplomat. In the piece, Wilson argued that there was no evidence to suggest that Iraq tried purchasing yellowcake uranium from Nigeria.[12] Notes from Cheney's meetings on the subject were marked *Treated as Top Secret/SCI*.[13] According to Leonard:

> That's not a recognized marking. I have no idea if it was the intent, but I can guarantee you what the consequences of those markings are. When any of this material eventually does end up at a presidential library and access demands are being made, or it's being processed for release, when some poor archivist sees material marked *Handle as SCI*, it's going into the bottom of the pile, and it is going to get much more conservative review. Whether it was the intent to retard the eventual release of the information, I know that's going to be a consequence of it.

The Office of the Vice President clashed with Leonard and the ISOO over its handling of classified information. Cheney's office had filed routine annual reports on its classification activity in 2001 and 2002 but stopped doing so in 2003. A year later, the Office of the Vice President rebuffed an attempt by ISOO officials to inspect it. The office argued that since it had both executive *and* legislative functions, it was therefore not bound by an executive order on the handling of classified information.[14]

This offended Leonard. "Putting aside the constitutional position of the vice president, the very concept that nonelected government officials working in the White House, accessing the most highly sensitive information, and weren't obligated to follow the rules set forth by the president, I found chilling, to tell you the truth."

Addington would later argue that the Office of the Vice President is not an agency and thus not subject to ISOO's oversight, a position the White House concurred with.[15] The vice president managed to evade ISOO's eyes through the end of the Bush presidency.[16]

In general, Bill Clinton's record on declassification and secrecy is quite good, and he doesn't get much credit for it. A billion documents were bulk-declassified during his tenure. Similarly, there were few leaks of sensitive information—and there was plenty of sensitive information to be leaked, including virtually everything about Clinton's secret war against al-Qaeda.[17] But habits remained hard to break. John Podesta, one of the architects of the modern Freedom of Information Act (FOIA) law and one of Clinton's chiefs of staff, recalls a battle he "won once out of every ten times." He said, "Sometimes, someone from the NSC would come into my office and hand me a newspaper article from overseas. It was marked 'C' for Confidential. I was quite an asshole about this, I admit," he said. "I would go to the NSC executive secretary down the hall and ask, 'Why is this classified at all? It's a newspaper article.' Then inevitably they would come back and say, 'It's classified because the president's interested in it and that is strategic information.' Okay. Yeah, right."

The FOIA is an effective counterweight to government secrecy. It is also a much-abused law, overburdened by communities of conspiracy theorists who overwhelm FOIA offices with requests for information on space aliens and such. This frustrates professional historians and reputable transparency advocates, whose FOIA documents are simply added to the back of the not inconsiderable queue.

By design, the FOIA process is cumbersome for both the petitioner and the government. To ensure that no actively sensitive material is released, an FOIA officer must often submit the request to colleagues at multiple agencies for review. And though there are written standards defining what exemptions are appropriate, every federal agency interprets them differently. This inconsistency, especially concerning matters of national security, frustrates researchers, and comes back to the fundamental question of what exactly constitutes harm to national security and who gets to decide? And if different people given interpretive authority make different conclusions on the same data (inter-rater disagreement, as sociologists call it), does that not undermine the intellectual edifice of both the FOIA process and national security classification itself?

The National Security Archive at George Washington University has made a sport out of finding examples where one government agency considers something too sensitive to declassify, oblivious to the fact that another agency has already released the material. For example, many Cold War–era memos related to missile defense and nuclear war planning have been held back by the Defense Department, even though many have not only been declassified but actually published by the government in official, unclassified histories. The problem, as university researchers see it, is that the government refuses to establish uniformly enforceable standards for historical and legacy information and often refuses to revisit earlier classification decisions. According to William Burr of the National Security Archive, "Neither historians, taxpayers, nor the secrecy system itself are well served when declassification reviewers treat historical classified information in the same way as today's secrets."

The more secrets an agency holds, the better it is at frustrating the FOIA process, intentionally or otherwise. The CIA, for example, regularly denies requests under the "(b)(3)" exemption, which gives the government a way to protect things not formally classified as national security information but legally protected from disclosure. (FOIA does not force the government to reveal ongoing and vital national security secrets.) There are many statutory exemptions that make sense. Sometimes government documents contain private information about U.S. citizens, such as Social Security numbers. Others might reveal a company's proprietary information. Some might contain facts pertinent to an ongoing criminal case. It's not hard to imagine exemption power being so broadly construed so as to nix the release of virtually every document requested. But the genius of the FOIA is in one of its final clauses, flowing directly from a quirk of the classification system itself.

Suppose that a single sentence in this paragraph contains national security information classified as Secret, and that a sentence or two around it contains modifiers or clauses that provide details from which the secret can be inferred. That still leaves a large number of sentences that in and of themselves, and even taken as a whole, do not contain classified information. Under the law, the government must segregate unclassified parts of paragraphs. The FOIA works because the state cannot reasonably argue that every sentence in every paragraph in every classified document is itself properly classified. The FOIA officers are sworn to uphold the statute, so while they might be biased in favor of whatever agency they represent, they are obliged to segregate.

The (b)(3) exemption is tricky because of its vagueness. For example, federal rules of procedure prevent the release of information obtained by grand juries. The law seems clear: testimony and evidence presented during grand jury sessions are never to be released. But in some notable cases, judges have ordered the release of information, usually because it might be of significant historical value. So is the grand jury testimony exemption in fact absolute? And if it isn't, what criteria should FOIA officers use when making decisions? There are no easy answers to these questions and few forums outside of a courtroom to establish precedent.

The (b)(3) exemption also requires FOIA officers to know the intent and meaning of virtually every federal law proscribing a process for withholding information. The officers must also keep up with changes to these laws. And, once again, standards across agencies are markedly different. Often information will be denied under (b)(3) on the basis of a law that has expired or that has changed.

To help matters, as of 2009, new bills before Congress must specifically state if certain information is subject to the provision. But reform will be slow going. The CIA's use of (b)(3) has prevented the disclosure of even the most basic information about how the agency works. Furthermore, the director of the CIA is legally empowered to protect the sources and methods by which intelligence is gained. But in 2004, that responsibility officially shifted to the Office of the Director of National Intelligence (ODNI).

The CIA, however, points to the National Security Act of 1947, which both established the CIA and appointed its director as head of the intelligence community. As such, the CIA continues to protect its sources and methods as if the ODNI did not exist. In theory, the ODNI could redelegate this power to the CIA, but it hasn't done so, which means the CIA has been using a "sources and methods" exemption that, technically speaking, it no longer possesses.

A few litigators, such as the National Security Counselors firm and the American Civil Liberties Union, along with news organizations like ProPublica, have tenaciously explored the exemptions issue, and thankfully so. Attention must be paid to the finer strands of the FOIA process precisely because the law is so powerful. The FOIA is a tremendous check on government power, and the stronger it becomes, the more incentive the government will have to treat it respectfully. Researcher Jeffrey T. Richelson has been able to get entire National Reconaissance Office imagery satellites and their products declassified with a single FOIA; the catch: he knows what to ask for.[18]

There is also the powerful Mandatory Declassification Review (MDR), established in 1972 and revised and liberalized by Presidents Clinton and Obama. The MDR process allows anyone (a reporter, a citizen) to formally request the declassification of a document. The originating agency still gets to determine whether the document was properly classified, and the CIA has special powers to protect its information. But MDR provides an avenue for petitioners to twice appeal the decision to a review board, called the Interagency Security Classification Appeals Panel. In theory, the review board has a broader perspective on classification matters than do individual agencies, and its decision is binding. It is a formidable mechanism by which the issue of declassification can be forced (especially for documents written before 1966, when the FOIA was passed).

The catch is that petitioners must fully develop information about the classified subjects for which they are requesting documents. And agencies can still deny requests, on the basis that confirming or denying the classification status of a secret document would itself reveal the existence of the document. (There is a similar exemption called the Glomar Response that is used to protect highly sensitive compartmentalized intelligence programs. It is named after the *Glomar Explorer*, the ship built by Howard Hughes to try and recover a lost Soviet nuclear submarine.) While MDR does not have any direct bearing on the classification process itself, repeated reversals of an agency's decision might provide incentive to the agency to make better decisions about what gets classified in the first place.

# CHAPTER 14

# Partisan Transparency

W e are facing a [missile] gap on which we are gambling with our
survival," said Senator John F. Kennedy on February 29, 1960,
during his campaign for the presidency. "Time is short. This situation
never should have been permitted to arise. But if we move now, if
we are willing to gamble with our money instead of our survival, we
have, I am sure, the wit and resource to maintain the minimum conditions for our survival, for our alliances, and for the active pursuit of
peace."[1]

There was no missile gap. President Dwight D. Eisenhower's
obsession with image intelligence had paid dividends, and photographs from the U-2 spy plane program confirmed that if there was
in fact a gap, it was in favor of the United States.[2] Still, Eisenhower
couldn't publicly state such a concrete fact for fear of revealing what else the United States had gathered over Soviet soil.[3] But
the president feared that Kennedy, now owning and leading on the
defense issue, was taking Congress and the electorate with him. Stuart
Symington, senator from Missouri, was especially forceful in his denunciations. "A very substantial missile gap does exist and the Eisenhower
Administration apparently is going to permit this gap to increase."[4]

The president dispatched General Earle Wheeler, director of the
Joint Staff for the Joint Chiefs of Staff, to give Kennedy a classified

176

briefing on intelligence gathered over the Soviet Union. But Kennedy wasn't going to let facts stand in the way of a winning campaign theme.[5]

"By getting into this numbers racket," Eisenhower would fume throughout the campaign, "and by scaring people, they are getting away with murder." "Deterrent" had become a code word for unbridled military spending, enriching arms makers at the expense of the nation's wherewithal. "Did they just want to build more and more Atlases for storage in warehouses? It was unconscionable."[6]

As early as 1951, Eisenhower fretted over the growing defense industry. He considered the economy to be a national security issue and argued that "our system must remain solvent, as we attempt a solution of this great problem of security. Else we have lost the battle from within that we are trying to win from without."[7] In his first State of the Union address, he remarked, "To amass military power without regard to our economic capacity would be to defend ourselves against one kind of disaster by inviting another."[8] And leaving office, shaken by this debate that he had clearly lost, he gave his famous speech warning, "In the councils of government, we must guard against the acquisition of unwarranted influence, whether sought or unsought, by the military-industrial complex."[9]

When President Kennedy assumed office, his rhetoric collided with a solid, apolitical intelligence assessment. Eisenhower's men had been telling the truth. There was no missile gap. The president greeted the news with a single dismayed expletive.[10]

It's hard to imagine something similar happening today. Presidential administrations seem more cavalier with classified material. The political incentives to leak are simply too great, and the press is very willing to accommodate. The chances of a leaker getting caught are slim at best, and the government doesn't have the resources to investigate a tenth of the cases presented to it.

In 2002, Thomas Fingar was the senior intelligence analyst who got Iraq right. He judged, correctly, that there was no evidence that Saddam Hussein had reconstituted an abandoned nuclear weapons program. In accordance with the axiom that holds the absence of evidence not being the evidence of absence, he put the prewar pattern of facts together in a way that suggested that Saddam kept to a policy of deliberate ambiguity despite having no weapons.

Others in the intelligence community fiercely resisted his conclusions. His expertise, and the expertise of Department of Energy (DOE) specialists who actually *build* centrifuges, was simply disregarded. Fingar and the DOE analysts had contacted the company that made the centrifuge Iraq had been found with, and they told him in no uncertain terms that the centrifuges could not be used to enrich uranium at a rate that would produce weapons-grade material. There were ring magnets too, which the Office of the Vice President was obsessed with—magnets that might be part of a centrifuge assembly. They had many applications. "If you didn't assume they were for centrifuges, you could have judged them to be used in many other places. In fact, we know now, they were used for their missile program."

What galled Fingar, though, was that the National Intelligence Estimate was "terrible," as he put it. Very few people read it. (Fingar knew this because the highly classified document had to be signed out by any official who wanted to do so.) So in his view, policymakers were acting like lawyers when it came to secret information. Find the precedents; build the argument; make a clear case. Saddam was evil; he had a nuclear program; he'd had a missile program; if he had *one*, he must have *one*. But intelligence isn't like that, and the information had to be respected for what it was.

There is a reason the U.S. government spends so much time training analysts about the fragility of information. The methodology of intelligence analysis is a cultivated skill; its subtleties are not self-evident. Politicians bring to the table a set of prejudices and predispositions, as was illustrated during a "missile gap" exchange between Allen Dulles and Stuart Symington. In declassified transcripts from closed congressional hearings, the director of central intelligence explains to the senator from Missouri that the intelligence community cannot *estimate* raw information:

> "When I saw you with other people who know their subject," said Symington, "we offered you what we thought were evidences of more [missile] testing."
> "But gave me no evidence," said Dulles.

"Well, we thought it was evidence," said Symington. "Let's not get into that."

"You gave me assertions," said Dulles. "I want to make that point perfectly clear."

Later, tensions rise as Symington again asserts that the opinions of his advisers constituted information. Dulles responds, "I want some of the background on which this information was adduced. I mean, the—if someone says there are 55 [missile] firings, there must be some evidence of those firings. What is the evidence?"

When Secretary of State Colin Powell presented the case that Iraq possessed weapons of mass destruction, the "facts" were based on a bad source, and assertions followed. (Echoes of Dulles: "You gave me assertions. . . . What is the evidence?") It is dangerous when policymakers abuse their access to classified information. But in the case of Iraq, it was even more dangerous that they used the information without really knowing what they were doing.

The obvious solution to the misuse of intelligence was to broaden access to it so that analysts from many different perspectives could use their unique lenses to arrive at a conclusion. The experts had to be trusted and empowered. And the information itself, being that it formed the basis for National Intelligence Estimates (NIEs), which formed the basis for policy that could lead the country to war, had to be processed in a way that took nothing for granted.

As the deputy director of national intelligence for analysis and chairman of the National Intelligence Council from 2005 to 2008, Fingar would be the administration's point person for writing the NIEs. In 2007, he was a principal author of an NIE on Iran. He knew quite plainly about the policy divide inside the administration. He also knew that once a piece of information made it into the brain of a policymaker, it would stick.

The process of crafting an NIE under Fingar could be interminable and exacting. First, analysts would come up with the assignment parameters: what is the puzzle to be assembled here, and what are reasonable questions that can—and can't—be answered? If analysts needed more information, they would go to the collectors (CIA, DIA) and ask if more was available. If it wasn't available, analysts would be asked if it could be acquired. Sometimes the answer was yes, in which case the NIE would wait on the new information so long as it didn't push the time frame too far to the right.

Slowly, the framework of the estimate would come into form, as bits and piece of evidence were analyzed and validated, or rejected, or rejected or validated with caveats—whatever the iterative process showed. Often this entire process would be repeated if the information seemed incomplete and the analysis unsatisfactory. After a preliminary hypothesis was formed, the NIE would be distributed to the analytical arms of the U.S. intelligence community, and based on their feedback, the NIE staff would carefully note where the analysts agreed and disagreed. If the CIA disagreed about a certain conclusion, their analysts would be invited to hash it out. Often, Fingar found, agencies disagreed with the analogies or metaphors that were used to illuminate a conclusion. The NIE, after all, is a story written for policymakers. The metaphors had to be precise.

Fingar didn't like his NIEs to have caveats. Better to draw a conclusion that incorporated the doubts by using language precisely rather than to say that agency X simply disagreed. At the end of the process, the staff would create several different versions: one for the White House, one for Congress, and one for senior officials elsewhere in government. Congress didn't get to see as many sources and methods as the White House did. The final NIE, one hundred pages long, had fifteen hundred source citations.[11]

In the case of the 2007 NIE, Fingar was ordered, to his surprise, to create a fourth version—one specifically for public consumption.[12] The order came straight from President George W. Bush. Fingar never knew precisely what the motive was, though he suspected that the Oval Office wanted to preempt the vice president's office from making rash remarks about Iran policy.

So Fingar created an executive summary with sources and methods excised. One of the conclusions that he published for public consumption was that, with a high degree of confidence, Iran had "halted its nuclear weapons program" in 2003. He added the important caveat that

> we also assess with moderate-to-high confidence that Tehran at a minimum is keeping open the option to develop nuclear weapons. We judge with high confidence that the halt, and

Tehran's announcement of its decision to suspend its declared uranium enrichment program and sign an Additional Protocol to its Nuclear Non-Proliferation Treaty Safeguards Agreement, was directed primarily in response to increasing international scrutiny and pressure resulting from exposure of Iran's previously undeclared nuclear work.

What Fingar could not publish was that the United States possessed evidence that Iran had started up a new, undeclared uranium enrichment facility at Qom. If that point had been published, it would have raised the question, How does the United States know this? The answer was a combination of human sources, signals intelligence, and imagery analysis. Fingar won't say why the sources were too sensitive at the time, but in the judgment of the intelligence community, the fact simply could not be compromised.

Fingar added a footnote to his published conclusion stating that the NIE's conclusion here referred to "Iran's nuclear weapon design and weaponization work and covert uranium conversion-related and uranium enrichment-related work; we do not mean Iran's declared civil work related to uranium conversion and enrichment." Indeed, as he later noted, "The declassified portion of the estimate did not address how long it would take Iran to convert highly enriched uranium into a weapon but the classified text did. What I can say here is that we judged Iran has the scientific, technical, and industrial capacity to produce a weapon if it decided to do so."

Iran wasn't building bombs, but it still was converting uranium at a rate that could be used for bombs.

The previous NIE had concluded that a military option was probably the only viable one, given the time frame it would take for Iran to make an actual nuclear weapon. The new NIE suggested that although Iran had not abandoned its goal of possessing a weapon, it would take some time to actually build one, if they decided to do so. It did not mean *at all* that Iran was out of the nuclear business.

But the White House went out of its way not to clarify, and the press jumped on the conclusion that the weapons program had been shut down. Take that, Dick Cheney!

Fingar told the authors that "they wanted this out, and then they refused to take responsibility for it." Even transparency can be used as a political weapon. To Fingar it was a reason to treat the privilege of accessing secret information with humility.

Wearing his other hat, as deputy director of national intelligence for analysis, he tried to change the culture of firewalls within the intelligence community that often provided for stovepiped, inaccurate, rushed, or just plain stupid analysis. The "need to know" habit long drilled into analysts turned into a "responsibility to share." That is, if a report was produced from raw data, it would have to justify its use of caveats and compartments. Reports were to be written for as many people as possible to see. All information that is disseminated, he believed, ought to be discoverable to analysts working on the subject. If part of an analysis was based on an extremely sensitive source and had to be excised, the analyst would have to certify that whatever he or she kept from other analysts would not change the conclusion.

Fingar encouraged the creation of A-Space, a cross-agency collaborative database of classified and unclassified information that was easily searchable. He is also responsible for another innovation—one that the Obama administration has done away with. He allowed his National Intelligence Officers (NIOs) to brief members of the press on background about their subject areas. To him, it was useful for the press to understand the thought process of policymakers who were wading their way through a difficult subject. So long as his NIOs didn't share classified information—and he trusted they would not—they could provide guidance to a reporter who was writing on, say, North Korea, or China.

Stephen Hadley, national security adviser to President Bush, knew that a pleasant spring morning in April 2008 would not become a pleasant spring day. A month after Israel had bombed what was believed to be a nuclear weapons manufacturing plant, Hadley was going to acknowledge to the House and Senate select committees on intelligence that the United States had provided Israel with intelligence well before the raid, knew for weeks in advance that Israel planned a strike, and (according to one official who remains in government) helped Israel disable part of Syria's air defense system along its northern border with Turkey. (Other published sources dispute this account, suggesting that the United States did not know in advance and had asked Israel not to disclose it even if they wanted to.)

The September 6, 2007, raid caught the world by surprise. The White House refused to shed any light on the subject for months after. Slowly, details about what the site was, or wasn't or might have been, began to appear in the press. Hadley had given the congressional Gang of Eight (four leaders from each party) a verbal briefing a week before. But the committees, controlled by Democrats in the throes of debating intelligence about the necessity of a surge in Iraq, demanded a full briefing. Why hadn't the White House briefed Congress before? After all, a team of White House advisers had been meeting weekly to discuss the impending Israeli action, and at least some U.S. intelligence resources were involved.

It wasn't, as some later speculated, that the United States didn't agree with Israel's interpretation of the intelligence. Hadley had simply made a judgment call about secrecy. Technically, since the United States was not running the operation, it was not an "ongoing and current" covert activity. Practically, he simply did not trust Democrats on the committee to keep their mouths shut. Many Democrats on the committee were haranguing the Bush administration on a daily basis, and Hadley wasn't about to pull them aside and share one of the most sensitive counterproliferation secrets in the world.

The Democrats had good reason to be upset, however. As the CIA later admitted, the United States had been observing the site with a spy satellite for more than a year before the raid, and secretly shared intelligence on the reactor site with Turkey in an effort to preempt the necessity of an Israeli attack. As a Bush White House official later conceded, "We were monitoring the site. That was an ongoing operation under almost any definition. But we didn't trust them and they didn't trust us, and this is the situation we found ourselves in."

Indeed, any hope the Bush administration had in using the formal disclosure of U.S. participation to advance its nonproliferation policy or rally opinion against North Korea was dashed by the tribal emotions unleashed by Democrats on the Hill. Though the increased partisanship in Washington is rarely discussed in this context, it is a driving force in the secrecy debate.

To be clear, relations between the secrecy apparatus and Congress have never been cordial. Bill Casey, former director of central intelligence, referred to congressional intelligence committees as "those assholes on the hill," and as Trevor Paglen noted, would mumble "incomprehensibly through his briefings, when he bothered to brief the intelligence committees at all."[13]

Fairly or not, Congress has long had a reputation for leaking classified information. (Frederick Hitz disagrees with that assessment. "Since [1975], the most damaging leaks have come from the executive branch, from intelligence officers or administration operatives who disagree with the policy behind the spying or covert action, rather than from a more vulnerable Congress.")[14] In a preemptive move against careless revelations, on October 5, 2001, President Bush issued a memorandum stating that the need "to protect military operational security, intelligence sources and methods, and sensitive law enforcement investigations" was too great to entrust to 535 members of Congress and their staffs.[15] The memo decreed that all such information would be restricted to the eight senior members of the legislative branch. Congress publicly balked, and five days later this policy was rescinded. Though "Gang of Eight" briefings became a regular occurrence (the NSA terrorist surveillance program being one such example), congressional oversight committees resumed regular hearings on national security.

According to *The 9/11 Commission Report*, in 1998 Osama bin Laden, ever on the move and tracked by satellite phones, stopped using this "particular means of communication almost immediately after a leak to the *Washington Times*. This made it much more difficult for the National Security Agency to intercept his conversations."[16] Jed Babbin, deputy under secretary of defense for George H. W. Bush, blamed an unnamed Republican senator for "blurting out" the information. CIA veteran Michael Scheuer, who ran the bin Laden program at that time, said in a 2005 speech that "a direct causal line from the publication of that story to the attacks of September 11" could be drawn.[17]

Even in instances where Congress is kept appraised of black operations, often and for political reasons knowledge of such briefings is later denied. Notably, in 2002 eventual Speaker of the House Nancy Pelosi was one of four members of Congress briefed on the

CIA's use of enhanced interrogation techniques. As described by the *Washington Post*, "Among the techniques described, said two officials present, was waterboarding, a practice that years later would be condemned as torture by Democrats and some Republicans on Capitol Hill. But on that day no objections were raised. Instead, at least two lawmakers in the room asked the CIA to push harder, two U.S. officials said."[18] Pelosi denies such details were revealed.

For a decade after 9/11, largely because of feverish levels of mistrust between Democrats and Republicans, congressional skepticism turned into defiance.* This damaged the intelligence community, Congress, and public trust in those institutions, and it had the perverse effect of weakening incentives for the secret keepers to exercise their power appropriately. Democrats will argue, with some justification, that Congress could not effectively fulfill its oversight functions in a political atmosphere where questions about counterterrorism policies were confused with (or deliberately turned into, by the White House) doubts about the righteousness of the American cause. This is true. So true, in fact, that the Bush administration's own penchant for secrecy and its determination to keep Congress out of the loop ultimately wound up undermining even some of the less controversial but highly effective secret policies it put into place.

The partisan instinct deserves its opprobrium. At ill-timed moments, both Democrats and Republicans screamed solely because their activist bases demanded such screaming. At least five committees in each chamber have some piece of the oversight mix, and the most important of the lot, the select committees on intelligence, hold special status. In the House, their members aren't appointed (as most members of most committees are) by steering committees. A single person, in other words, cannot overload a committee with allies. Instead, the Speaker of the House and the minority leader make the appointments.

---

*Vice President Dick Cheney writes that when he briefed members of the Gang of Eight on the NSA surveillance program in March 2004 (after the Justice Department's objections threatened to curtail the operation), the Gang agreed that Congress could not be trusted with writing legislation because it would leak. Another official present at the meeting recalls the Gang's objection differently: they didn't think Congress would pass something so controversial.

During the height of hyperpartisanship post-9/11, the intelligence committees, particularly in the House, were treated as sinecures and, even worse, platforms for the airing of grievances. Sometimes the grievances were well formed. When members of the intelligence community brief Congress on highly classified programs, they're incentivized to do so in a way that provides the necessary amount of detail to satisfy the legal and administrative requirements, and not a shred more. Since most members of the intelligence committees aren't experts, an imbalance is built into the system. The briefers will use technical language, knowing that members often can't share with their staffs enough information to develop follow-up questions. Members know this and tend to be on the alert for weasel words or any hints or indications that there are depths to the particular program that might not be visible in a briefing. The less trust there is between institutions, the more games are played in the briefings. These games have become endemic, which for oversight is troubling. The less trust we have in government, the more likely it is for free-lancers and hobbyists, people who traffic in classified information that is expressly often pulled from its context, to decide whether to publish secrets. Don't blame this on the lone wolves. Blame it on the gatekeepers for failing to maintain credibility.

CHAPTER 15

# Open Source
# Strikes Back

Once upon a time, the federal government's response to existential emergencies (known as Continuity of Government procedures, or COG) was the holy of holies. There was a time when the FBI wouldn't even inform members of Congress about their designated relocation site in the event of a catastrophe (the Greenbrier Resort in White Sulphur Springs, West Virginia). Instead, the Bureau entrusted the heads of its local field offices with that knowledge and instructed them to impart it to members when FBI headquarters in Washington cabled them permission. The cover organization for COG activities, the Defense Mobilization Programs Support Activity, remained a secret for two decades, until journalist Ted Gup exposed it in 1982. (It would be replaced by the National Programs Office, which used the same office space and did the same thing.) After COG programs atrophied in the 1990s, the Bush administration reconstituted many of them after September 11, 2001.

At first, stories appeared about an "undisclosed location" where Vice President Dick Cheney would spend much of his time. This was a secret in name only, as most everyone in Washington assumed that Cheney was either at Site B, the Mount Weather bunker on the border of Virginia and West Virginia, or Site R, the enormous underground compound near Maryland's border with Pennsylvania. Then Bob Woodward and his colleagues at the *Washington Post* wrote about a "shadow government" that was replicating the functions of senior military and civilian officials, ready to step in and take over in case of a decapitation attack. The story offered little in the way of specific detail but created an unmistakable aura of gravity about the new post-9/11 reality—the Bush administration was really *that* worried about the threat of a nuclear explosion or a catastrophic biological attack.

As the COG programs expanded, so too did the number of open positions. Jobs that officially did not exist had to be filled somehow. Job solicitations were posted on websites that cater to those seeking government employment. In July 2011, government contractor SAIC advertised for a "Continuity of Operations Watch Officer" who would monitor incoming national intelligence data and be prepared, on a moment's notice, to provide intelligence analysis to senior policymakers. The officer would monitor the "health" of the intelligence community and provide daily updates to the director of national intelligence about the status of critical intelligence systems.

Notably, the advertisement mentioned that the "actual work location is on the VA/WVA border." That meant that the analyst was destined for the Mount Weather bunker and would actually be a part of the government-in-waiting. If the headquarters of the director of national intelligence were to be destroyed and its analysts incapacitated, this analyst would be among a small team of surviving, fully cleared all-source analysts who could jump in and provide the analytic support that would otherwise be unavailable. (The job posting also provided a list of some of the classified COG computer systems that the officer would use, including "the PCT," "ADAPT V2," and "the SPURS system.")

Open source job postings for classified functions and organizations are ubiquitous and create a headache for counterintelligence. One recent posting sought a civilian "director for mobility" at the U.S. Joint Special Operations Command (JSOC) and described, in excruciating detail, the classified special mission unit that transports special operations forces to and from their secret missions. The entity that currently provides cover for Continuity of Government contracting and acquisition services (we shall not disclose the name, although it is distinctly unmemorable and therefore enormously powerful) operates out of a highly secure facility in Elkridge, Maryland.

Tracking job postings can give interested parties a pretty good idea of where the government hides its dozen or so continuously operating secret bunkers. These open source security breaches are self-inflicted intrusions, but they are arguably necessary in order to efficiently staff critical government positions. Still, the level of detail that can be found on social networking sites like LinkedIn is often astonishing. One former program manager of the Ground Applications Program Office (GAPO), a secret office of JSOC, bragged openly that his five-hundred-million-dollar portfolio included acquisitions for U.S. Special Operations Command's most secretive units. Though the "U.S. Army Ground Applications Program Office" can be found in Fort Belvoir's telephone directory, its existence and function is classified.

If you're interested in the budget levels for satellite programs, a LinkedIn search for the National Reconnaissance Office or "Air Force satellites" will be illuminating. Résumés often include the names of intelligence databases that the job seeker is familiar with, along with operating locations. (The NSA, for example, has an enormous facility near Denver that is not classified, but plenty of LinkedIn resumes matter-of-factly report unusual NSA deployment locations, such as Jordan.)

Then there's the swarm of gadflies, obsessives, and good-government critics who consciously, conspicuously, and boastfully watch the watchers. Some do it for fun. The day that NATO launched bombing operations against Libya, for example, a Dutch scanner enthusiast named Huub posted to Twitter the identities of military planes his commercial software setup was able to track. He even recorded a U.S. information operations drone, Commando Solo, as it broadcast messages urging Libyan troops to surrender. By monitoring the transponder codes of the planes (Libya is too close to Europe for military jets to operate invisibly, as civilian planes might otherwise inadvertently get too close), Huub and his online followers were able to track French Air Force jets as they closed in on Benghazi. The enthusiasts got a remarkably close look at how the United States operates its airborne reconnaissance and command and control platforms, like the RC-135 Rivet Joint.[1]

Using websites (and even iPhone apps) like Flightradar24.com, a gaggle of Google Groups regularly monitor the progress of U.S. military aircraft across this country, scraping their ADS-B transponder codes and listening in as they interact with air traffic controllers. They send logs of their daily monitoring to sites like RadioReference .com, allowing enthusiasts to compile fairly accurate databases of training flights and even overseas troop deployments. With remarkable precision, members of these groups (a lot of them former aviators) report the location of U.S. nuclear command and control command posts, from the TACAMO E6-Bs (which are tasked with sending war orders to submarines in the event of a nuclear war) to the various Boeing jets that serve as transports for high-ranking U.S. officials in the event of emergencies. On a frequency of 111.75 megahertz, on the high-frequency band, they listen and transcribe the Emergency Action Messages that are transmitted by the main STRATCOM nuclear communications hub at Andrews Air Force Base, as well as strategic detachments around the world that are testing the system. (MAINSAIL is the call sign for "Is anyone out there?")

They've even monitored U-2 pilots. On March 28, 2011, Jody in North Georgia reported, "Currently have DRAGON 69 working CHECKER OPS on 381.3 requesting they call their ops and let them know that they are in the green. Wonder where the U-2 is headed?"

On May 30, Monitor Ed L. in Maine tracked Air Force One and its backup, two aerial refueling aircraft, a Boeing E4-B nuclear command post plane, and two large cargo planes as they flew President Barack Obama and his entourage to Europe.

Earlier that month, tracker and aviation geek David Cenciotti caught the Boeing 757 used by the Foreign Emergency Support Team, a semicovert rapid response team of U.S. nuclear technicians and experts, flying into Andrews Air Force Base and using a call sign reserved for the FBI. He first noticed the flight on a free tracking website. It had no official call sign—indeed, it was tagged as "NO CALL SIGN"—but when he cross-checked the tail number of the plane, he discovered its base squadron. When the plane maneuvered into an area where he could use a radio scanner to pick up its transmission, he recorded it and posted the audio on his website. The planes, and others operated by the government, try to change their call signs and their transponder codes, but the Federal Aviation Administration makes it almost too easy to subvert the feeble efforts at cover. "Don't you believe it is somehow weird that such elusive aircraft, deploying U.S. teams in response to terrorist attacks or (as someone speculated) to transport prisoners, was transmitting full ADS-B over the U.S.?" Cenciotti wondered.[2]

At Cryptome, a website run by retired architects named John Young and Deborah Natsios, users delight in "reversing the panopticon," as Natsios once put it. They've compiled a cache of data about the secret geography and archaeology of national security, welcoming contributions for publication "that are prohibited by governments worldwide, in particular material on freedom of expression, privacy, cryptology, dual-use technologies, national security, intelligence, and secret governance—open, secret and classified documents—but not limited to those." They write, "Documents are removed from this site only by order served directly by a U.S. court having jurisdiction. No court order has ever been served; any order served will be published here—or elsewhere if gagged by order. Bluffs will be published if comical but otherwise ignored."[3]

Using imagery provided by Terraserver, Google Earth, and MSN Maps, their "Eyeball" collection includes detailed, annotated photographs and maps of everything from nuclear storage depots to secret CIA training facilities to former vice president Cheney's house. In early October 2012, the two found that Microsoft Bing's commercial satellites had photographed the still-standing, full-sized mock-up of Osama bin Laden's lair in Abbottabad.[4] It was there that Navy SEALs trained for their eventual assault.

Using commercial news photographs, the two created a series of pages—forty-four to date—devoted to "Obama Protection" and filled with specific references to the location and methods of the U.S. Secret Service. The Secret Service is aware of the site and probably has opened a watch file on Young and Natsios, but there's nothing illegal about what the two are doing, which is using protected speech to expose the secrets of the president's guard, simply because they can. The FBI has twice contacted the site owners about specific content but hasn't done anything else. Microsoft threatened to sue the site's ISP after Cryptome posted an internal guide about its cooperation with law enforcement, but later backed down.[5] In 2011, apparently under pressure from the government, PayPal briefly stopped processing financial contributions to the site.

Cryptome went live in 1996, well before Julian Assange ever contemplated his crusade against government secrecy. It has spawned dozens of other websites, ranging from publicintelligence.net to WikiLeaks rival OpenLeaks.


Among the best chroniclers of the secret state has been John Pike, formerly of the Federation of American Scientists and now the director of GlobalSecurity.org. His original purpose was to bring transparency to the decision-making process and to the policies guiding nuclear weapons deployment, dispersal, and disposal. For years, through Freedom of Information Act requests, guesswork, and sheer doggedness, he managed to compile an open source repository of secret programs, policies, and images that almost certainly rivals anything our government has on any other government. And he's still at it.

This public domain information—even that which is fragmented and rudimentary—provides a decisive check against the secrecy apparatus. The men and women tirelessly piecing together the great puzzle of the deep state are only getting better at what they do and their tools more effective. Advancements in public databases and information technologies are outpacing government tools and thinking by orders of magnitude. As proven with Primoris Era and the Osama bin Laden raid and government flight patterns and military operations, the real-time crowdsourcing of data as events unfold is an overwhelming and unstoppable force against a lumbering, compartmentalized bureaucracy that's only scarcely capable of internal communication, to say nothing of interagency cooperation. The intelligence community is damn good at what they do, but one man and his flash drive can throw into disarray the fundamental dynamics of the system on whose behalf they work.

It all adds up to the inescapable truth of today and the reality going forward: the American deep state as we know it is over. There are simply too many amateur but interested parties; too much public data and too many tools that help that public drill down to deeper truths; too many news outlets and too much connectivity, where a secret can circle the globe femtoseconds after revelation; too many people with access to secrets; too many ways to steal those secrets; too many people with reasonable reasons to leak.

The system will plod on because a century of inertia doesn't stop overnight. The government will reel and overreact and prosecute with impunity. (Already we are seeing signs of this. In only three years, the Obama administration has charged six whistleblowers—not spies, but people interested in good government—with violating the Espionage Act.) And methods for safeguarding state secrets will see the occasional leap forward, just as the Soviet Union "disappeared" in 1948.

But every day, the public knows more and the picture clarifies. The press is useful but no longer essential. Today, it wouldn't matter if Allen Dulles implored Arthur Hays Sulzberger to spike a story. It would get out anyway, on a blog or an activist site or Twitter. It doesn't matter where, because users—not only activists, but mild-mannered men and women—would cross-post and click "Like" buttons and retweet.

Days after it was reported that an al-Qaeda airline bombing plot was foiled, the world learned that the "bomber" was actually a spy working for Saudi intelligence who had penetrated al-Qaeda, gained its trust, volunteered for the martyrdom operation, and secured the new type of bomb for the CIA. We learned how the bomb was worn and that testing revealed that it would have slipped through Transportation Security Agency checkpoints. An operation that in any other time in history would rank as a triumph of tradecraft, counterterrorism, and international cooperation, and remain as close and treasured a secret as the nuclear launch codes, became public knowledge not just for newspaper readers but for everyone with a Facebook account and interested only in pictures of the grandkids.

The deep state doesn't stand a chance.

CHAPTER 16

# Resistance

In 2005, Pirouz Sedaghaty (Pete Seda) and Soliman al-Buthi, two principals of the Oregon affiliate of the Saudi Arabia–based Al-Haramain Islamic Charity Foundation, were indicted by a federal grand jury. They were accused of conspiring to funnel money from their charity to Chechen rebels engaged in jihad against Russia. The government had obtained evidence that the two men were regularly in contact with an Egyptian who was raising money for the Chechens. Sedaghaty and al-Buthi operated one of several U.S. bank accounts that the charity—designated an official sponsor of terrorism by the Treasury Department in 2004—was using to hold its money.[1] Al-Buthi spent most of his time in Saudi Arabia.

What they didn't know at the time was that the NSA was intercepting their telephone calls to see who else might have been involved in their particular (and alleged) nexus of terrorism. The men learned of this when, early in the discovery phase of the administrative hearings to confirm the terrorism designation, the Justice Department accidentally provided the defendants with a transcript of conversations between them and a variety of people, including their lawyers. (All parties would hence refer to this bit of work as the Sealed Document.)

The FBI retrieved the Sealed Document from the various attorneys and parties involved in late 2004, a few months after its disclosure. In 2005, the *New York Times* revealed the NSA orderless wiretapping program.* In 2006, the charity lawyers filed suit against the government, alleging that they had been subjected to surveillance without a warrant.

The government then asserted the state secrets privilege, meaning the defense attorneys couldn't reference the potentially illegal wiretaps, as they were a state secret. The defense attorneys said they didn't need to see the retrieved file—the attorneys and the judge had seen the document. They knew what it said. They knew what it proved.

No, no, said the government. You saw nothing. The state secrets privilege applies *even to your memories.* The government insisted that the charity lawyers could not possibly establish a case without referencing the classified information now retroactively erased from the public record. And even if the lawyers *could* prove that they had been surveilled without referencing the document, they wouldn't have known to even think about the potential of being surveilled had the (nonexistent, of course) document not been disclosed. The government was, in other words, extending the state secrets privilege to infinity.

The case would become terribly important to the American Civil Liberties Union and other groups trying to pry open the sealed jar of secrecy.

Of course, no one can prove what they can't know. But when it came to being the subject of government surveillance, Al-Haramain was a case where they knew. *They knew.*[2]


While the Bush administration made extensive use of the state secrets privilege, they did not invent it. For fifty-seven years, it has allowed the executive branch to bar sensitive evidence from use in courtrooms. In 1953, the Supreme Court formalized the privilege with *United States v. Reynolds.* The government successfully prevented widows from seeing the official accident reports after their husbands died piloting U.S. Air Force experimental planes. When the women first requested the report, the Air Force said it would violate national security to provide them. Fifty years later, it emerged that the government had been

---

*Technically, "warrants" are not required; court orders are.

lying—there was nothing secret in the accident reports. (Again, it's not hard to see where skepticism about government secrecy comes from.) This raised obvious questions about the legitimacy of the state secrets privilege, but the solicitor general under President Bush stuck to a historical argument: although nothing in the case was truly a secret to modern eyes, and even though the government at the time turned to the state secrets privilege only when every other tack failed, the executive branch would not go about second-guessing security decisions made fifty years ago.

The privilege remained effectively sacrosanct. Its origins in common law actually reach back much earlier. In 1876, the court said it had no jurisdiction to hear cases involving spy contracts. (The spy in question worked on behalf of Abraham Lincoln and was seeking compensation for services rendered.) The CIA still invokes that decision as a means to block employment disputes from going to trial. The government likewise used a privilege-like argument to squelch disclosure of the technical details of armaments in litigation between military contractors in World War I.

In *United States v. Reynolds*, the Supreme Court rejected the government's argument that it alone should be able to decide whether to withhold information. Instead, it gives judges the final say—in part. The nub of the issue is that the *Reynolds* decision seems to allow a judge to determine whether national security information rises to the level of a state secret in need of protection without presuming that the judge will automatically have access to that information. How a court can independently determine whether the privilege was properly invoked without seeing what the privilege is actually protecting has been the subject of years of scholarly articles and debate, with no real resolution.

In practice, the government cannot win a state secrets case unless it provides classified information ex parte and in camera to a judge. Modern cases never involve documents containing information that everyone would agree should be protected. Rather, the issue is always whether a secret has become so public that it's no longer really a secret, or whether the matter forfeits protection because it might involve government illegality.

Consider: secrets are now so commonly and quickly revealed that we've encouraged extensive legal theorizing over how "leaked" is completely leaked, how "known" is widely known. The executive branch has found itself repeatedly closing the proverbial barn door after the horses are out and then saying to the judicial branch, "What horses?"

To be sure, the executive branch has asked for, and received, substantial deference from the courts. During the Bush administration, the privilege was invoked by the Justice Department at least a dozen times, often to dismiss without hearings potential cases involving secret interrogation, rendition, and surveillance programs. The number of invocations was not unusual with other administrations. What generated controversy was the aggressive use of the privilege to prevent cases from reaching the discovery stage.[3] But if blame should be placed, it belongs to the judges. In 2006, Judge T. S. Ellis threw out a case brought by a German citizen who had been "rendered" from Macedonia to Afghanistan and tortured. Khalid El-Masri wanted economic redress; civil libertarians cottoned to his case as a way to force information into the public domain about the state secret that allowed his rights to be violated so egregiously.

Judge Ellis's reasoning: one cannot simply bring a civil case with the primary purpose of forcing disclosure of a state secret. This opinion has resonance. Though no one disagrees that aggrieved victims of torture have every right to have their day in court, courts tend to be skeptical of those cases where major civil liberties groups have attached themselves. Their direct interests differ from the interests of the plaintiffs.[4]

An irony in this case: El-Masri's case for redress had been tacitly endorsed by Secretary of State Condoleezza Rice when she apologized to Germany's chancellor for the way that the United States handled El-Masri in custody. (Rice even mentioned handling such cases in "proper" courts.) This would seem to undercut any claim of privilege—the government could not argue that the rendition program was still a secret because it had already acknowledged its existence. El-Masri could point to evidence in the public domain that he was the victim of a specific CIA program. Still, Judge Ellis, relying on precedent, would not budge, accepting the government's argument that acknowledgment of a program in general does not compel the government to acknowledge specifics of a program that may have significant national security implications. And because the government enjoys, thanks to *Reynolds*, the presumption that its definition of "national security harms" in particular cases is correct, Ellis had no choice but to rule against El-Masri.[5] As Robert Chesney, a University of Texas law professor who served in the Obama administration, has written, the case exposes an extreme version of the basic secrecy tension. Quoting U.S. attorney general Edward Levi, who was speaking after the Supreme Court had rejected Richard Nixon's executive privilege assertion a year earlier, there is "on one hand, a 'right of complete confidentiality in government could not only produce a dangerous public ignorance but also destroy the basic representative function of government.' On the other, 'a duty of complete disclosure would render impossible the effective operation of government.'" But it seems wrong that the American system of justice could not have found a way for El-Masri to receive some measure of relief.

Obama the campaigner had pledged to treat secrecy as an operational need as opposed to a constitutional prerogative. Obama the president embraced secrecy with alacrity. Inside his national security cabinet were many different stripes of politicians and military officials with varied opinions on executive power. Obama promised to be sparing in the use of the state secrets privilege. He vowed to usher in a new era of transparency, where government operated less in the shadows.

Still, he was not unaware that there are bad people in the world. In the summer of 2007, he said he wouldn't hesitate to violate Pakistan's sovereignty if he knew that the country knowingly permitted terrorist training camps within its borders. During the campaign, on advice from John Brennan, former director of the Terrorist Threat Identification Center, Obama supported the controversial immunity provisions built into the new Foreign Intelligence Surveillance Act (FISA) law. (If, as a civil liberties activist, you held the view that government surveillance was inherently bad, then you did not share Obama's view.)* Government surveillance was fine, Obama believed, so long as it was conducted within the norms of constitutional law.

---

*One prominent critic of Obama, Glenn Greenwald, was never convinced that Obama would be the beacon of hope that some of his fellow liberals thought he would.

Nevertheless, the expectation among liberals was that Obama would be less secretive than President Bush, and that he would use executive power more judiciously.

What concerned Obama, however, was not the perception of secrecy vis-à-vis the public. Rather, it was the perception of secrecy vis-à-vis the other branches of government. He was determined to more fully inform Congress and the judicial branch about secret activities—partly to get their buy-in, but also because he understood, as a constitutional law lecturer, that a vigorous executive branch requires an active and independent check on its power.[6] Where the public was concerned, he would reform the Freedom of Information Act (FOIA) procedures that agencies used, reversing the Bush-era bias in favor of secrecy. He would take full advantage of a congressionally mandated panel on civil liberties and privacy that was created in 2007 but had yet to be staffed. He pointedly promised "the most transparent administration in history." From transparency to Guantánamo Bay, there was hope among civil libertarians that Obama would find a better way to balance competing equities for what his lawyers would call the "classified information privilege." Then reality intruded.

Obama's first three months were spent dealing almost exclusively with pressing cases inherited from the Bush administration. "Almost every day, [White House counsel] Greg Craig would pop into the Oval Office with a sheet of paper and say, 'Oh, the Justice Department has a filing deadline tomorrow in this Bush-era case. We need to know whether we should continue the opinion or reverse it,'" a former senior administration official recalls "The president would roll his eyes at first, but this stuff really agitated him. He had a lot less discretion than he thought he would." In many of the cases, without having the time to think through the ramifications, Obama would ask for briefing books with the relevant information, take them to bed with him, and return the next day having concluded that he hadn't been able to come up with a new way forward, or that he'd deal with the consequences down the road. It was, in a way, the curse of the Twenty-Second Amendment: presidents are limited to two terms, and there's always unfinished business left for their successors.

It was no easier on his close friend Eric Holder, the attorney general. On February 3, 2009—the day he was sworn in—Holder got his first classified briefing on a state secrets case, *Mohamed et al. v. Jeppesen Dataplan*, where the plaintiffs sought redress from the company, which had allegedly helped the government organize the flights that "rendered" them to foreign countries to be tortured. (Mohamed himself endured electric shocks and genital mutilation.) The case came to Holder smartly wrapped in an orange folder marked Top Secret, having been teed up by career officials in the civil division long used to litigating it. Holder had no deputy attorney general, no solicitor general, and no associate attorney general to help him out. And the response was due in six days.[7] Even the court expected the administration to change its position. During the campaign, Senator Obama had called warrantless wiretapping illegal.[8]

Here's what happened when Justice Department attorney Doug Letter informed the court that the administration was sticking with the privilege:

> "Is there anything material that has happened" that might have caused the Justice Department to shift its views, asked Judge Mary M. Schroeder, an appointee of President Jimmy Carter, coyly referring to the recent election.
>
> "No, your honor," said Mr. Letter.
>
> Judge Schroeder asked, "The change in administration has no bearing?"
>
> Once more, he said, "No, Your Honor." The position he was taking in court on behalf of the government had been "thoroughly vetted with the appropriate officials within the new administration," and "these are the authorized positions," he said.[9]

There are many different reasons to hold umbrella secrets that have nothing to do with the actual secrets themselves. When Obama's Justice Department first asserted the state secrets privilege in the Al-Haramain case, many observers concluded that it was forced to do so because of standard legal procedure. The argument went like this: if Justice Department lawyers had retracted the privilege in this case, they would be sending the signal to judges handling other highly sensitive cases that the Obama administration did not consider the executive branch sole decider of what constitutes national security information, or how best to protect that information. The day that Obama's Justice Department asserted the privilege, therefore, critics asserted that Obama had been captured by the culture of secrecy or had been tempted by the allure of unchecked executive power.[10]

But when the decision to reassert the privilege was first made public in March 2009, a senior Justice Department official told one of the authors that the national security equities at stake in the Al-Haramain case were "more than the privilege itself." Later that year, Attorney General Holder released guidelines for future assertions of the state secrets doctrine. Meanwhile, a senior Justice Department official handling state secrets cases said that where the Obama administration extended the Bush administration's privilege assertions, it was doing so not to protect the principle—precedent would take care of that—but because there were legitimate and valid reasons for each case in question.

In the Al-Haramain case, what so rankled civil libertarians was the notion that President Obama seemed determined to permit use of the state secrets privilege even in cases where the plaintiffs could prove that something illegal had happened. Judge Walker had no problem with the plaintiffs using the classified document, but the Justice Department fiercely resisted. Walker tabled the issue and asked the plaintiffs to make their case using public evidence. In March 2010, he found that the state secrets doctrine did not trump the FISA law requiring warrants. The surveillance had been illegal.

The decision was good for the lawyers and the charity, but to civil libertarians and critics of warrantless wiretapping it seemed a pyrrhic victory, as Walker did not rule on the merits of the program. (But he had already done that in July 2008, holding that the president's authority to conduct domestic surveillance was circumscribed by no other statute but the FISA.) Another reason Walker ruled so narrowly was that the Department of Justice under Holder did not argue that the surveillance program was lawful and constitutional, but rather that parts of it were so secret (indeed, *still* so secret) that any courtroom proceeding—even with the most stringent security measures—would significantly jeopardize national security. This line of reasoning was curious to Judge Walker, who had grown increasingly impatient with the government's claim that it simply could not and would not go to trial. It seemed equally specious to the plaintiff's attorneys. After all, their clients wanted justice. They had no intention of forcing the government to reveal state secrets. Several times, in fact, the plaintiffs' attorneys had informally attempted to resolve the case by asking the Justice Department to admit that the two lawyers were surveilled, and provide relief. "Work with me," Jon Eisenberg would tell Anthony Coppolino, the lead government attorney, and we'll end this matter to everyone's satisfaction without revealing state secrets or harming national security." But Obama's lawyers continue to press.

In a casual conversation in 2009 with a senior administration official sympathetic to the arguments against the constitutionality of warrantless wiretapping, the assertion of the state secrets doctrine was defended in general as a way of "protecting our relationships with allies." Never before had anyone connected the Al-Haramain case with allies.

But those relationships *are* worth protecting. Institutionally, the U.S. government takes a mother hen approach to foreign relations. In other words: don't you *dare* touch our chicks. (Such an approach was also seen in the aftermath of WikiLeaks.) It is hard to quantify the actual damage to national security that would result if liaison relationships were compromised. There is some logic behind the government's maternal approach. However, if the state secrets privilege is asserted primarily to avoid signaling to allies that the U.S. government can't keep things secret from its own court system, then the privilege is being used to recursively justify itself. The national security harm is secondary.

The United States relies on France, Egypt, Morocco, Jordan, and Israel for the bulk of human intelligence information about al-Qaeda targets in the Middle East. Meanwhile, published reports suggest that the United States, the United Kingdom, and Canada collaborated very closely on the controversial renditions of terrorist suspects to Third World countries that subsequently tortured them. (This accounts for relationships with less-than-friendly countries in North Africa, in the Middle East, and even occasional collaborations with countries like Syria and Libya.)

The United Kingdom, in particular, has a highly advanced signals intelligence capacity, run by an agency called the Government Communications Headquarters (GCHQ). It routinely sends technicians and officers to the United States for missions; hundreds of NSA personnel work directly from GCHQ's headquarters near London. Under a seventy-year-old agreement known colloquially as UK-USA, five countries—the United States, the United Kingdom, Canada, Australia, and New Zealand—cooperate extensively on all matters of intelligence collection programs.* A superintending panel of senior executives from each country's signals intelligence agencies regularly meets to decide collection priorities and divvy up the tasks.[†,11]

The agreement has given rise to a classic conspiracy theory, appropriated from a technical collection program called Echelon: allegedly, when the United States needs to spy on its own citizens without a warrant, it can call upon the resources of one of its allies to do so, and vice versa. All five UK-USA member states have strenuously denied that they do this—though there is nothing in the agreement itself that would prevent them from doing so. But as one former senior NSA official who worked often with the British put it, UK-USA is just "a gentleman's agreement." Still, Michael Hayden and others insist that it would be patently illegal for the United States to ask the British to spy on an internal target if the NSA wasn't allowed to do so. And it is also true that while the GCHQ gets most U.S. SIGINT product, it does not get everything—nothing derived

---

*In the 1980s, New Zealand essentially broke the ANZUS defense treaty with the United States by banning nuclear weapons in the region (and consequently, a large part of the U.S. Navy). As part of a larger response, the United States withheld UK-USA imagery intelligence from New Zealand until very recently. According to a diplomatic cable released by WikiLeaks, intelligence sharing has been "fully restored."

†A remarkably comprehensive description of the meshing of the NSA and GCHQ can be found in the testimony of former GCHQ chief David Pepper to the United Kingdom's commission investigating Iraq War intelligence.

from FISA monitoring goes overseas or into databases accessible by the British.

The relationship that exists between the various allied SIGINT organizations is a very important one, and the risk of its potential use as a "work-around" in monitoring possible terrorists on U.S. soil perhaps isn't given sufficient attention. While every member of the National Security Agency signs an oath promising not to spy on U.S. citizens without a warrant, collectors from the UK's GCHQ are not bound by such obligations. Unlike American intelligence agencies, they don't have to follow the dictates of Executive Order 12333, which prohibits, in no uncertain terms, domestic intelligence collection without extensive oversight and warrants. (Notably, NSA managers did not ask U.S. soldiers to participate in the earliest incarnation of the terrorist surveillance program.)

This raises larger questions and issues. If liaison worries were behind the government's extraordinary concerns about Al-Haramain, what would that mean? Is it something as seemingly innocuous as the usage of a particular GCHQ-controlled communication channel—with or without that agency's knowledge—by the NSA to surveil these two (or more) U.S. persons? Did GCHQ knowingly participate in the program? Was the program farmed out to GCHQ collectors or to American collectors operating out of any of the four other member countries' intelligence agencies? All of this is unlikely. Because of British domestic politics alone, a disclosure that the GCHQ intercepted the communications of U.S. citizens could cause a row of massive proportions. (Phone hacking scandals often obliterate careers in London.) The disclosure of such activities would certainly lead to a significant curtailing of intelligence sharing between the United States and Britain. It would also, quite probably, cause other U.S. allies to withhold cooperation as well. If the United States cannot keep its arrangements with the UK secret, can less friendly governments expect any better treatment? A senior intelligence official revealed to the authors that in the wake of revelations in the United States about its secret rendition programs, relationships between the British Secret Intelligence Service and the CIA required mending when Obama assumed office. And earlier in the year, a UK court forced the British government to disclose information about the rendition of one of its own citizens. As a result, the United States warned that intelligence cooperation could be jeopardized.[12]

The British Communications Act of 1985 would seem to prohibit the targeting of citizens under the blanket of the UK-USA agreement, but the laws make exceptions for the general processing of communications that flow through the country. American law does this as well; FISA permits the NSA to collect undifferentiated information incidentally. As a 1998 article on British surveillance in the *New Statesman* archly concluded, "Whether or not a British government warrant can legally allow American agents to intercept private British communications, there is no doubt that British law as well as British bases have been designed to encourage rather than inhibit the booming industry in international telecommunications surveillance."*

It is more reasonable to guess that the secret liaison relationship the government is protecting in the Al-Haramain case is with Saudi Arabia.

In the case, Judge Walker was openly skeptical of the classified evidence being used to justify the state secrets privilege, even as he acknowledged the privilege's reach and grounding. But the Justice Department assumed that Walker would put a quick end to the proceedings. Walker did not, and indeed at one point he told a government lawyer that he was "not impressed" with the classified evidence. (When the Ninth Circuit heard oral arguments in the case of several detainees who alleged that Jeppesen Dataplan assisted in their illegal rendition to other countries where they were tortured, the government's attorney, Doug Letter, mentioned the Al-Haramain case as a way of boosting his argument that its secrecy was warranted. But one of the panel judges—Michael Daly Hawkins, who was also on the panel that sent the Al-Haramain case back to Walker—slapped him down, responding that the government knew very well why the Ninth

---

*In 2008, ABC News reported on the case of David Murfee Faulk, a U.S. Army soldier who worked at an NSA satellite in Georgia. Faulk told ABC News that he had seen evidence that the United States was collecting information about then British prime minister Tony Blair. This accusation triggered denials from all parties, all around. The CIA's spokesman called it "utterly absurd" and rejected "any notion that the CIA spies on the British government."

Circuit had not ruled entirely in favor of the plaintiff and implied that it had nothing to do with the quality of the secret evidence.)

On page 14 of the government's third motion to dismiss the Al-Haramain case, attorneys wrote that "it bears emphasis that nothing plaintiffs cite would establish that any alleged surveillance of plaintiffs (if any) would necessarily have occurred on a wire in the United States in violation of the FISA." The motion continues, "The Government has many means of surveillance of al Qaeda–affiliated organizations and individuals at its disposal, including surveillance under authority of the FISA itself, surveillance information obtained from foreign or human sources, or surveillance undertaken overseas—that is, collected outside the United States and not on a wire in this country."[13]

In the government's opening brief filed in the Ninth Circuit in July 2011, when suggesting various other ways the NSA might have gotten information about Al-Haramain, there is this: "Alternatively, surveillance abroad may be conducted by foreign intelligence services, which may then forward information to their American counterparts."

Were government attorneys alluding to something they might have said in a secret filing before Judge Walker or to the Ninth Circuit?—that parts of the Terrorist Surveillance Program were outsourced to a "foreign or human source," meaning a foreign government, or to another federal agency? The government, in the same motion, noted that it had "previously provided the Court, for *in camera, ex parte* review, classified information in support of the state secrets privilege which sets forth the actual facts regarding whether or not plaintiffs have been subject to surveillance." Is this what the government said in those filings about the "actual facts" regarding plaintiff's surveillance? That it was outsourced? That part of it was? In other words, maybe the Saudi government was "up" on al-Buthi and passing the communications to the United States, or was working with the NSA to allow NSA personnel to eavesdrop on both the domestic and international end of the conversation. If that's the secret, it's not a big one. Either the United States was illegally intercepting phone calls (from the Saudi perspective), or it was intercepting them with the help of the Saudis. That's how the whole thing got started anyway.

Eisenberg (the lawyer for the plaintiff) and his co-attorneys had never raised the possibility that any entity other than the United States was involved in conducting the surveillance, and from the standpoint of their case it really didn't matter. They did suggest it obliquely in a separate filing, explaining how the government would still be liable for damages even if it hadn't directly conducted the surveillance. Walker did not address the matter in his ruling. Eisenberg has been cautious about speculating on the secret. But in 2007, he felt compelled to post an item on a relatively obscure liberal website, asking whether it was "possible a foreign government—perhaps the United Kingdom—has colluded with the Bush administration in conducting warrantless electronic surveillance of American citizens?" He was on to something, but the fact of surveillance wasn't an issue; the evidence suggests that the originating country, and the political implications that could result from that country's participation being exposed, was the actual secret. And that country was (probably) Saudi Arabia.

On a broader level, Obama had to figure out what to do with its "legal IEDs"—what many on his side considered to be actual crimes of the Bush era: the torture inflicted on detainees; the rendition of prisoners to other countries that tortured them; and the NSA surveillance program. Many decisions involved whether to keep things secret. Others involved whether to reopen investigations and prosecute cases. Obama stuck to a thin piece of ground in the middle of two very polarized sets of elite opinion. The left wanted Dick Cheney tried as a war criminal. The right would seize upon any hesitancy as proof of weakness and was ready to prod agencies like the CIA into going to war with the president.

Outside the Beltway, these issues carried little resonance. Even while the public's faith in government has steadily declined, as part of the implicit bargain it tends to allow the government to do pretty much whatever it wants in the realm of national security. (Not to say these issues aren't important—they are, which is why a predilection to cover them is not necessarily a bad bias for the press to have here.)

But Obama's decision-making satisfied no one, save for a tiny, Washington-based clique consisting largely of middle-of-the-road

Democrats, centrist Republicans, and the political press corps, all of whom understood Obama's reasoning because they operated under the same impression about how the U.S. government really worked. There are many complicating factors in deciding whether to prosecute CIA officers for following an order to torture a prisoner. So far as the CIA is an important instrument of U.S. national security power, a young Democratic president could not be seen as taking a firm stand against field operators simply doing their jobs. This was the argument advanced by Rahm Emanuel, the White House chief of staff. Holder and Emanuel did not see eye to eye from the very beginning.[14]

Obama was swayed by the pleadings of former directors of the CIA, who said that retrospective prosecution would turn every CIA officer in the field into a lawyer, making ad hoc decisions that were potentially subject to criminal prosecution. This would largely render them powerless. The bureaucracy relied on faithful adherence to executive branch orders. At a higher level, when it came to possibly prosecuting policymakers, the reasoning was more clear: Obama refused to set a precedent that would be hard to undo, no matter how egregious the policies had been. Bloodless transitions of power in the United States are nontrivial; Obama would much later in his first term remark upon this when most of the countries involved in the Arab Spring turned to prosecuting their respective former presidents as the first order of business.

Politically, too, Obama felt he was hamstrung. Had he aggressively made an issue of Bush-era intelligence activities, he would have ensnared the country in debates on policies already undone, incited a partisan frenzy in a polarized atmosphere, and found that his own ability to get things done was crimped. Despite all of these caveats, however, Obama did not entirely step away from the controversies. He told his attorney general that he would defer to him about whether to prosecute CIA interrogators. (Actually, Holder, in pondering whether to take the job as attorney general, asked Obama for independence as a condition of accepting the offer.) He would neither order a new investigation nor step in the way if Holder decided to reopen some cases, despite the urging of his chief of staff.

Holder and Obama agreed to consider prosecuting only those cases where CIA officers acted beyond the strictures of what even John Yoo, author of the memos guiding enhanced interrogation

techniques, felt was acceptable. And over the objection of the intelligence community, Obama released redacted versions of Bush-era
Office of Legal Counsel opinions on enhanced interrogation techniques. On his first day in office, he signed a memorandum restricting interrogation methods to those prescribed by the Army Field
Manual, wagering that secret and potentially immoral techniques
were less desirable than legal but potentially beatable ones. The
predicate of Obama's decisions was that these actions would be the
end of the "looking back." He would not endorse congressional calls
for an investigation or committee of inquiry. In walking this middle
line, Obama would find himself tied to policies he did not necessarily endorse. And an implicit message was sent: however bad the torture stuff had been, it couldn't have been *that bad*, because the need
to move forward outweighed the need for direct accountability. As a
result, the left would continue to be suspicious, the right would never
allow Obama to move forward an inch, and the middle was too impotent to do anything else.

Obama was furious with this depiction. Contrary to the assertions of his staff, he *did* read some of the law blogs that savaged him.
Whenever a state secrets case arose—like when the family of Anwar
al-Awlaki, the American-born cleric who from his post in Yemen
called for the murder of Americans, sued the government to remove
his name from a list of allowable targets—Obama spent hours reviewing the case, even though there was almost no question that the government would assert the privilege. According to one source, Obama
asked his White House counsels whether there was a way to litigate at
least some of the case without using the privilege peremptorily. In al-
Awlaki's case, the Justice Department offered the court four reasons
the case wouldn't stand; the state secrets privilege was their firewall
option.

The judge decided the case in the administration's favor, finding
that Al-Awlaki's father had no standing to challenge the alleged assassination order on his son's behalf. Inside the Justice Department and
the White House, this was a victory—the right way to do things. The
privilege would be used as a last resort, and judges would always be
provided with classified information to prove that the government
wasn't trying to cover up wrongdoing. Holder hoped that, at the very
least, the policy decision to provide judges with ample classified

information would set the bar very high for any future administration that tried to litigate state secrets cases while keeping judges in the dark.*

On September 30, 2011, a U.S. drone targeted and killed al-Awlaki in Yemen. Senior administration officials, briefing reporters, said that they had concrete evidence that al-Awlaki had directly facilitated several terrorist attacks and provided technical assistance and logistical guidance for two failed terrorist attempts on U.S. soil. This made him a legitimate target under the Authorization for Use of Military Force, according to the administration, regardless of whether he still considered himself a citizen. The ACLU and other civil rights groups rightfully questioned the integrity of the administration's pronouncements and accurately called his killing the "first targeted assassination of an American citizen" by the American government.

Holder's reasoning and careful approach to the privilege butted up against a very powerful counterargument. According to Ben Wizner, the lead ACLU attorney for Binyan Mohamed (he of *Mohamed et al. v. Jeppesen Dataplan*), "Remember, the state secrets privilege was invoked—and the case was dismissed—before the plaintiffs had made a single request for evidence." He adds, "In fact, all we were seeking was the opportunity to present our claims with evidence already in our possession." But the Ninth Circuit Court of Appeals ruled that even if they could prove the case with the evidence they had, it had to be dismissed because the trial itself would create what the court felt was an "unjustifiable" risk of compromising the government's ability to keep a needed secret.

Wizner notes that there is a weird and absolute contradiction at the heart of this ruling, and many others in state secrets cases—one that even defenders of the privilege have trouble with. "The state secrets cases stand for the proposition that *no amount* of public evidence can overcome a government secrecy claim so long as the 'privileged' content has not been officially confirmed." What does it mean that something can be universally known and yet not confirmed? We have already encountered two examples: the U.S. Joint Special Operations Command, and the CIA Predator drone program.

---

*Interview with Matthew Miller, former spokesman for Holder.

Indeed, when the ACLU recently asked the CIA for documents about the drone program using FOIA, the CIA said that to respond to the request would require them to confirm or deny the existence of a program and said confirmation or denial would itself irredeemably harm national security. The argument then dissolves into circularity: everyone knows about the drone program, the lawyers say. But the CIA says, "Nothing is known until we confirm it." In other words, if we confirm something, then the enemy will react to it. There's a difference between what they read in the *New York Times* and an official declaration of the CIA.

This is a legal fiction. Pakistan acknowledges the CIA's drone program. The president has *joked* about it. Leon Panetta, as the Secretary of Defense, joked about how he missed the drone tools he had available as CIA director. The CIA talks to journalists "on background" about the drone program. Former CIA officials, like general counsel John Rizzo, have described it in detail.[15] The enemy knows. But technically, the program is classified at the Top Secret level.

And that makes levelheaded people like Mike Rogers, the chairman of the House Permanent Select Committee on Intelligence, do weird things, like tell an audience of policy professionals at the Woodrow Wilson Center in Washington, D.C., in September 2011 that the "Title 10" "airstrike program" was a vital tool of national security. Title 10 activities are military activities; "airstrike" implies a manned airplane. Yes, the Air Force had a drone program too, but the question wasn't about that, and he knew it. He had been asked about the CIA's drone program, but technically he would be disclosing classified information if he even *acknowledged* the antecedent of the moderator's question.

So even if there is a legal distinction between what's known and what's confirmed, Wizner contends, with some consternation, that there is no material difference. His conclusion: "This legal fiction is essential to ensuring that no one from the CIA or NSA will ever face prosecution for lawbreaking. So long as courts honor the distinction between what is known (and can be proven!) on the one hand, and what is confirmed on the other, the intelligence agencies will hold the keys to their own immunity." And Wizner, by the account of those who assert the privilege, is correct.

Obama will be forever lonely in his position. He may see himself as a civil libertarian, but so long as the only possible government argument to the public about state secrets cases is "trust me," civil libertarians will not claim him. Interest groups generally determine the reference points in debates like these. The American public was highly polarized even before September 11, 2001. (How many Democratic activists really believed that President Bush had been legitimately elected in 2000?) And many Republicans spent that decade politicizing terrorism in order to scare people for political gain. The following decade saw Democrats "spiking the football." A second civil war of hyperpartisanship predated the Obama presidency, and continues to be waged during it.[16]

CHAPTER 17

# The Flicker of a Piercing Eye

In the early part of 2000, the National Security Agency was "up" on a known al-Qaeda safe house in Yemen. It had intercepted cell phone calls between a known terrorist and persons unknown in San Diego. Because the conversations were not themselves evidence of terrorist plots, and because the identities and locations of the persons inside the United States were not known, the NSA did not have the probable cause necessary to seek a Foreign Intelligence Surveillance Act (FISA) warrant. (Had the other numbers been known, the FBI could easily have figured out who these guys were. But the collection platform in Yemen was acoustic and not electronic; the NSA had no data about the target cell number.)

Then 9/11 happened.

The calls in question went to two of the airliner hijackers living in San Diego. As Lieutenant General Michael Hayden, director of the NSA, would explain to President George W. Bush and his cabinet, it was unconscionable that he lacked the authority to ask a telecom for the transactional records associated with the numbers in question. He could have connected the dots, but FISA was being interpreted in such a way that kept his hands tied. As a practical matter, telecoms were all but off-limits, and time was of the essence.

In the aftermath of 9/11, Hayden and other American officials believed, with good reason, that further attacks were planned. Hayden could help find those missing dots—the U.S.-based ends of telephone conversations emanating from Yemen, Afghanistan, and Somalia—but he would need to do things he hadn't done before. Things that didn't necessarily track with FISA. He would need to be able to proactively monitor the outgoing calls of people inside the United States—possibly even citizens—who regularly made foreign calls to "dirty numbers" or confirmed terrorist targets.[1]

He needed transactional records from the telecoms so that he could immediately identify who was on the other end of the telephone call or who was the recipient of an e-mail. Noting that the two San Diego terrorists changed their cell numbers frequently and regularly opened new e-mail accounts, Hayden needed access to credit records and bills that would tie one person to a series of communications transactions. And he needed to be able to see the calling circles of those called by the U.S-based persons. He needed a way to know, instantly, when one of those persons received or made a call associated with terrorism to a number outside the United States or to an e-mail associated with jihadists. And he needed to find a way to do all of this without intercepting the telephone and web traffic of innocent Americans.

Hayden would get what he needed. (It helped that Vice President Dick Cheney; his chief of staff David Addington; and William Haynes, the Pentagon's top lawyer, had already identified the NSA's collection problems as a major obstacle to find extant al-Qaeda cells inside the United States.)[2] But as Hayden later described it, the President's Surveillance Program was simply a gap-filler, albeit a crucial one that would allow the government to thwart terrorists before they could act.

The NSA is the largest factory of secrets in the world. Instead of giant brick chimneys billowing out smoke, the NSA works from a colossal mirrored-glass building at Fort Meade, Maryland, where it collects the world's digital detritus, refines it into a digestible product, and sends it to policymakers for consumption. For sixty years, the NSA has turned whispers into shouts. It is the anchor of the deep state.

What older Americans know about the NSA was gathered from a different era in American espionage, when the intelligence community was more pliant to the oftentimes nefarious whims of politicians. The NSA followed directives to spy on U.S. citizens. Younger Americans, on the other hand, often view the agency through a cinematic lens. At the NSA, they called it the "Enemy of the State problem"—a reference to the 1998 movie portraying the agency as an amoral panopticon able to follow anyone anywhere. (Not a few NSA managers at the time saw the movie and privately thought, "If only!")

For many years, it did not matter how the NSA was portrayed in the media.[3] Congress willingly funded its ambitious projects and asked few questions. Then came the end of the Cold War and an era of relative peace. The president no longer depended on intelligence collected by the NSA. Furthermore, the way signals traversed the earth changed as telecommunications shifted from satellites to fiber and the global communications infrastructure exploded in size.

At the dawn of the millennium and the height of the dot-com boom, the NSA faced a budget crunch; its technological capabilities could no longer keep pace, and its mission seemed less relevant.[4] Policy entrepreneurs in Congress, to include then representative Porter Goss, a former CIA case officer who would later serve as director of central intelligence, wanted to siphon money from the NSA for their own pet intelligence projects. In a private meeting before Hayden was sworn in, he told the incoming director that the NSA had a "reputation problem."[5]

When Hayden, a bracing and admired U.S. Air Force general, became the NSA's director in 1999, he tried to show some leg. Greater openness, he suspected, would lessen anxiety about the agency and maybe even generate positive publicity, which would feed back into Congress's perception of the NSA. With his general counsel, Robert Deitz, he set up SIGINT 101—a class for reporters who covered the agency, which included trips to NSA labs and even a brief chance to put on the headphones and hear what an intercept sounded like. General Hayden cooperated with author James Bamford—who theretofore had written the only contemporary history of the NSA—on a second book.[6] He made himself accessible to reporters, hosting dinners at his home. He even joked about the agency's alleged prowess. "Despite what you've seen on television," he told college students in 2000, "our agency doesn't do alien autopsies, track the location of your automobile by satellite, nor do we have a squad of assassins."[7]

The agency—once the closest held secret in the United States, if not the world—even established an official children's website called CryptoKids, for "America's future codemakers and codebreakers."[8] Hayden knew how to work the system. Like J. Edgar Hoover and Walter Bedell Smith a generation removed, he recognized that it really did matter what the newspapers printed about secret agencies, and he was determined to put the NSA on solid footing. His strategy worked, something for which even his fiercest detractors give him credit.

Politically, Hayden had no doctrine but Goldwater-Nichols: the civilians proposed and he disposed. He followed the law and followed orders. That may be why he had no problem with secrecy— even the "weird secrecy," in the words of David Kris, former associate deputy attorney general for national security issues.[9] Part of that weird secrecy included what would become known as the Terrorist Surveillance Program (TSP), one of the larger sets of secret surveillance activities authorized by President Bush in the weeks following the September 11, 2001, attacks. (We will refer to these activities as the "special programs" to distinguish them from regular NSA signals intelligence collection and analysis.)

After 9/11, in an effort to build a virtual fence around the country, the NSA deliberately began collecting certain types of data generated by U.S. citizens and tapping directly into the vein of communications that originated in the United States. It did so with the tacit, uneasy, and provisional approval of Congress—or rather, of the small fraction of congressional leaders given early briefings about it. Members of the judiciary were also involved; the two Foreign Intelligence Surveillance Court (FISC) chief judges who were "read in" to the program also did not object.

After it was partially exposed by the *New York Times* in 2005, a consistent number of polls suggest a majority of Americans believe that the program—to the extent that they know about it—was right. In keeping with the implicit bargain, Americans give their presidents wide latitude to do secret things so long as their security is enhanced and their blood is not shed. So maybe we shouldn't talk about it all. Where's the right to keep digging?

For one thing, an accurate accounting of the special programs—extraordinary extensions of executive power, and something that Hayden described to Congress during their initial briefing as "very, very different" from what the NSA had been doing before—has never been published in an unclassified format, so far as we can tell. But plenty of current and former government officials—in congressional testimony, in official reports, and in published and broadcast interviews—have described parts of the program that technically remain a secret. The information is already out there, and a jumble of data points exist for anyone with a bit of time to put together. It's not that hard to simply (and correctly) guess what the special programs were (when they were first authorized by President Bush), and what they are now (formalized under FISA). Confusion and mythology may have helped the government keep its secret, but they have not helped the NSA repair the damage its reputation sustained in the breathless aftermath of the *New York Times* piece.

Though Americans cede great authority to the president during wartime, they become more skeptical of that authority as the war recedes from view. Accepting the general premise that the president ought to be allowed to listen to conversations between one person in the United States and one person overseas *where one party has a probable connection to terrorism* is one thing. Accepting that a computer is sifting through an ocean of phone records to try and connect dots—and, oh, *your* phone records *might* be in that data set—is another. Accepting that the laws permitting this were interpreted and reinterpreted in secret (and for the most part still are) is even harder. As the fine teeth of the NSA's combs move closer to *your* data—the telephone numbers you dial, the e-mail addresses you use—the more nervous you are, especially if you don't know what the NSA is doing with them. In the future, Americans will be asked to allow the NSA to sift through the Internet traffic they generate solely to detect and mitigate the threat of massive cyber attacks.

The NSA's collection activities increasingly overlap with the digital detritus that Americans generate. For that reason alone it is worth the effort to put together an accurate account of what the agency does when no one is looking. The NSA has a story to tell and an argument to make. So do critics of its role. In the case of the special programs, excessive secrecy has contributed to several fundamental misunderstandings that undermine any debate about what the NSA's role ought to be.

Secrecy allowed the special programs to exist when they were absolutely crucial—in the days after September 11, 2001, when the government had lots of information but was legally restricted from assembling the toolkit to deduce if even greater terrorist attacks were forthcoming. At the same time, the type of secrecy bolted around these programs—exceeding even the extremely high level of secrecy that accompanies regular NSA activities—undermined the special program's efficacy and legitimacy. At various junctures, the motivation to keep the program so secretive provided the main justification for decisions about how best to modify it, and even which laws would serve as its basis.

Suspicion about NSA motives and operations may be an inevitable historical fact given its range and scope. But fallout from the controversy over warrantless wiretapping has drifted into the NSA's other missions as well. The "puzzle palace" is responsible for information assurance (which basically means it protects the Defense Department from cyber threats), and it creates and breaks codes. These tasks remain more difficult today because of, again, a legal system on a heightened state of alert against the NSA, so to speak, and a Congress less likely to write checks without certain assurances.

Here we tell the story of what we think, to a reasonably degree of certainty, the NSA did after 9/11. We have omitted a number of sensitive details because we (alone) do not possess the knowledge to determine what would and would not compromise national security. We have relied on the guidance of people who know about the program to help achieve an appropriate balance.

Ten years after 9/11, Hayden, now retired, remains accessible. He answers questions sent to his AOL e-mail address. "Can the UK task the US with listening to British citizens? Can the US task the Brits with collecting on US citizens?"

"Absolutely not," he replies.

"Does the NSA maintain a database of potential political undesirables in the event of martial law in the US?"

"An urban legend," he says.[10]

Did the NSA illegally eavesdrop on American citizens?

Though the intelligence community esteems Hayden—indeed, it's hard to find someone he has worked with who will speak ill of him even in private—in public he becomes quite defensive about the special programs. Of course, he cannot be *too* defensive, because he can't present a defense. The program, discontinued and then revived under the FISA Amendments Act of 2008, is ongoing and has expanded beyond what even he envisioned for it. It remains Top Secret and compartmentalized as SI, or "Special Intelligence." If that wasn't enough, the program is stovepiped into a special compartment whose name itself is classified.[11]

The basic reasoning behind such draconian secrecy measures is that if Bill the Plumber knows roughly how the NSA intercepts communications originating within the United States, then Michelle the Terrorist will likely also know this and change her communication methods accordingly. The United States, collectively, will then find it harder to figure out where the bad gals and guys are. So far as national security arguments go, this one is fairly basic. Still, it's not inherently persuasive, being predicated on a condition that there are terrorists who assume the U.S. government *doesn't* have a method of listening to telephone calls or reading e-mails.

That said, when the *New York Times* printed details of the NSA surveillance program in 2005—whatever one's feelings about the special programs and their legality—there is evidence that the bad guys weren't making these assumptions. The *Times* bowed to White House pressure to sit on the story for a year but reversed course shortly before the publication of a book by one of the story's lead reporters. Though the *Times* story itself did not contain any details that intelligence officials could later tie to any American lives placed in jeopardy— and indeed, the NSA thanked the *Times* in private for its discretion, while publicly flailing it—the percussive effect led to a disclosure that made it harder for the NSA to perform basic functions: that American companies were cooperating with the NSA, mostly by providing them with reams of data about foreign communications that happened to touch (or "transit through") an American wire. "This, by far, was the worst disclosure," Hayden said in an interview. "It actively stopped collection that no one anywhere had any problem with."

Ironically, the first public confirmation that President Bush had authorized the acquisition of information from these domestic junctions came courtesy of Bob Graham of Florida, chairman of the

Senate Select Committee on Intelligence, who mentioned it to the *Washington Post* after the *Times* first reported the domestic terminal portion of the story. Graham had been told about the cooperative arrangement between the government and the telecoms in October 2002. Not long after that the NSA and the telecoms had figured out how to sift through reams of metadata in real time. Earlier that summer, the NSA had started to set up splitters at key telecom network nodes across the country, including one in San Francisco that was exposed by a whistleblower.[12]

The special programs (of which the Terrorist Surveillance Program is a part) reside at the intersection of two very complicated and overlapping bodies of law, each with its own language and legislative history. Laws circumscribing the practice of domestic law enforcement and statutes proscribing the country's flexibility to respond to existential military threats are not always reconcilable— nor were they designed to be. Where laws governing domestic law enforcement tend to minimize powers and focus on the traditional balance of self-government and security, the larger body of national security laws often justifies its own existence with the need to give the executive branch a normative foundation for extraordinary actions.

The NSA operates collection platforms in more than fifty countries and uses airplanes and submarines, ships and satellites, specially modified trucks, and cleverly disguised antennas. It has managed to break the cryptographic systems of most of its targets and prides itself on sending first-rate product to the president of the United States.

Inside the United States, the NSA's collection is regulated by FISA, passed in 1978 to provide a legal framework for intercepting communications related to foreign intelligence or terrorism where one party is inside the United States and might be considered a "U.S. person."

Three bits of terminology: The NSA "collects on" someone, with the preposition indicating the broad scope of the verb. Think of a rake pushing leaves into a bin. The NSA intercepts a very small percentage of the communications it collects. At NSA, to "intercept" is to introduce to the collection process an analyst, who examines a leaf that has appeared in his or her computer bin. (An analyst could use computer software to assist here, but the basic distinction the NSA makes is that the actual interception requires intent and specificity on behalf of the interceptor.) A "U.S. person" refers to a U.S. citizen, a legal resident of the United States, or a corporation or business legally chartered inside the United States.[13]

Before the Terrorist Surveillance Program went live, the system was designed to work something like this: When the FBI or CIA developed information about foreign espionage or terrorist plots that tied legitimately bad people to U.S. persons (citizens, corporations, charities), the government, through the Justice Department's Office of Intelligence Policy and Review, applied for a FISA warrant. This allowed the NSA to collect all electronic communications that directly emanated from, or were directed to, that specific U.S. person—so long as one side of the conversation was known to be overseas.

In practice, the process went like this: If an NSA analyst decided that one party of a conversation she was about to monitor (or had just intercepted) might be inside the United States, she would have to convince her superior that there was probable cause to believe that the person inside the United States was connected to the foreign intelligence purpose that the analyst was tasked with collecting on. The superior would go the NSA general counsel, who could veto the request. If the general counsel approved, however, a packet of materials would be created for the Justice Department to review. Again, Justice could say no, but if they said yes, they (that is, Justice) would have to draft a document demonstrating probable cause for the duty judge on the FISC. This process could be done quickly, but often was not, and certainly couldn't be scaled sufficiently so that potentially urgent situations could be approved. Even accepting that FISA allowed for orderless interceptions in emergencies, the bottleneck of processing applications would be significant. The government was required to have probable cause to believe that the person overseas was a member of, or significantly associated with, a foreign government or terrorist entity. Also, intention mattered. The primary purpose of surveillance had to be to gather foreign intelligence.[14]

What the special programs did, from a 30,000-foot level, was remove the multiple layers of lawyers. Analysts could decide for themselves whether probable cause existed to intercept a communication. Their work was subject to regular review by the inspector general of the NSA, who would sample target folders to see if the analyst's operational standard of probable cause met hers. The special programs allowed the NSA to determine much more quickly whether a flashing dot somewhere in the world was worth paying attention to or could be safely ignored. It allowed the NSA to directly acquire a raw feed from telecoms—AT&T, BellSouth, and Verizon—and merge it with data collected from a number of other sources (e-mail servers, most of which were based in U.S. credit bureaus; credit card companies; passport records)—to identify the U.S.-based target of a foreign communicator with ties to terrorism, or, in some cases, to identify the foreign-based communicator based on a live intercept. The telecoms provided bulk data in the form of CDRs—Call Detail Records, which included the destination number, the duration of the call, and the location of the call (a home switch, a cell tower, an IP address). The NSA and the telecoms widened secure data channels already constructed for the purpose of allowing law enforcement to monitor to-and-from telephone information in real time—a requirement of the Communications Assistance for Law Enforcement Act.

There was quite a bit the agency could monitor in real time.[15] Based on a scrap of paper collected somewhere overseas with a U.S. phone number on it, the NSA could figure out what other numbers that number called and even determine whether any of those domestic-terminal numbers were in contact with numbers associated with others on the watch list. (This form of analysis is called Community of Interest collection.) To be clear, at this stage of the process the NSA is not actively intercepting communications. It is collecting and analyzing metadata to determine whose communications to intercept. The equipment the NSA reportedly used at the telecom switches (the places where Internet traffic gets routed from one company's system to another) allowed them, in theory, to query e-mail traffic for content. The NSA insists that performing such semantic analysis on content was not done until the target was established.*

The effectiveness of the special programs of the NSA is a mystery. There are a couple of cases where they provided real assistance to

---

*Narus, a company now owned by Boeing, sold AT&T several of its STA-6400 Semantic Traffic Analyzers, which AT&T used to detect worms and infections in data streams but which could also be used to search through the content of e-mail for keywords.

investigators. But the FBI claims that early on the NSA added need-less complications to the Bureau's efforts to determine whether sleeper cells actually existed inside the United States. It was difficult to segregate data that came from the special programs from data that came from normal NSA FISA intercepts. Today, the NSA is more judicious with the information about domestic targets that it provides to the FBI.

Operationally, the NSA keeps secret what internal checklist must be satisfied before it asks telecommunications companies for stored data sets; how quickly it can drill down on a target after identifying it; how, precisely, it uses target and link analysis (also known as data mining) to develop probable cause; what equipment it uses; what auditing tools it uses; and more.[16]

What *is* known is that the NSA's special programs are larger than they were when they first existed as a presidentially authorized intel-ligence collection tool. Inside the government there is a consensus that the programs are critical to national security. This consensus did not come easily, and from a civil libertarian standpoint the checks and balances are insufficient. It could be that the Justice Department, the courts, and Congress previously objected to the program only because they weren't let in on the secret. Now that they're in on it, they're willing participants in its perpetuation and expansion.

In the days after September 11, 2001, Vice President Dick Cheney and David Addington, his legal counsel, both of whom inti-mately knew the habits of Congress and the executive branch, had assumed the opposite would be true. They ordered that details of the special programs remain so tightly compartmented that lawyers for the NSA were forbidden to discuss the matter with lawyers from the Justice Department. The barest minimum number of congressmen received briefings. So tightly stretched was the secrecy blanket that even the National Security Council's legal team was kept in the dark, as was the president's chief homeland security adviser and the Justice Department's chief liaison with the FISA court.[17]

Only one attorney in the Justice Department's internal legal office, John Yoo, was providing the legal guidance. Yoo had no one to help him. He was formerly a constitutional law professor at the University of California, Berkeley, with a strong interest in national security. At Justice, he wrote several opinions that read like law articles but in practice would serve to justify a wide range of practical actions. His boss, Jay Bybee, had been confirmed but could not assume his post as head of the Office of Legal Counsel (OLC) until his teaching term ended. But he would never be read in to the program.[18] Nor was *his* boss, the deputy attorney general. When this later came out, it appeared that Cheney and Addington had hand-selected someone they knew would be sympathetic to their case. But the truth is more prosaic: Yoo was simply the go-to guy for national security in OLC at the time. Had Bybee been at his Justice desk, he would have been the one to decide who would formulate the opinion.

At the NSA, Hayden immediately consulted his general counsel. "Here's what the president wants me to do under 12333," he told Robert Deitz, referring to the executive order authorizing intelligence collection. "Can we do it?" This was a Thursday. Deitz spent a sleepless night trying to figure it out, but came in on Friday morning with an answer: there was no constitutional question at stake—but yes, the NSA could probably do this either under an implicit exemption in FISA, or, if not, the act itself had suddenly revealed itself to be unconstitutionally constraining on the president's power. As Deitz read court opinions going back decades, he noted that even where judges explicitly limited the president's reach, they always tacked on a footnote implying that nothing in their opinion was designed to constrain the president's ability to perform his main Article II functions. Deitz and Hayden agreed on two things: if the programs were revealed, they wouldn't lie to Congress about them, and Hayden would inform at least the chief of the FISC and the Gang of Eight from the start. Both used the same metaphor: they wanted to make Congress "pregnant," too. The programs were legal, in Deitz's view, but very close to the line.

Hayden then asked his SIGINT chief, Maureen Baginski, to figure out how many people would be needed to run the programs. Given the sensitivity involved, he had a hand in personally selecting everyone who would participate. Early the next day, a Saturday morning, Hayden, Deitz, and about fifty unsuspecting NSA analysts and engineers filed into a conference room in the main headquarters building. Hayden has several times since recounted the directive he gave to the staff: they would carry out only what the president authorized "and not one photon more." At the time he did not know, he now concedes, how realistic that promise was, given that the NSA had never attempted this type of thing before. But he knew that it would send a message to those who would operate the program: over-collection (which is inevitable) in a program like this is more than a minor sin.

Before 9/11, there was plenty of secrecy associated with the FISC. Its decisions were never public, and the subject of the surveillance would be—so far as the government was concerned—blissfully ignorant.[19] In 1999, engineers brought a program to Hayden called ThinThread. It looked quite promising to an agency that was struggling to keep up with its core intelligence-gathering mission. Hayden's analysts were hearing a lot of chatter about millennium-related terror plots, and ThinThread was a $20 million computer system that could do what the NSA admitted it needed to do better—tap into the ever-changing global telephonic and network architecture.[20]

One thing that the NSA could not do without a court order was acquire—the verb is important—communications that did not fully bypass the United States. If both ends of the conversation came from sources outside the United States, the NSA could intercept it, even if the wires through which the electrons and photons flowed physically went through the United States. But it was very hard to segregate these conversations from domestic traffic, and the NSA couldn't collect everything and then segregate it. That the NSA had the authority to do this at all was itself a necessary secret, and it remains redacted in official NSA regulations from the 1990s and the early part of the 2000s that were obtained by the authors under the Freedom of Information Act.

ThinThread's proponents believed they had figured out a way to intercept conversations without technically "acquiring" them, where one terminal might indeed be in the United States. NSA signals intelligence operations managers believed that by subjecting the content of these communications to encryption they could analyze the *metadata* for suspicious patterns. The response from the NSA's lawyers was unanimous: the agency could not acquire communications inside the United States without a warrant whether they were encrypted or not. The lawyers had asked the Justice Department for its view; President Bill Clinton's team found no basis in law for it. Therefore, the neat technology of ThinThread was not something the NSA could use. After the special programs began, the NSA used a program called Trailblazer to do link analysis on the data provided by telecoms and other sources. Trailblazer did not encrypt communications, which raised a red flag for many NSA SIGINT teams who weren't read in to the program. Why wasn't ThinThread being used? Trailblazer, by comparison, seemed more Orwellian and more expensive.*

The reason was that Hayden now had the authority to acquire communications inside the United States (where one terminal was reasonably believed to be outside the United States) without an order. From his perspective, he didn't need ThinThread. And in any event, his software engineers told him that it wouldn't scale. It would later emerge, as Hayden acknowledges, that the system ultimately used to acquire U.S. communications didn't work as well as it could have, but that was no reason to replace it with an untested, entirely different system.[21]

A few weeks after the programs began, Deitz called Addington's office and asked to see the Justice Department's legal opinion on the special programs. Addington refused to provide it. The president was entitled to private legal advice, and the OLC's opinions were not designed to be shared even within the executive branch. Deitz asked him for a summary, so Addington gave Deitz the gist: the president had inherent authority under Article II of the Constitution to—well, it was Article II *über alles*. He could do anything he wanted. Deitz did not agree.

We don't know what John Yoo wrote exactly, because his initial opinion and many subsequent memoranda remain classified. But

---

*In 2010, an NSA manager, Thomas Drake, would be indicted for allegedly improperly storing classified information about the two systems and then giving information to a *Baltimore Sun* reporter. Drake has since become an active public critic of government secrecy and the NSA. Drake was never actually convicted of leaking.

there are clues in a September 25, 2001, memo prepared by Yoo for David Kris, who was then an associate attorney general trying to figure out whether FISA could be interpreted to allow collection in cases where foreign intelligence was merely *a* purpose, rather than *the* purpose. The change of an article might allow FISA orders to be issued for the purposes of terrorism cases, Kris reasoned. What he did not know was that the creators of the program had already decided against asking Congress to modify FISA in any substantial way.[22] Yoo responded to Kris in such a way as to suggest that Congress and the courts wouldn't mind a little participle switcheroo. "The factors favoring warrantless searches for national security reasons may be even more compelling under current circumstances," concluded Yoo after analyzing circuit court decisions. "After the attacks on September 11, 2001, the government interest in conducting searches related to fighting terrorism is perhaps of the highest order—the need to defend the nation from direct attack."[23]

During interviews about the topic years later, Yoo basically confirmed that he had argued in favor of inherent presidential authority to protect the nation and that the congressional authorization to fight al-Qaeda at least implicitly authorized aggressive surveillance during this war. In any event, FISA was simply not applicable to the post-9/11 terrorist threat.[24] He argued, in other words, that FISA was okay until existential events rendered it irrelevant.

The NSA's initial opinion on the "Presidential Authorization for Specified Electronic Surveillance Activities during a Limited Period to Detect and Prevent Acts of Terrorism within the United States" was much more cautious.* The opinion remains classified, and Deitz would not discuss its contents with the authors. Several who have read it say that it did not draw the same conclusion as Yoo did. Instead, it read in to FISA as an applied exemption that would permit surveillance without a court order if it had direct bearing on imminent threats—particularly if the type of war incorporated the United States as a battlefield, and if a combatant or terrorist was receiving orders from another country. The NSA lawyers viewed the

---

*The formal unclassified name for the presidential order as disclosed by the Justice Department in 2005.

Congressional Authorization for the Use of Military Force against al-Qaeda and its affiliates as a safe harbor. Intelligence collection was clearly a part of the process of going to war.

Deitz added one thing that displeased the White House: he insisted that the analysts stick to the probable cause threshold, and not simply a "reasonable suspicion" threshold. In practice, it might not have altered the decision chain. The analyst would decide independently and the collection would begin immediately. NSA lawyers and the attorney general could stop it if they didn't think the threshold was actually met.

Had Congress been aware that the NSA and the Department of Justice (DOJ) had different, somewhat contrary, legal justifications for the program, they might have had greater reservations. But Addington argued that the OLC opinion was tantamount to internal deliberations and could be—indeed *should* be—withheld. It is possible that he was aware of how the two opinions conflicted and knew that their commingling would create problems. Regardless, he argued that if FISA didn't apply, it didn't apply. The NSA could collect on phone calls and read e-mails if it wanted to, he believed.[25]

That said, the threshold to tap into any phone was fairly inviolable when it came to U.S. persons: the government had to show probable cause that a U.S. person was connected to terrorism before any interception could begin. Anticipating the objection that FISA expressly allowed for emergency wiretapping, both the NSA's and the Justice Department's legal briefs argued that as a practical matter, because the probable cause standard *as the court would define it* could not possibly be met to the satisfaction of a court, all wiretap activities would be halted by the FISC as soon as the exemptions ran out, which would be disastrous if the NSA were in the middle of tracking someone.

Context is crucial here: as all of this was playing out, lower Manhattan was still covered in ash. The lawyers were trying to figure a way to allow the executive branch to discover whether any additional plots were imminent or whether conspirators were working on U.S. soil. A secondary priority was to learn whether other al-Qaeda sleeper cells were preparing for later plots. Neither the White House nor the NSA viewed the surveillance as a police investigator would. Instead, this was an intelligence operation that by design and urgency had to be carried out pursuant to the laws governing a covert operation.

And that's basically how the White House played it. Within a week of this determination—on October 1, 2001—Hayden went to Capitol Hill and gave a briefing to the Gang of Eight on the program. He did so over the objections of Addington and Cheney, which itself provides some evidence that, contrary to a shared belief among the program's critics, the two men did not make all of the decisions about it and were occasionally overruled.[26] There were no notes taken during that briefing, so it is not clear whether the congressional leadership was forthright in later complaints that what they were told was less egregious than what the NSA actually did (or possibly just described to them as technically as possible in order to obscure the egregiousness).[27] Associates of Hayden's say that the target analysis component of the surveillance program—identified as STELLAR WIND—had not yet been set up when he first went to Congress, though engineers were working on it.[28]

Although terrorism was on the minds of NSA managers before September 11, 2001, the agency was not on a war footing. It had few linguists capable of translating intercepted phone calls, much less a good system of figuring out how to determine which calls to intercept. (Its SIGINT directorate tried to ascertain how many skilled Urdu and Pashto speakers it had on staff; the NSA's own internal count was off by a factor of three.)

Still, pretty much any phone call originating from Afghanistan and from the tribal regions of Pakistan was suspicious in September 2001; very few people in Afghanistan had satellite phones capable of making calls, and those who did were either terrorists or drug dealers. "You could figure out that if someone turned on their Iridium, bounced a call off an Intelsat satellite to a number in the United States, they probably had something to do with terrorism," says Matthew Aid, a former NSA signals intelligence analyst turned historian who wrote *The Secret Sentry*, a definitive history of the agency.

By Afghanistan's standards, Pakistan had a fairly modern technological infrastructure. The NSA had spent a significant amount of money on a secret program to tap into the private cell phone network used by the country's civilian, military, and intelligence leaders. The priority of U.S. intelligence was to collect as much information as possible about the Pakistani nuclear program; terrorism was a secondary concern. When thinking about the scope of potential domestic targets, the NSA ran into a problem of scale. In one of New York City's "Little Pakistan" enclaves, about ten thousand immigrants speak a dialect of Urdu that the NSA could not properly decipher. Even if they had found some legal or technological way to monitor all international communications to telephone numbers and e-mail addresses associated with these Pakistani Americans, they could do nothing with the intercepts.

One of the NSA's foundational secrets is the result of two historical accidents. First, early worldwide telephone treaties made it much less expensive to route calls through the United States than through other, smaller countries. This made the telecommunications infrastructure an American creation—the product of American engineers and American equipment. Second, the U.S. Department of Defense created the Internet. Americans like to think of ourselves as central to the smooth operation of the world, and so far as communications are concerned, we are.

For the most part, telecommunication "switches," or central hubs, where packets of data stream through are either physically located in the United States or built in foreign countries by U.S. companies.[29] This is highly inefficient for someone in Latin America trying to send an e-mail to a friend in Europe, but it is a boon to the National Security Agency.[30] According to NSA officials, before 9/11 as much as 85 percent of the world's telecommunications traffic (cell phone calls, satellite calls, Internet traffic) coursed through a fiber optic cable inside the United States at some point during its transit. When it "hit the wire," the NSA had the right to intercept it, provided there was no reason to believe that it was a purely domestic transmission. The NSA therefore found it fairly easy to convince U.S. telecom providers to allow them access to the international portion of that traffic, although, as we have noted, the technology to segregate the data was not very mature. Where it had gaps, it negoti-ated secret agreements with friendly countries like India, which con-tained the largest telecom switch for e-mail and phone calls for the Middle East.[31]

The NSA also has a daring unit of secret wiretappers known as the Special Collection Service (SCS), or internally as "F6," which operates in the field with CIA officers. In 1999, to give one example, the NSA tasked SCS with secretly tapping the communications net-work used by the Pakistani military to communicate with its civilian leadership about nuclear weapons.[32]

This fiber optic idyll for American eavesdroppers contains many hidden thorns, however:

- How do you separate packets involving U.S. persons from packets that don't, if it all flows through the same node?
- Many countries don't want the United States to be able to listen in on their traffic, or don't want their citizens to know that the United States has such easy access to it. As a result, these coun-tries are often difficult to deal with.
- Telecommunications companies might not wish to cooperate. Because no law compels them to, there are gaps in data.
- The volume of raw signals generated by the world each day is increasing, and not even Google has the computing power to sample more than a fraction of it. How is the NSA supposed to know what is important?
- Routing calls and emails is an art of economy. Telecoms don't operate according to the protocols of an intelligence agency. Rather, they're primarily concerned about cost. Communications, and especially email, are commonly routed in groups without distinction, which makes it difficult at times to separate the domestic from the international.
- Because of the way email works, locating the origin of an email by IP address is difficult. Using the old Information Superhighway metaphor, email is like a motorcade. The com-puter disassembles files into a series of discrete vehicles, each of which contains a portion of the original entourage. (These vehicles are called packets.) But no worries: every car in this

motorcade has the same map so no one will get lost. Each packet includes directions about where it needs to go; Internet hardware reads this metadata and determines the easiest route. Still, the motorcade often gets split up. There may be too much traffic on one road, forcing some packets to divert to another. As long as the packets don't lose their metadata maps, the computer waiting for their arrival will be able to reassemble everything in the right order. The process of travel often makes it difficult to determine precisely where in the world the email came from, because each packet collects a different souvenir from all the hubs and switches it transits through. Spammers have figured out how to spoof the unique twelve-digit addresses that serve to identify the original computer.[33] The NSA has an ISP Geolocation Cell that does nothing but track down the physical locations associated with IP addresses. Its computers are unable to do this automatically.

Even before 9/11, collecting foreign intelligence required a massive amount of post facto deletion of data inadvertently collected about U.S. persons. And that's okay. Congress accepted that in the course of daily SIGINT hunting, domestic traffic would creep into the bins. Provided that the NSA got rid of it quickly—unless there was some emergency that threatened someone's life—eavesdroppers were none the worse for wear.

But then events changed the NSA's mission, and accordingly, its mind-set. Technology simply wasn't ready for these changes, its progress being dependent on, but agnostic to, the goals of human beings. The agency lacked linguists, equipment, policy, and legal guidance. And it was under extreme pressure. The White House needed product the NSA could not produce. The SIGINT directorate would have to create databases of its own and massively reorient its collection program.

After 9/11, The White House asked Hayden to treat any communication that terminated in Afghanistan or Pakistan as potentially intelligence-bearing. That meant the NSA had to figure out how to sift those communications from all the rest. It had to determine how best to geolocate email senders using Internet Protocol addresses, something that to this day it has trouble doing.[34]

Email was easier in theory. The NSA could program its computers to search through electronic messages and maintain them with much greater ease than phone calls, which required significant server space. Immediately after 9/11, an NSA assessment concluded that terrorists would likely communicate with one another by embedding data in PDF files. So it proposed an expanded program to determine whether emails passing through its systems had PDF attachments. Its analysts would focus on those items first.

The work was divided into compartments—perhaps as many as a dozen, each given their own classified code word.[35] A technical team would figure out how to modify computers and equipment to allow for the type of collection that was required. One team of analysts would review all pocket litter (that is, things found in a terrorist's possession) coming back from the battlefield. Another would try to use data-mining programs and statistical methods to search patterns of telephone calls and emails of specific targets. Suspicious sets were given probability scores, which, if high enough, triggered an interception. Another team of engineers worked to draw a map of the world's telecommunications pipes to see whether there were any access points inside the United States that the NSA was not yet able to monitor.

The NSA still had to sanitize the content of messages and phone calls—there was no way around U.S. law here.[36] Only after the interception standard had been reached could the actual calls and emails themselves be monitored.

The compartment of the program revealed by the New York Times allowed the NSA to intercept conversations between a U.S.-based target and a person overseas, provided that there was probable cause to believe that at least *one side* of the communication was involved in terrorism. Usually, the NSA knew the foreign target; it didn't know the domestic target and used the bulk data analysis to figure out who it might be. (FISA, of course, required that if one side terminated in the United States, an order had to be issued, with few exceptions.) The collection had to be directed at a target, which under the new standard could be almost anyone or anything—an unknown person living in Detroit whose identity (but not a name) was collected from an al-Qaeda detainee in Afghanistan; a group of people; even people whose behavioral patterns resembled those of a terrorist. In other words, the "other side" of this war on terrorism could be anywhere, and that meant the program's definition of a target could be anything that reasonably *resembled* an enemy.*

Regardless, it turned out to be difficult to accurately pipe exact conversations to the NSA analytical teams. Ironing out these technical wrinkles, which a former senior NSA official likened to a building engineer trying to figure out which valves to open to properly heat a building, meant that a lot of unrelated data was sent to the analysts. They ignored it (or "minimized" it), which is what they're supposed to do when they encounter a U.S. person unrelated to the target.

Because of technological limitations, getting to the target required the collection and conflation of many unconnected and innocent phone numbers and email or text message metadata. Some intercepted communications originated and terminated inside the United States.[37] To the NSA, this was all right because nothing was done with those conversations once the correct "valve mix" was determined. To those later read in to the program, intention was now irrelevant; what mattered was the very *fact* of collection.

President Bush acknowledged only one part of the program—the Terrorist Surveillance Program—after the *New York Times* publicly disclosed it. The president did not reveal the "other intelligence programs," as a government report later called it, that he had ordered.

It would be reasonable to assume that the TSP itself prompted hand-wringing and objections and almost, in 2004, led to the near resignations of the director of the FBI and the entire top turret of the

---

*In 2007, Yoo was asked by PBS whether the government could do "blanket surveillance" under FISA. Here is how he responded: "No. This is a good example of where existing laws were not up to the job, because under existing laws like FISA, you have to have the name of somebody, have to already suspect that someone's a terrorist before you can get a warrant. You have to have a name to put in the warrant to tap their phone calls, and so it doesn't allow you as a government to use judgment based on probability to say, 'Well, 1 percent probability of the calls from or maybe 50 percent of the calls are coming out of this one city in Afghanistan, and there's a high probability that some of those calls are terrorist communications. But we don't know the names of the people making those calls.' You want to get at those phone calls, those emails, but under FISA you can't do that."

Justice Department. But it was not. Something about the way these "other intelligence programs" were presented to Justice was the real problem.

When acting attorney general James Comey was read in to the program for the first time, he relied on the advice of the OLC head, Jack Goldsmith, who had growing concerns about Yoo's legal analysis, particularly with regard to the Other Intelligence Activities (OIAs)—not the TSP.[38] One of the OIAs, for example, directly contravened a statute of Congress. (The statute in question was not FISA.) Comey has never publicly disclosed exactly what he objected to, but people briefed on the program and who have spoken to Comey say it was the legal rationale giving the NSA quick access to telecom-collected metadata that "drove him bonkers. There was just no way to justify this."

To quickly acquire communications inside the United States, the NSA needed the cooperation of U.S. telecommunications companies. The Stored Communications Act of 1986 (SCA) would not allow the provision of historical data without an order or warrant. The Electronic Crimes and Privacy Act (ECPA) banned real-time monitoring without an order or warrant. Furthermore, because the types of communications that the NSA wanted were considered "consumer proprietary information," telecoms couldn't turn them over to a third party for profit, law enforcement, or at the government's request. (This latter point was rejected by the NSA's lawyers, who said that the FCC, which enforced it, misread the statute.) But the SCA had language that seemed pretty clear: "[A] provider of remote computing service or electronic communication service to the public shall not knowingly divulge a record or other information pertaining to a subscriber to or customer of such service . . . to any governmental entity."[39]

The rest of the act basically adds "without a warrant." So assuming that citizens of the United States count as customers, telecom companies are forbidden from voluntarily turning over records to the federal government. But what counts as a "record"? Anything the telecom keeps in storage and anything involving the customer's past communications. In other words: everything it knows.

One of the OIA authorized by President Bush seemed to provide a blanket feel-free-to-ignore-the-Stored-Communications-Act-and-ECPA card to telecom companies. It was a certification signed by the attorney general attesting that the government would not criminally prosecute the telecoms for their cooperation.

So what did the telecoms turn over to the NSA?* Millions of transaction records that included millions of instances of domestic telephones dialing other domestic telephones. Other companies sent over tranches of email messages. The volume itself is material; the NSA would ask for telephone logs from a certain time at a certain place (that is, a company, a neighborhood, a mosque), and telecoms would transmit those records upon request.

By law, the NSA had no right to do anything with such data at that point other than try to deduce their significance without reading them. (Again, reading them would be both illegal and time-consuming.) The agency used several computer programs to scan the pen register logs (the lists of phone numbers that called other numbers) and the metadata associated with emails (for example, To; From; subject lines; IP addresses; lengths; frequencies; and so on). If a group of people associated with an entity (like an Islamic charity) had (or appeared to have) a connection with an entity connected to foreign terrorism, all three were subject to the interception protocols.

To go back to the example that leads this chapter, the NSA would have used this data and correlated it with the bulk radio data they intercepted from Yemen to see which calls overlapped. Then they could (and would) task an analyst with an interception of the U.S. end of the call. Mike McConnell, a former director of the NSA and the second director of national intelligence during the Bush administration, would later describe to a group of intelligence industry professionals what happened next: "If the U.S. end of the call was Grandma, and they were talking about cakes, we would minimize it. If it was operationally significant, we would keep it. If that U.S. number were to call another U.S. number, we would have to get a FISA warrant."[40]

---

*The Senate Select Committee on Intelligence's report concluded that "we have seen no evidence that Congress intended the AUMF [Authorization for Use of Military Force] to authorize a widespread effort to collect the content of Americans' phone and e-mail communications," implying that the NSA had done just that.

At no point, so far as we can tell, did the NSA ever perform link analysis on a data set without having a specific target in mind. They did not use the data sets to discover "both" ends of a communication. In all instances—and the NSA's inspector general would certify this—the NSA had a specific thing, such as a person, a telephone number, or an address, and used the data provided by the telecoms to figure out whether the thing was significant enough to warrant actual interception. Maybe two flashing red lights were linked, or maybe several numbers were associated with one person, but without synthesizing the data it was hard to tell.

We are fairly certain that Comey was refusing to sign the authorization for these activities. The Stored Communications Act and the Electronic Crimes and Privacy Act had exceptions, but Comey didn't think they applied.

Initially, the White House was ready to have the president's counsel, Alberto Gonzales, sign his name to it. They tried to use Congress as a lever. In a hastily organized briefing, a member asked whether any ongoing operations would be jeopardized if the telecoms refused to hand over data without a warrant. A senior NSC official brought up a major counterterrorism investigation code-named CREVICE. The United States, British MI5, and German intelligence were working closely together on the case, which involved al-Qaeda-linked jihadists in Europe who were communicating with Americans. One was caught on a wire musing about blowing up an airplane.[41] At least some of their communication was transiting through the United States. Without the program, the White House insisted, the ability to disrupt CREVICE would be significantly reduced. The FBI and the Justice Department representatives in the room who had been working CREVICE for months knew that wasn't true. FISA warrants had already been issued and MI5 had its own technical surveillance operation under way. The bulk provision of data was just not that necessary anymore.

The White House really wanted to advance a practical argument to Congress but declined to do so. They want to say that the lawyers who handled the program for the telecoms would have panicked if, after months of seeing the signature of the attorney general—the nation's top law enforcement officer—they saw instead the scribble of the president's in-house guy. They not only would have questioned any past cooperation with the NSA but also probably would significantly curtail their cooperation in the future. Practically, even though Comey *had* signed off, certifying that it was legal to intercept the U.S. side of an international communication connected with terrorism, the companies might balk at providing even this basic service.

This was why the White House changed course after the now-famous hospital room confrontation whereby Gonzales tried to persuade an ailing Attorney General John Ashcroft to affix his signature. The White House had to; it simply could not send a document to the telecoms with *anyone else's signature*. It took six months before the NSA was able to develop procedures that fit the interpretation of the metadata provisions promulgated by Jack Goldsmith and his successor, Daniel Levin.

It's worth noting that it was President Bush himself who actually stopped the program. Bush felt he had been misled by his cabinet about the degree of support for it. As time went on, the president became convinced that the program had to be brought in from the cold and written into law. His next attorney general, Gonzales, would agree.[42] Bush wrote in his memoirs:

> I had to make a big decision, and fast. Some in the White House believed I should stand on my powers under Article II of the Constitution and suffer the walkout. . . . I was willing to defend the powers of the presidency under Article II. But not at any cost. I thought about the Saturday Night Massacre in October 1973, when President Richard Nixon's firing of Watergate prosecutor Archibald Cox led his attorney general and deputy attorney general to resign. That was not a historical crisis I was eager to replicate.

As Bart Gellman, Vice President Cheney's best biographer, would later write, "The Bush-Cheney relationship never fully recovered from that day. Bush wrote, without naming Cheney, that he 'made clear to my advisers that I never wanted to be blindsided like that again.' March 11, 2004, was the day the president of the United States discovered that the vice president's zeal could lead him off a cliff."[43]

• • •

Comey was not beloved at the White House. Dick Cheney in particular was not a fan of his from the start. Comey first met the vice president the same day he appointed Patrick Fitzgerald to investigate the Valerie Plame leak—an investigation that would culminate with the indictment of Cheney's chief of staff for lying for the government. When Comey introduced himself that day, Cheney replied, without looking back, "Oh, I know you from television." He wasn't smiling.

But Comey would come to the rescue of the White House later that year, helping dissuade the *New York Times* from publishing details about the special program before the 2004 election. He did so by keeping his mouth shut. In October of that year, Condoleezza Rice, the national security adviser, invited Phil Taubman, the *New York Times*'s Washington bureau chief, and Jill Abramson, the *Times*'s executive editor, to a private meeting in her office.* Hayden and Comey attended. On Rice's cue, Hayden gave the two editors a fairly comprehensive briefing on the program—virtually the same briefing Comey received when he was read in.

At one point, Abramson asked if the program was on a solid legal foundation. Rice said that some lawyers, including Comey, she said, gesturing, had expressed concerns, but the program was on solid footing now. *Is this true?* Abramson asked Comey. Comey replied that it was. The *Times* editors did not pursue the matter. Hayden invited Taubman to Fort Meade at one point, brought him to a conference room, sat him down with two SIGINT analysts who were part of the program, and then left the room. The idea was to give Taubman a chance to question these analysts without the boss present. Hayden was very aware of the way that journalists thought—and knew that the gesture would gain him credibility with the *Times*. He was right.

A year later, Comey was not happy that the *New York Times* had disclosed the TSP's existence. He believed that the paper's reporting had also compromised the NSA's capacity to conduct *legal* surveillance. Still, Comey did not feel particularly aggrieved for those who set up the programs—the good ones and the bad ones. They created the mess by refusing to do it properly in the first place.

---

*Abramson would not comment on the meeting.

But where did the leaks come from?

Some former Bush administration officials blame Comey (though Hayden explicitly does not). At least one Justice Department official, Terrence Tamm, and Russell Tice, a former NSA analyst, have admitted to talking about the program to the *New York Times*. Neither has been prosecuted. (A senior Justice Department official said that Tamm was considered a legitimate whistleblower and that he planned to use then senator Barack Obama's declaration that the program was unconstitutional in his defense.)

According to a report provided by the White House to the Justice Department's inspector general, the Bush administration believed that as of 2005, fewer than a dozen people outside the NSA were read in. This satisfied Addington's desire for strict compartmentalization. But the White House was delusional. It has never been harder to keep secrets than now. For example, Chuck Robinson, chief of staff to Comey, was never counted as having been read in, but he had been by the FBI—by a security officer named Mike Fedonchick. A senior FBI agent later estimated that as many as six hundred from the agency were briefed on some part of the special programs.

True, most field FBI agents didn't have a full handle on every detail, but more than enough special agents were sufficiently knowledgeable to talk. And inside the FBI, everyone talks to each other, and everyone assumes that everyone else knows about big programs. The FBI was getting lots of leads from the NSA. People heard things. There was plenty of noise getting out of the compartment. The tighter the White House tried to grip the water, the more easily it spilled from its hand.

The White House tried to use the *Times*'s partial disclosure to publicly advance a theory of presidential power. Practically, though, it was only a matter of time before the rest of the program's details leaked out in one form or another. The NSA had legitimate worries. If more details about the program were known, the bad guys might learn about how difficult it was to rapidly acquire a target and how the agency had solved that problem. The NSA's liaison relationships with other governments might also be jeopardized. If derivative information was ever disclosed in a court, many of those governments would probably alter the degree to which they cooperated with the United States. The intelligence community did not want the press to disclose the degree to which the NSA monitored and was able to intercept virtually all telephone and email traffic originating from Afghanistan and later from Pakistan and Iraq. This might also compromise the technological methods that the NSA legally used overseas.

Finally, the holiest of holies: a large percentage—one former intelligence community lawyer put the figure at 90 percent—of international telephone and email traffic passed through a server or node associated with an American-owned telecommunications company. If terrorists had known this, they could have tried to use those rare networks that were entirely geographically constrained. But the bigger fear, which proved to be entirely valid, was that disclosure of this would lead companies and countries to demand that their communications pipes not pass through the United States. These entities were worried not about terrorism but about geopolitics: the NSA easily intercepting their diplomatic and industrial communications and the reaction of their citizenry to the fact.

The scene at the hospital marked a turning point for the program but did so in a way that may well have hastened the day that Congress would officially deem it sound and legitimate. Immediately after he became attorney general in early 2005, Alberto Gonzales asked the new head of the OLC, Steve Bradbury, to reexamine whether there might be a different legal approach to the NSA activities authorized by the president that would put those activities on a stronger legal footing (even though all aspects of the program as then conducted had been approved in a comprehensive legal opinion issued by Jack Goldsmith and the OLC in May 2004). Starting in March 2005, Bradbury crafted a novel legal analysis that, if approved by the FISA court, would permit much of the NSA program to be based on the FISA statute. Bradbury presented his new approach to the White House in the late spring of 2005, and the White House approved without hesitation the Justice Department's proposal to move forward with the concept, provided that the director of national intelligence and the NSA were confident that the new approach would not materially compromise the value and effectiveness of the program. The DNI and the NSA expressed support, and over the next several months, the OLC, working with the Office of Intelligence Policy and Review, developed a detailed analysis and proposal intended to be submitted to the FISA court in late 2005 or early 2006.

The *New York Times* article in December 2005 sidetracked the legal effort that the OLC was pursuing under FISA. Bradbury and others in the DOJ spent much of their time and attention in 2006 explaining to the public (and in private to Congress) the legal basis for the NSA activities, which were now publicly acknowledged by the president following the *Times* article, as well as addressing other alleged activities and rumors swirling around those allegations. As a consequence of the catastrophic distraction, it wasn't until January 2007 that Gonzales told Congress that the DOJ had succeeded in obtaining from the FISA court an order authorizing under a novel interpretation of FISA.

Then, just as quickly, it went away. A FISA judge refused to sustain the same legal approval in its full scope. In late spring or early summer of 2007, this new legal hurdle in the application of FISA became a serious impediment to the continued effectiveness of the surveillance activities, and thus spurred Congress to enact substantial FISA reform legislation, which occurred first in the form of stopgap legislation in 2007 and in 2008 as a permanent and fundamental restructuring of FISA.

This drove Mike McConnell, the DNI at the time, crazy. He told members of Congress that if he had been the director of the NSA on 9/11 he would have asked Congress to simply change the FISA law. He disagreed with Hayden that doing so would have made it easier for terrorists to communicate.

Although President Bush could have ordered the program's continuation under his signature alone, Congress would doubtless have responded in a way that might have precipitated a constitutional crisis. Bush was convinced by Bradbury, Gonzales, and Stephen Hadley, his national security adviser, that the best way to make sure the program lasted was to allow Congress to rewrite the FISA law. That the entire program was nonfunctional remained a secret until John Boehner, then the minority whip, told Fox News that "there's been a ruling, over the last four or five months, that prohibits the ability of our intelligence services and our counterintelligence people from listening in to two terrorists in other parts of the world where the communication could come through the United States."[44] Republicans had at the ready expansive legislation that Democrats wouldn't accept—this the public knew. But no one outside government knew that the program had ended. Regardless of whether one views Congressman Boehner's revelation as a kind of whistleblowing or a partisan leak, one year later Congress passed the FISA Amendment Acts.

Hayden, now the director of the CIA, found himself delighted and felt vindicated. The FISA Amendments Act allowed the president to do more than ever before. Now anyone associated with terrorism could be subject to surveillance. For the most part, the only restriction placed on the NSA was that they could not surveil Americans overseas without an order. The telecoms had their official congressional writ of immunity. Bulk collection began to flow again, as did NSA access to real-time telecom data. The big difference? More people knew the secret.

Presently, the executive branch is not (that we know of) hiding anything from Congress, the judiciary branch, or (more weirdly) itself. Everyone has been read in to the program. And Congress moved to align the law with the president's exercise of executive power. The courts, by and large, have not objected. And most details about the current program remain classified.


But the question remains: Does the NSA read my email? Based on what Hayden, Yoo, and others have said publicly, as well as confidential information provided to the authors and verified independently by officials read in to the programs:

- If you regularly call people in Afghanistan, Pakistan, or Yemen, your telephone *records* have probably passed through an NSA computer. Most likely, however, if you've been calling rug merchants or relatives, no one at the NSA knew your name. (A computer program sanitizes the actual identifying information.) Depending on the time, date, location, and contextual factors related to the call, a record may not have been created.
- If you've sent an email from an IP address that has been used by bad guys in the past (IP addresses can be spoofed), your email's metadata—the hidden directions that tell the Internet where to send it (that is, the To and From lines, the subject line, the length, and the type of email) probably passed through a server. The chances of an analyst or a computer actually reading the

content of an email are very slim. (If you're a journalist who writes about the Secret Service, it ought to be more disconcerting to you when Google customizes advertisements for weapons and commando courses based on search queries.)

- If you are or were a lawyer for someone formally accused of terrorism, there is a good chance that the NSA has or had—but could not or cannot access (at least not anymore)—your telephone billing records. (N.B.: A Senate Select Committee on Intelligence report notes that the FISA Amendments Act does not require material erroneously collected to be destroyed.)
- If you work for a member of the "Defense Industrial Base" on sensitive projects and your company uses Verizon and AT&T, your email has likely been screened by NSA computers for malware.[45]
- Before 2007, if you, as an American citizen, worked overseas in or near a war zone, there is a small chance that you were "collected on"—that is, actively listened to—by a civilian NSA analyst or a member of the NSA's Central Security Service (the name given to the military service elements that make up a large part of the NSA's workforce).[46]
- If you, from September 2001 to roughly April 2004, called or sent an email to or from regions associated with terrorism and used American Internet companies to do so, your transaction records (again, without identifying information) were likely collected by your telecommunications company and passed to the NSA.[47] The records were then analyzed, and there is a tiny chance that a person or a computer read them or sampled them. The NSA would ask telecommunications companies for tranches of data that correlated to particular communities of interest, and then used a variety of classified and unclassified techniques to predict, based on their analysis, who was likely to be associated with terrorism. This determination required at least one additional and independent extraneous piece of evidence.
- There is a chance that the NSA passed this data to the FBI for further investigation. There is a small chance that the FBI acted on this information.[48]
- If you define "collection" in the broadest sense possible, there is a good chance that if the NSA wanted to obtain your transactional

information in real time and knew your direct identity (or had a rough idea of who you are), they can do so, provided that they can prove to a FISA judge within seventy-two hours that there is probable cause to believe you are a terrorist or associated with a terrorist organization.

- If the NSA receives permission from a judge to collect on a corporation or a charity that may be associated with terrorism, and your company, which is entirely separate from the organization in question, happens to share a location with it (either because you're in the same building or have contracted with the company to share Internet services), there is a chance that the NSA incidentally collects your work email and phone calls. It is very hard for the agency to map IP addresses to their physical locations and to completely segregate parts of corporate telephone networks. When this happens, Congress and the Justice Department are notified, and an NSA internal compliance unit makes a record of the "overcollect."

- If any of your communications were accidentally or incidentally collected by the NSA, they probably still exist somewhere, subject to classified minimization requirements. (The main NSA SIGINT database is code-named PINWALE.) This is the case even after certain collection activities became illegal with the passage of the 2007 FISA Amendments Act, the governing framework for domestic collection. The act does not require the NSA to destroy the data.

- If you are of Arab descent and attend a mosque whose imam was linked through degrees of association with Islamic charities considered as supporters of terrorism, NSA computers probably analyzed metadata from your telephone communications and email.

- Your data might have been intercepted or collected by Russia, China, or Israel if you traveled to those countries. The FBI has quietly removed from several Washington, D.C.–area cell phone towers, transmitters that fed all data to wire rooms at foreign embassies.

- The chances, if you are not a criminal or a terrorist, that an analyst at the NSA listened to one of your telephone conversations or read one of your email messages are infinitesimally small given the technological challenges associated with the program, not to mention the lack of manpower available to sort through your irrelevant communications. If an unintentional collection occurred (an overcollect), it would be deleted and not stored in any database.

What safeguards exist today? From what we could figure out, only three dozen or so people inside the NSA have the authority to read the content of FISA-derived material, all of which is now subject to a warrant.[49] Can the NSA share FISA product on U.S. persons with other countries? By law it cannot and does not. (The FBI can, and does.) What is the size of the compliance staff that monitors domestic collection? Four or five people, depending on the budget cycle. How many people outside the NSA are privy to the full details of the program? More than one thousand. How can you find out if you've been accidentally or incidentally surveilled? You can't. You can sue, but the government will invoke a state secrets privilege, and judges will probably agree—even when you can prove without any secret evidence that there is probable cause to believe that you were surveilled. The NSA's general counsel's office regularly reviews the "target folders"—the identities of those under surveillance—to make sure the program complied with the instruction to surveil those reasonably assumed to have connections to al-Qaeda. They do this by sampling a number of the folders at random. How do we know the program isn't expanding right now, pushing the boundaries of legality, spying not just on suspected terrorists but on American dissidents? We don't. But if it is, and over a thousand people are involved, how much longer can that secret last?

As of September 2011, ten years after the terrorist attacks that set a new course for the NSA, the special surveillance programs are institutionalized. The code name for the special access program is RAGTIME. In reports it is abbreviated as "RT." There are four components. RAGTIME-A involves the U.S.-based interception of all foreign-to-foreign counterterrorism-related data. RAGTIME-B deals with data from foreign governments that transits through the United States. RAGTIME-C focuses on counterproliferation activities. Finally, RAGTIME-P (P stands for Patriot Act) is the remnant of the original PSP—the interception where one end of the call or email is inside the United States. FISA certifies a slate of approved targets for RAGTIME-P, and a certain amount of bulk data can be collected around those targets. An NSA spokesman said the agency had "no information to provide" about the existence of RAGTIME.[50]

At Fort Meade, a program called XKEYSCORE processes all signals before they are shunted off to various "production lines" that deal with specific issues. PINWALE is the main NSA database for recorded signals intercepts. It is compartmentalized by keywords (the NSA calls them "selectors"). Metadata is stored in a database called MARINA and is generally retained for five years. "Finished reporting," or transcripts and analysis of calls, is accessed through the MAUI database. (Metadata is never included in MAUI.) There are dozens of other NSA signals activity lines, or SIGADS, that process data in parallel. Among the active databases and systems: ANCHORY, an all-source database for communications intelligence; HOMEBASE, which allows analysts to coordinate their searches with DNI mission priorities; AIRGAP, which deals with priority DOD missions; WRANGLER, which focuses on electronic intelligence; TINMAN, a database related to air warning and surveillance; OILSTOCK, a system for analyzing air warning and surveillance data; and many more.[51]

It's almost an axiom of the age that citizens are willing to give corporations almost unlimited access to our data. That we don't even mind when these businesses use our data against us to manipulate us into buying things we didn't know we needed or voting for politicians and policies we didn't know we wanted. But there is a kind of clear-mindedness about the government. It is different. It has the power to kill and jail, and thus its surveillance powers must not go unchecked. Even if the president possesses inherent powers to collect intelligence or to perform surveillance under Article II of the Constitution, the mere fact that he is doing so might encroach upon the rights of Americans to associate with whomever they wish, might chill controversial but protected speech, and might blur the boundary between rights that are secure (like the ability to say in an open forum that one supports the right of Hamas to bomb Israeli citizens) and activities that are illegal (like soliciting funds for Hamas to do precisely that).

Combating terrorism requires a subjective judgment about when protected speech crosses the line into something that threatens the nation-state. In its investigative guidelines, the FBI uses a certain line repeatedly: "No investigative activity, including preliminary investigations, may be taken solely on the basis of activities that are protected by the First Amendment or on race, ethnicity, national origin or religion of the subject." The key word is "solely." There has to be something else.

In early 2002, the FBI and the Department of Energy (DOE) created a secret program to detect radiation in American cities. Vans were outfitted with sophisticated sensors and deployed when the Homeland Security threat level rose. In the absence of information about a specific threat, the FBI would often task the vehicles to check rail depots and airports, tourist hubs and malls—but also, frequently, mosques.[52] Another ongoing program uses DOE helicopters to create radiation maps of American cities and then regularly remap the cities to test for subtle differences. The rationale for these programs is self-evident, but it does raise certain questions. We don't really mind (mostly) when a police officer, sensing something suspicious, runs our license plate through the National Crime Identification Center. Even when she finds nothing, a record of that search remains in a computer somewhere forever.* When the FBI does the same thing in the context of a terrorism investigation—it calls this first step a "threat assessment"—the lines blur and most reasonable people get nervous.† It's also worth considering that the police thresholds for obtaining warrants and arresting citizens for ordinary criminal acts are a matter of open record. The rules of cops and robbers are known and accessible to criminals, victims, and

---

*The snipers who terrorized Virginia, D.C., and Maryland had their license plates run quite often during their spree, which allowed prosecutors to prove that their car had been close to the scene of several of their crimes.

†Until 2011, the FBI could not run names through investigative databases without creating paperwork to do so during an assessment phase; the classified guidelines change this requirement.

bystanders. The legal justifications for these thresholds are similarly public.

The FBI, on the other hand, won't release even the full *definition* of a terrorist threat assessment.[53] The Bureau's Domestic Operations Investigations Guide is unclassified, but nonetheless redacts information about what constitutes this type of stranger danger. In the normal course of abnormal events, an FBI counterterrorism squad receives intelligence from FBI headquarters about a vague and undefined threat.

For example, say the NSA intercepts a phone call from someone in Somalia who mentions training a Minnesotan named Jason for Jihad. Under the FBI's classified guidelines, it must open a file (thereby leaving a record) and use the bare minimum of tools (for example, open records searches, surveillance of a building, querying Customs databases) to see if there is someone named Jason who traveled to Somalia and back to Minnesota within the time frame specified. If the tip doesn't pan out, or if there are too many Jasons and no evidence connecting any of them to Somalia, the assessment case closes, generally after thirty days of inactivity. After ninety days, a formal review takes place. If the FBI develops evidence leading it to a particular target or place ("adequate predication" is the standard), a preliminary investigation is launched.[54] If not, the data collected during the assessment *still* goes into the FBI's massive Investigative Data Warehouse (this it redacts from its public guidelines) for later use in data and link analysis.[55] Under the guidelines, FBI section chiefs have a year to develop enough evidence ("an articulable factual basis") to convince the counterterrorism section chiefs to open a *full* investigation, which can stay open until there's an arrest, or forever.

To investigate a crime that is yet to be committed is to create a typology of thin distinctions. After 9/11, Congress quickly provided the FBI with a larger set of precision tools, among them the expansion of certain types of information that businesses and individuals are required to give the Bureau without a court order. These "National Security Letters," which are basically an administrative subpoena for counterterrorism and counterintelligence, allow the FBI to collect and analyze financial records of specific persons or entities, telephone logs, credit histories, and rudimentary information about email messages.

To examine the actual content of emails, to record telephone conversations, or to physically follow or search someone, the FBI needs a FISA warrant. The exact threshold for obtaining one is classified—again, a difference that adds to the mythos of what the FBI actually does. But here it is: the FBI must be able to convince the FISA court that the U.S. person targeted is directly connected to a terrorist group or an agent of a foreign government. The FBI has seven days to start surveillance before it goes to the court—which in theory could lead to abuses. To wit, what if the FBI starts and stops surveillance before the court ever hears any evidence? Admittedly, it's unlikely that this happens often, as the FISA court is made aware of the surveillance regardless of whether the affidavit for a warrant is submitted. And an affidavit is almost always submitted, in term-paper form, with footnotes and heavy documentation. On occasion, the FISA court will find the evidence lacking and order the surveillance stopped until the court is satisfied, and the FBI is disallowed from retaining records of what they've already collected. If the court is satisfied, however, it grants G-men permission in blocks of 180 days, with the option to renew.

There is another important caveat that limits the FBI's authority in such matters. The terrorist group to which the person (our man from Minnesota, for example) is connected must be on the State Department's list of terrorist entities. If the cell is not, the surveillance may only continue if the FBI deems the person to be acting alone, without instruction from anyone. (This is the "lone wolf" provision. According to officials, it has rarely been used.)

At FBI headquarters, surveillance requests are processed by the Communications Analysis Unit, which has not thus far acquitted itself well. An inspector general's investigation found that from 2003 to 2006 it essentially fabricated the pretexts for what might be thousands of National Security Letters (NSLs), allowed representatives from telecommunications companies to point out suspicious patterns, and promised to send businesses actual National Security Letters in the future in exchange for data immediately—so-called exigent letters that had no basis in law.

The inspector general found no evidence of ill intent but did find a Bureau overwhelmed with suspects, tips, and leads and under intense pressure to perform. It found that few standards had been enforced internally and that many special agents specializing in criminal cases had trouble following the complex counterterrorism legal guidelines that, by the way, the Justice Department refines constantly. This is one reason that Robert Mueller, director of the FBI, agreed to fairly stringent limits on evidentiary standards for FISA warrants, and for extended oversight of the NSLs—Congress intended to bind the FBI to tighter standards if he refused to write his own.

Within the Communications Analysis Unit, the FBI's Electronic Surveillance Operations and Sharing Unit (EOPS) has an organizational mission that, for some reason, the Bureau redacts from public reports. EOPS is, in fact, responsible for liaison with the NSA, other government agencies, and even foreign countries. EOPS gets the tips from the NSA's surveillance and passes along FBI product to allies (the Brits get everything), friends (Israel gets many things), and occasionally even strategic opponents (China might get a report or two).

So the FBI uses FISA to develop probable cause to arrest terrorists inside the United States, and it uses NSLs to develop the evidence that results in those FISA warrants. The number of NSLs issued since September 11, 2001, is astronomical in comparison to the number of investigations opened. This is mostly because a single case can often require hundreds of letters. Presently, the FBI is running a large investigation (code-named "SP") into whether mainline Middle Eastern terrorist groups are inserting agents into the United States in order to target synagogues, or are using Islamic charities inside the United States to raise money to target Israel. SP has required more than four hundred NSLs.

Meanwhile, it's also true that the FBI has a lot of open cases on people who may have no connection to terrorism whatsoever. Because each NSL includes a gag rule on the recipient, most subjects are unaware that they're under investigation. After the assassination of Osama bin Laden, the attorney general ordered enhanced surveillance on hundreds of these suspects. (Most had existing FISA warrants; some had to be renewed.)

It is hard to assess the FBI's record. Many cases brought to court do not seem to have been worth a nationwide surveillance dragnet. Of the 508 who've become defendants in terrorism-related investigations, about half were charged with terrorism-related crimes, while the rest were charged under unrelated statutes. A plurality of those arrested had no connection to any terrorist group—or no seeming connection. Here officials have an unusual explanation. They say that a lot of evidence that could have been introduced is purposefully withheld. In cases where an NSA tip had been given to the FBI (a "GUARDIAN Tip"), the chain of logic that led the FBI to begin looking at the bad guy in the first place might seem to begin abruptly in the absence of an acknowledgment that the NSA had intercepted a conversation.*

Quite often, as with the case of Mohamed Osman Mohamud, a Somali arrested in Portland, Oregon, the U.S. attorney and the intelligence community decided to obscure, not reveal, evidence they'd gathered about his alleged ties to al-Shabbab (a Somalia-based adjunct of al-Qaeda), because to do so might compromise the method that was used to identify him in the first place. It should be assumed in this case that other alleged terrorists who know Mohamud would change their communication methods if they knew that the NSA had been able to intercept their end of the conversation in Somalia.[56] Officially, the FBI told reporters that Mohamud was not being directed by a foreign terrorist organization. That was a partial truth—he had not been ordered to perform this specific task. But the FBI was first alerted to him based on information derived from an NSA operation in Somalia.[57] Mohamud's status from person of interest to suspect changed when he allegedly raped an Oregon State University student. Still, the Bureau has concluded that the circles between domestic and international terrorism don't overlap as much as it seemed they did after 9/11.

A healthy 333 defendants arrested by the FBI have pleaded guilty. And though the FBI arrested more than 150 of them in sting

---

*Early on, the FBI and U.S. attorneys were loath to use any of the NSA-derived information because they didn't know where it came from, and the secrecy associated with the program raised suspicions about the legality of the interception. This problem grew acute when an informal system emerged for segregating the regularly acquired NSA FISA data (which under the Patriot Act should have easily gone to the FBI) from data acquired through the PSP. There was contamination-enough, in the minds of some Justice Department officials, to not use the data at all. From the NSA's perspective, the contamination was the inevitable consequence of the technical challenges associated with the program, and the idea wasn't to prosecute terrorists, but rather to prevent terrorist acts.

investigations—the type where one might accuse the Bureau of pushing people over the edge—at least 243 were arrested based on dealings with FBI informants, according to a *Mother Jones* analysis of data collected through the middle of 2008.[58] Many of the cases closed by the FBI seem quite small. How many actual threats has the FBI prevented? How many people would not have resorted to violence had the FBI not bothered them? Does the FBI, in aggressively using informants and sting operations, create a climate that allows a disaffected but otherwise harmless person to want to act on his impulses?

# CHAPTER 18

# Olympic Games

In June 2012, the *New York Times* published an article by journalist David Sanger unequivocally stating that the National Security Agency, with Israeli assistance, created Stuxnet, the Internet virus that disrupted operation of nuclear centrifuges in Iran. The article's sourcing was an all but official confirmation that the United States had preemptively attacked critical Iranian infrastructure with a sophisticated cyber weapon. The article came in advance of a book by Sanger that contained a granular, step-by-step account of how the United States and Israel pulled the operation off. Sanger even had the program's unclassified nickname: OLYMPIC GAMES.

Congressional response to the story was swift and angry. Members of Congress accused the Obama administration of leaking the story and promised investigative hearings and new legislation. Dianne Feinstein, senator from California, compared the cyber attack to the German invasion of Austria in 1938.[1] John Kerry, senator from Massachusetts, called it "amazing" that journalists like Sanger "get a lot of people talking about things they shouldn't be talking about." He specifically objected to the level of detail that Sanger published — too much "nitty-gritty," he said.[2] Interestingly, the intensity of congressional outrage served as further confirmation of Sanger's account.

Regardless, because of the credibility of the *New York Times*, the Stuxnet story was assumed to be true anyway. Iran certainly wouldn't need better confirmation; nor would China or Russia, both of whom are aggressively testing America's cyber defenses on a daily basis. Ironically, most of Sanger's disclosures were already public knowledge. When Stuxnet moved from the Iranian uranium refinement network and onto the Internet, experts quickly determined its purpose and noted that its complexity suggested authorship by a nation-state. A very detailed account of precisely how the program worked had been published in *Vanity Fair* more than a year earlier.[3] Internet security firms Symantec and Kaspersky Lab reverse-engineered the virus and figured out how it worked; that there were two variants; that it targeted SCADA systems built by the German company Siemens (which supplied the software for the Iranian nuclear program); that it exploited a vulnerability in Microsoft Windows 7; and that it was introduced to Iran's system by way of a thumb drive. *Wired* later published the entire code with annotations.[4]

The Sanger story declared that the United States and Israel developed the code. Well, yes. Given that it was designed to disrupt Iranian centrifuges, and *only* Iranian centrifuges, who else would Iran think was behind it—Bangladesh? In short, the secrets disclosed by the *New York Times* were secrets *in name only.* The "nitty-gritty" that so concerned Senator Kerry was not in fact a consequence of Sanger's story. When is a secret not really a secret? Is it when everyone assumes something to be true, and that assumption is already priced in to the way states conduct their affairs? What is the value of authoritative confirmation when all it does is tell us that what we think we know is indeed what we know?

A U.S. official who was read in to OLYMPIC GAMES told us that only about thirty people had access to all of the program's compartments. Of the thirty, few would have had any reason whatsoever to brag to Sanger—that few, however, had motive and opportunity.

Confirming that the United States helped create the Stuxnet virus had several downstream effects on policy that are hard to extricate from politics. In an election year, President Barack Obama had a reason to show that his Iran policy had teeth. In building the argument for a "muscular" Obama policy, an overzealous senior

American official might have let it slip that President George W. Bush authorized the initial creation of the program and that President Obama ordered its expansion in spite of the dangers associated with discovery by Iran. Sanger, who specializes in counterproliferation, has enough sources to go from there. It's also possible that the official was acting in accordance with the president's objectives. A legitimate argument can be made that it's important for the world to know about America's incredible cyber warfare capability. From that standpoint, there might be policy justification for relaxing internal executive checks on the release of classified information.

But there are risks to this strategy. Privately, U.S. officials insist that for years now, China has aggressively probed U.S. cyber infrastructure for weaknesses and exploited those "holes in the fence." Most of China's penetrations have been passive—whatever bots the Chinese have planted inside American computer networks seem to be just sitting there, collecting data (maybe) or waiting for some signal to do whatever they are supposed to do. At this stage, it seems China is gathering intelligence. Alternately, perhaps the software is waiting for a signal—it's conceivable that a major cyber attack is part of China's contingency plans in the event of a war with the United States. Such are the scenarios that U.S. war planners must now game, just as they planned for nuclear exchanges with the Soviet Union.

Both China and Russia have gone on the record saying that they would view an operation like OLYMPIC GAMES—a military-led cyber attack against another country—as an aggressive act. (The NSA is a defense intelligence agency; the CIA, which is a civilian agency, almost certainly played a role in introducing the weapon into the Iranian centrifuge processing system.)

Senior U.S. intelligence and technology officials have long warned that the next "Pearl Harbor" may be electronic. As Noah Shachtman of the Brookings Institution think tank's 21st Century Defense Initiative has said, "But now we know that what they were talking about wasn't what other people might do to us; it was what we were doing to others."[5]

As a result, calls for laws that would give the government more control over the dot-com domain have new, sinister undertones. The legitimate concerns about how this protection scheme would work, or whether it would stifle innovation or compromise civil liberties, now must be paired with a fact: for every public expression of law, there is also a covert purpose being served.

Meanwhile, attempts to draw boundaries around the global cyber "commons" may become next to impossible. That isn't to say that there won't be cooperation—there are more than a dozen international organizations that already, in a way, regulate parts of the Internet. Countries actively cooperate on cyber crime. Even the United States and China quietly partner to thwart copyright violators. But from the standpoint of each country's political economy, there is little incentive to sign treaties that constrain action if the prime mover of those treaties has already violated the sovereignty of another country. (International laws, both formal and customary, obviously allow a country to protect itself using its military, but there is a real argument about whether they allow preemptive strikes.)

In the end, the U.S. officials who approved OLYMPIC GAMES decided that America's national security interests demanded an action that, if revealed, might hinder its long-term interests. Our enemies in the electronic battlespace will help determine whether it was worth it.[6] "I think there is a big difference between government-supported economic espionage (China) and geopolitical covert actions. I am not saying one is better or worse, but they are quite different and probably shouldn't be conflated," a former administration official insists. "But it is a distinction without a difference, at least for now."

One of the country's most senior experts on cyber warfare, a person who currently serves in a position to influence policy, gave an unequivocal answer to the question of whether the narrative change—from basically assumed to definitely confirmed—would make things more difficult for the U.S. government both militarily and diplomatically. "Certainly. The sad part is that it will be a nightmare for us whether or not it is true," the official said. "I think Sanger's article is a critical milestone regardless of its accuracy."

Long-serving intelligence experts like this one operate on a different time horizon than do the political appointees and staff who directly serve the president. It would surprise many Americans who are critical of the CIA that the Agency often resists requests from the executive branch for covert action because it has learned from mistakes. Generally, covert action should be the action of last resort, when all other alternatives have failed. Covert actions can span several presidencies. CIA directors are often the most hesitant. As former director Richard Helms wrote, "At its best, covert action should be used like a well-honed scalpel, infrequently, and with discretion lest the blade lose its edge."[7] The problem, as former director William Colby wrote, is that covert operations often involve a lot of people, and "one man has the power to frustrate the whole thing."[8]

A week or so before Sanger's story hit the press, researchers in Europe announced the discovery of a highly sophisticated computer bot that sat undetected on several hundred seemingly deliberately chosen personal and business computers. It was dubbed "Flame." State sponsorship was a given. A former U.S. intelligence official said that the Flame was the NSA's first major cyber exploitation effort after President Bush signed a finding allowing the intelligence community to do "whatever is necessary to bring down Al Qaeda and its leadership."[9] The virus took years to code and test. In 2008, using conventional spear-fishing techniques by way of email, it was unleashed on several targets, including Iranian proxies in the al-Qaeda network, and more than a thousand suspected peripheral players and financiers. (How did the NSA get their email addresses? Even cursory attempts to answer that question point to the cooperation of companies that store and process email, most of them based in the United States.)

By tracking the software's progress from targeted computer to, perhaps, the computer of someone theretofore unknown, Flame traces the flow of money and resources and people who, whether for reasons of virtue or vice, associate with terrorists. Given the sophistication of the viruses, it is hard to imagine that the computer scientists and managers who wrote up the extensive read-aheads that go along with any major covert action did not anticipate the reality that each program would operate until—*not if*—it was publicly disclosed. It is hard to hide anything from anyone on the Internet. But more on Flame in a moment.

On its face, the collective response by Congress to Stuxnet would seem to be an overreaction. But there are institutional reasons such a response is merited. For one, human beings who are asked to keep something secret do not react well to a double standard that allows others to disclose it without consequence. Members of Congress are just such human beings. Their access to secrets of the executive branch is contingent upon whether they prove responsible with that information. Who determines whether Congress is "responsible"? The executive. The same people, in other words, who leaked the details of Stuxnet. (Concerning the legal obligation of the executive branch to brief the legislative branch on covert operations, once a finding has been transmitted to Congress, the CIA can basically tell overseers that the covert action is working, or working well, or not working very well, and get away with providing little supplemental detail.)

Tension between the branches flared up after the bin Laden raid, when the armed services and intelligence committees received very little information that didn't make its way almost immediately into the press. To some on the congressional intelligence committees, the administration is simply too proud of its own accomplishments and President Obama so sensitive to the notion that he is not tough when it comes to fighting terrorism, that post facto disclosure (for example, successful drone strikes, thwarted terrorist attacks) are seen as legitimate ways of messaging.

The charge is not without evidence. The administration did in fact provide filmmakers Mark Boal and Katherine Bigelow with a special briefing about the raid, and their movie about members of elite special operations forces suddenly had a new ending.* Meanwhile, the U.S. Special Operations Command cooperated extensively with Nicholas Schmidle of the *New Yorker*, allowing his article to accurately channel the thoughts of Navy SEALs who were on the raid's stealth Black Hawk that night. In both cases, a deputy commander of SEAL Team Six was offered as a source of guidance on the orders of Mike Vickers, who was, at the time, the chief civilian special operations manager in the Pentagon. When a Freedom of Information Act request uncovered internal emails testifying to this fact, the SEAL's name was redacted.[†]

In a hyperpartisan state run by men and women seeking validation wherever it might be found, and an aggressive press corps running a twenty-four-hour news cycle watched and read by a society

---

*Marc Ambinder and Mark Boal met once to exchange details and thoughts on Neptune's Spear. Boal did not tell Ambinder who his sources were.

[†]The Special Operations Command asked the authors to avoid revealing his real name.

embracing openness with heedless abandon, and technology that allows Libraries of Congress worth of classified material to be moved from the deep state to the public domain in a matter of minutes, it is clear that secrecy as we know it has reached a precipice. The modern state now faces serious implications as a result of leaks not as an aberration, but as inevitability.

Computer scientists at Kaspersky Lab analyzed Flame and compared it with Stuxnet. They discovered a common section of code that proved conclusively that the two viruses were developed in tandem *by the same organization*. Because the story of Stuxnet leaked, we now know that the NSA is also responsible for Flame.

This makes the work of our cyber warfare group more difficult, because any future cyber weapons will now have to be engineered from scratch in order to allow for deniability, which is essential to covert operations. In the coming years, this will become a serious problem. In the real world, it would be like having to reinvent the sniper rifle every time we have to quietly kill someone.

CHAPTER 19

# The Next Battlespace

On April 30, 2009, during a national security symposium at the Ritz-Carlton in Tysons Corner, Virginia, Melissa Hathaway, then acting senior director for cyber-security policy at the National Security Council, enthused about the "unprecedented transparency" of her soon-to-be-unveiled review of federal cyber policies. President Barack Obama had promised to elevate the issue within the bureaucracy and had suggested a new age of open discussion about the technological and security challenges posed by the age of ubiquitous, instantaneous communication. Hathaway said that the administration would even release a legal appendix to the report that laid out the complex web of authorities governing cyber law, as well as the gaps that Congress had to address.

But when an unclassified version of Hathaway's report was released several months later, there was no legal white paper. A footnote in the appendix of the main report notes that the legal analysis was not intended to be of the type that would or could influence policy, and the report itself calls for a new interagency legal review team—a team that would produce products for internal, executive-branch-only deliberation. A senior administration official explained that although the cyber policy questions that the lawyers debated were obvious and common, the "mere fact that we recognize them could be of use of the enemy." In other words, merely because the review sought the formal opinion of lawyers from the Department of Defense, the CIA, Homeland Security, the Justice Department, and the National Security Agency, releasing it might somehow provide those with nefarious intentions a guidebook to exploit the gaps in U.S. law. (It was also true, as another official later explained, that the lawyer responsible for clearing the paper for publication was tied up with other matters—he was also the chief NSC attorney in charge of approving covert action, and simply let the cyber issue slide.)

Hathaway had left the government by then, but her successor, Howard Schmidt, did not understand why the review had to be classified at all. He told a colleague that there was nothing in there that the government hadn't already acknowledged. Hathaway made it very clear that the White House overruled her decision to release the legal annex. Administration officials dispute the idea that it was her decision to make in the first place.

The partially finished classified legal annex—a copy of which was obtained and read to us by a consultant outside of government—was written for public consumption. It makes scant reference to controversies about whether the government has the authority to, for example, unilaterally shut down a piece of critical cyber infrastructure during a major cyber attack, or what the rules of engagement should be if a nation-state uses a cyber weapon to attack the United States.

The classified review very closely tracks a PowerPoint presentation presented at a *Texas Law Review* symposium in 2010 by Sean Kanuck, a CIA consultant who would later become the first national intelligence officer for cyberspace. Kanuck's presentation had to be cleared for release by the CIA. It notes the various declarations of major countries on cyber aggression, as when President Obama declared critical cyber infrastructure to be a national security asset. The presentation notes that if country A attacks country B, the laws of country B will determine, absent an international consensus, what the proper response should be. Kanuck's unclassified presentation makes a point that the classified review finds too secret to be released: current technology is not sufficient to allow governments to set up, much less monitor, the activities of nation-states in the way they do for arms control treaties. Another obvious and unclassified point that Kanuck makes—another government secret in the White House review—is that the risk of cyber escalation is grave, because a country will be tempted to respond if it thinks another country is behind an attack, and that such escalation could be easily premised on false assumptions. It is not easy to pinpoint the source of an attack without first gathering intelligence. Assuming it's easy (and, to be clear, it's *not*) to attribute the cyber penetration of an American defense contractor to one of China's hacker schools, it is more difficult by orders of magnitude to prove that the Politburo in Beijing sanctioned the attack.*

With the exception of cyber warfare capabilities like OLYMPIC GAMES and the location of the central servers through which U.S. government traffic is screened, there aren't very many secrets associated with cyber security, and certainly not enough to justify the intense secrecy associated with federal cyber-security policy. Serious national security harm could come from the disclosure of particular government vulnerabilities or by revealing, for example, how the U.S. intelligence community tracks and archives jihadist websites, or precisely how it engages in offensive cyber warfare against enemies of the state. But that activity compromises a tiny fraction of what cyber-security policy covers. And America's strategic adversaries in the cyber domain—China, Russia, and occasionally Israel—know about them in detail, because they engage in the same practices. The U.S. government might well quarantine anyone it identifies as a hacker, so obvious are its cyber secrets to people who spend their days coding for fun and malice. Mike McConnell, the former director of national intelligence and now a senior vice president for the Booz Allen Hamilton consulting firm, wants to declassify almost everything cyber-related. He believes that secrecy significantly distorts the way the public comprehends the cyber problem and provides the wrong types of incentives to Congress. At a time when budgets are crunched, he wants more resources devoted to the cyber threat, which he believes at this point is primarily economic.

The overwhelming bulk of U.S. Internet traffic is commercial. The secrecy associated with cyberspace seeps into the public debate, engenders mistrust of government, and often blocks an

---

*Kanuck did not provide the classified report to the authors and declined to comment on its contents. The University of Texas Law School made his slideshow available.

honest discussion of what's at stake. On top of the formal secrecy associated with cyber policy debates, there is an informal, but perhaps more toxic, conspiracy of silence between the government and private industry when it comes to detecting, deterring, and responding to cyber attacks against the stuff that regular citizens rely on. Until very recently, thanks to a spate of state laws requiring companies to disclose when they've been penetrated by hackers, companies have been extremely reluctant to acknowledge that their Internet infrastructure has been compromised. That makes sense for public companies with fiduciary duties to shareholders, or for private companies with images to protect. Similarly, no bank would voluntarily disclose that it had been robbed. But when banks *are* robbed, customers find out about it because police investigations become part of the public record. Because the Federal Deposit Insurance Corporation insures accounts up to $250,000, customers don't lose money. Smaller banks have every incentive to spend more money on security up front to prevent or deter robberies in the first place, while large banks are able to spread the losses from a single robbery across other branches.

In the cyber realm, the incentives differ. The Secret Service and the FBI, which investigate most large cyber crimes, don't disclose their investigations. Companies don't have to disclose cyber attacks unless data they retain on private citizens is breached. (McConnell's own Booz Allen Hamilton, which is synonymous in government circles with cyber-security consulting, was conspicuously silent when some of its front-end servers were attacked in 2011. In 2009, Lockheed Martin tried to keep secret a penetration of data banks holding information about the F-35 Lightning II, the most expensive acquisition project in the history of the Air Force. In 2011, it bragged about detecting and defeating another attempt.)[1] An obvious consequence of this is that when the press discovers a cyber penetration, the company that didn't initially disclose it looks as though it had something to hide. Trust atrophies.

For the most part, the public cyber debate stalls because of secrecy. Civil libertarians worry about a so-called Internet kill switch—that is, whether the president can shut down parts of the Internet if it becomes infected in such a way that seriously compromises national security. They'd like legislation to address this. The White House doesn't think anything else needs to be said about it.

Does the president have that authority? Of course he does—he's had it for seventy-five years, since the 1934 Radio Communications Act, and well before the Defense Department even conceived of such a thing as the Internet. (Indeed, before the United States conceived of a Defense Department.) But the administration won't admit this—it's a secret—and so they only have themselves to blame if cyber legislation gets hung up on issues they're afraid to debate.

It turns out that the NSA has some pretty nifty tools to use in terms of protecting cyberspace. In theory, it could probe devices at critical Internet hubs and inspect the patterns of data packets coming into the United States for signs of coordinated attacks. It took the government a very long time to declassify another important cyber document: the Comprehensive National Cyberspace Initiative (CNCI), which is a road map for policy. It describes in general terms how the government plans to spend $40 billion to secure the Internet.[2] The main protection policy, informally known as Einstein 3, addresses the threats to government data that run through private computer networks. In declassifying the CNCI, the government admitted that the NSA *would* perform deep packet inspection on private networks.* Basically, the NSA provides the Department of Homeland Security (DHS) with the equipment and personnel to do to the packet inspection; the DHS (using NSA personnel) analyzes the patterns, sanitizes the data, and sends the information back to Fort Meade, where the NSA can figure out how to respond to threats discovered.[3] This cyber shield does not (and cannot, by law) be applied to regular Internet traffic.

The NSA has gathered a significant amount of intelligence on the ways sophisticated cyber actors—usually nation-states and, more often than not, China—have written their code. Sometimes the NSA is able, through its SIGINT collection, to get advance notice of a major attack on a major company. It has very recently begun sharing this information with the FBI, which in turn shares it (or a sanitized form of it) with the companies that might be affected. But it is NSA

---

*Among the other facts classified at the code word level for two years: that the United States needs more public-private partnerships and is falling behind India when it comes to generating and keeping computer engineering talent.

policy to keep its information private. They're an intelligence agency. They gather information in secret and use it to outfox the enemy. If the NSA were to share with the public what it knows about China's cyber capabilities, for example, then China would know what the NSA knows and would adjust its tactics accordingly, thus potentially rendering the Defense Department's Internet space more vulnerable. That's the argument, anyway.

The logical flaw is immediately apparent: the NSA apparently assumes that China won't already realize that their cyber attacks are ineffective. The NSA has either creatively spoofed them (by "allowing" China into a system and feeding it false data), or China might just assume that the United States has randomly varied its defenses. The NSA, in other words, assumes a static enemy. It also completely ignores the real problems—the vulnerability of critical infrastructure in private hands; the vulnerabilities of banks; the holes in major companies—each susceptible to government-sanctioned (or government-sponsored) cyber intrusions.

It's undeniable that Congress and the public probably wouldn't be comfortable knowing that the NSA has its hardware at the gateways to the Internet. And yet there may be no other workable way to detect and defeat major attacks. Thanks to powerful technology lobbies, Congress is debating a bill that would give the private sector the tools to defend itself, and it has been slowly peeling back the degree of necessary government intervention. As it stands, the DHS lacks the resources to secure the dot-com top-level domain even if it wanted to. It competes for engineering minds with the NSA and with private industry; the former has more cachet and the latter has better pay.

Some private-sector companies are good corporate citizens and spend money and time to secure their networks. But many don't. It's costly, both in terms of buying the protection systems necessary to make sure critical systems don't fail and also in terms of the interaction between the average employee and the software. Security and efficiency diverge, at least in the short run.

If the NSA were simply to share with the private sector en masse the signatures its intelligence collection obtains about potential cyber attacks, cyber security could measurably improve in the near term. But outside the space of companies who regularly do business with the intelligence community and the military, few companies have people with the clearances required by the NSA to distribute threat information. Also, because the NSA's reputation has been tarnished by its participation in orderless surveillance, and because telecoms are wary of cooperating with the NSA beyond the scope of the law, companies are afraid to even admit that they've asked the agency for technical advice. As a senior executive at Google admitted to us, "People don't really trust the NSA, and it will raise suspicions that we're letting them look at their search data, and other things. It's not in our interest." And though Google's cooperation with the NSA is well known in national security circles, "Our average customer does not know it and there is no reason for us to disclose how we secure our assets."

In 2011, the government disclosed that it had extended, on a "voluntary" basis, cyber intrusion protections to the Defense Industrial Base (DIB)—the collective name for those companies that regularly do business with the Department of Defense. Reasoning that it would be much easier to monitor threats from the enterprise level, the program would set up equipment at Internet service provider (ISP) hubs run by Verizon and other telecoms; packets coming into any of fifteen DIB companies would be screened by data sets distributed and updated by the NSA. The NSA itself would not perform the screening, although it is possible that NSA employees might dip into the private sector for short periods of time to help. It was an auspicious decision: the reaction from the privacy community was rather muted and even complimentary. If the NSA was going to partner with industry to protect cyber infrastructure, disclosure was a good first step.[4] "Because of its important partnership with industry, and given that defense contractors have already been targeted for cyber intrusion on their unclassified systems, DOD is concerned about the security of DIB networks," said Lieutenant Colonel René White, a Pentagon spokesperson. "Therefore, DOD has asked NSA to evaluate under what conditions it might be possible for the government to work with the DIB to better protect national security information and interests in the DIB systems."

White stressed that the cooperation was "purely voluntary." That's true—but the Defense Department is also writing new contracting rules that would require companies with sensitive contracts to secure their Internet space using pretty much the same technology that the DIB pilot uses. One reason the government is so sensitive about the DIB pilot is that there is a sensitive program attached to it. One way to prevent attacks is through a concept known within the government as "active defense." The NSA could use its platforms at the ISPs to prod and poke and ping places on the Internet where intelligence points to the threat of an original cyber attack. Such poking might lead those bad actors to respond in a way that reveals a pattern, allowing the United States to figure out the precise origin of the attack (called "attribution") or even to design creative ways to let the "attack" happen while not doing any damage. The NSA would scrutinize the attack in real time to learn how it works. There are legal limits to what the NSA can do, and within the telecom companies themselves there are diverging opinions about how much cooperation is acceptable. The legal teams are extremely wary of potential liability, but the government affairs teams, noting that the government has deemed the ISPs to be passive providers of a service, tend to encourage more direct cooperation. Where the balance is drawn depends on the companies involved.

As of this writing, there is still no single protocol or common procedure for letting companies, big or small, know about potential cyber threats. In 2010, the NASDAQ market was attacked, and it took the government several months to provide financial companies with prophylactic information about the penetration. There is no standard way for an employee at a financial, electrical, telecom, or cyber firm to obtain a security clearance. The government and industry are aware of this virtual air gap in security, and they've drawn circles around the problem for years without coming to a solution.[5]

Credit where credit is due: several officials in the Bush and Obama administrations have pushed for more transparency about cyber policy issues, and, in fits and spurts, Obama's national security team has managed some accomplishments in this area, all in the way of providing the public with a better grounding in what the actual threat is. In the summer of 2011, Howard Schmidt's office at the National Security Council released a long outline of cyber policy legislation that would be acceptable to the White House—something that had never been done before. William Lynn, the former deputy secretary of defense, became the ad hoc advocate for a shared sensibility inside Washington, even writing in the city's house journal of international relations, *Foreign Affairs*, about the Pentagon's vulnerability. The DHS began inviting journalists to its formal cyber-security response exercises.

These are encouraging signs, but the government needs to do more. In any event, the cyber-industrial complex is happy to talk about the issue. They want the business, after all. Shortly after he left government to join Booz Allen Hamilton, McConnell was on *60 Minutes*, telling Steve Kroft, "Can you imagine what your life would be like without electrical power?"[6] In February 2010, when CNN broadcast a cyber war game exercise sponsored by the Bipartisan Policy Council (and featuring several former senior government officials who worked for private companies with lucrative cyber con-tracts), the White House was not terribly thrilled with the hyperbolic and theatrical treatment that the "formers" (as folks who leave gov-ernment are known) gave the scenario, which involved a mass attack against cell phones.

This is not a debate the government would be wise to cede to industry. But unfortunately, the government hasn't gotten its act together. Even basic questions, like who is responsible for attacks against the United States, are unresolved. In theory, U.S. Cyber Command (stood up in 2009 after the DOD fell victim to a series of system-wide cyber penetrations by China in 2007) provides the resources, consolidating the various offensive cyber capabilities of the Air Force, the Army, and the Navy. In practice, aside from weekly phone calls, the services still pretty much do their own thing. Cyber Command is developing a doctrine and policy, and prac-tices attacking things quite often, but whenever anything needs to be done, the NSA, whose director is also the commanding general of Cyber Command, does the dirty work. Under the new system, it asks Cyber Command to write a "check" to authorize either cyber exploitation or an offensive cyber attack. Lest you think the NSA is regularly bombarding China with cyber penetrations, it's not. Most U.S.-generated cyber attacks are aimed at very specific targets within recognized battlefields, like Iraq and Afghanistan, and occasionally in countries where the CIA is conducting covert operations. (For example, the electricity was turned off in Abbottabad on the night of the raid that killed Osama bin Laden; either the CIA figured out how to temporarily cut the power from the ground or the NSA had long ago penetrated Pakistan's electrical grid.)

James Lewis, a longtime government consultant on cyber issues, is not especially given to hyperbole. He is an academic, not a consultant. But he is worried. "We're politically inept. It's like the Churchill quote: America always does the right thing after it's exhausted all other options. That's where we are," he says. "There is strong resistance from the business community for better cyber security. Some of that I don't understand. Some of it is pretty clear. They don't want additional costs, they don't want additional regulations. I understand that. National security is not something you can hand to the market or private sector and expect to have it work. But that's what we've been trying now for about fifteen years. So we've had ideological and political constraints that are slowly beginning to shift the equation in ways that favor our opponents."

What he means is that the Russians and the Chinese aren't going to do something crazy. First, they make (and save, through data theft) so much money off cyber espionage and cyber crime that they don't want to kill the golden goose. China, in particular, needs the U.S. economy to function so it can prosper and get its debts paid back. And second, they know that if they cross the line, Americans—well, we *are* a little bit crazy and may shoot a missile at them. Right now, our political system is willing to tolerate a significant amount of cyber espionage and the loss of billions of dollars per year. "It's like the mob in New Jersey," says Lewis of cyber invaders. "They're not going to close a business down; they're going to be parasites and suck money out of them."

A miscalculation could be costly, but the rules are unclear and secret. The possibilities for mistakes due to confused lines of authority are nontrivial. The U.S. electrical grid is uniquely vulnerable to cyber attack: its control systems are plugged in to the Internet, and the United States has successfully managed to shut down supposedly highly protected, air-gapped electrical control systems in tests at the Idaho National Laboratory.* As former DNI McConnell has admitted, the grid is probed regularly by the Chinese government, which maps its vulnerabilities.

---

*According to Lewis, "DHS has looked at twenty-two different power companies, and found that every single one of them said they weren't connected, when in fact they were. And believe me, if DHS can find it out, the Chinese are way ahead of them."

Suppose that during the course of one of these probes China trips over a cord somewhere and unplugs something. Boom: the United States is attacked; China has disabled part of the electrical grid. Technically, yes—but also not really. They were trying to spy. In the very unlikely event that the United States were to go to war with China, we would want to disable their electrical system and no doubt have used other intelligence means to figure out how to do so. What China is doing is not easily distinguishable from what a human source in Beijing might be doing for the United States.

A common vocabulary is first needed to address cyber security as well as an accurate sense of where the threat comes from and where it does not. We might want to start by reserving "attack" for really serious cases where critical infrastructure is endangered by a deliberate action. "Hack" can serve as a guide for the rest of what we read about. There are major hacks and then there are nuisance hacks. Most hacks are nuisance hacks. Because there is no requirement to report being hacked (aside from state data breach laws), hacks encompass everything from malicious infiltrations of British banks that siphon away tiny fractions of pences, to the political chicanery of Anonymous and LulzSec. It would be reasonable to require MasterCard to disclose when a hack compromises the way they exchange data with companies; it would not be reasonable to require them to disclose a denial-of-service attack to their public website. Congress, however, doesn't want to do any of this, because it violates a sacred rule of tech legislation: it should never betray a bias for or against a particular type of technology, and should always be as open-ended as possible so as not to prevent the development of better technology to address whatever the law is intended to regulate. This sounds sensible. But twinned with the lack of required disclosure, it provides an incentive for technology that is cheap rather than technology that is effective. Congress won't tell power companies how to protect their grids and doesn't require them to disclose when they've been attacked. It might want to do one or the other, or both. Tech neutrality turns into tech indifference, which makes everyone more vulnerable.[7]

Incidentally, the government could simply decide to report to the public when a company that handles a lot of data or protects something critical falls victim to a major attack. This wouldn't require any change to the law—only a change in attitude. In theory, companies could try to hide breaches from their regulators, but in practice it would be very difficult to do. The easiest short-term solution—one that might create incentives for industry to spend more money to protect the stuff we care about—would be to speak more openly. The problem also arises in thinking about the future architecture of the Internet.

On the other hand, it is very hard for the intelligence community to intercept mobile communications over packet-switched networks. (Reportedly, the NSA cannot penetrate VoIP [voice-over Internet protocol] encryption, although a senior intelligence official says that they *can*, with great effort, though they usually do not.) This type of communication is very secure. As Susan Landau, a former engineer for Sun Microsystems, has written, "The ability of the government to wiretap under legal authorization is an important tool for national security, but the ability of the government to wiretap under legal authorization is quite different than the government requiring that the network be architected to accommodate legally authorized wiretaps."[8]

Tech neutrality has another good argument going for it: by the time government catches up with a technology that the law proscribes, technology is someplace else. Indeed, the government's Einstein 2 solution imposed on the dot-gov domain by the DHS is about five years out of date, according to officials there. The speed with which the country's enemies adapt to technology is remarkable. Where it took al-Qaeda ten years after its founding to launch its first attack, it took al-Qaeda's loosely linked affiliate based in Algeria and Yemen less than a year from its founding to the near assassination of the internal security minister of Saudi Arabia with a highly sophisticated rectum bomb, and shortly thereafter, the near destruction of an airplane over Detroit on Christmas Day.[9] The threats of tomorrow are being engineered in academic laboratories today. If the technology has the potential to be transformational and disruptive, does the government have the right to keep it secret?

Quantum computing is a variable in the cyber-security equation. According to Tony Tether, former director of the Defense Advanced Research Projects Agency (DARPA), quantum computing in the wrong hands poses a threat comparable to advanced biological weapons.

The physics of quantum computing are quite elegant, which is why scientists are aware of its potential, but also terribly complicated, which is why no one has figured out how to make a workable machine. A quantum computer takes advantage of the weirdness of the quantum world, notably parallel processing, and single bits of information encoded as photons, or qubits, could be used to store two pieces of data. Quantum particles can be, like Schrödinger's cat, in two states at once. The more qubits a quantum computer has, the more operations it can perform.

There is a quantum computing arms race of sorts under way. China, Israel, and Russia have advanced quantum computing programs with the direct aim of gaining geopolitical advantage, as does DARPA itself. The U.S. government monitors the activities of physicists and mathematicians who work on the subject, and the government even went so far as to require scientists who worked on quantum computing for Bell Labs when it dissolved into Baby Bells to remain in the United States if they wanted to pursue the subject.

Tether told *Wired* magazine that quantum computing is one reason he does not always agree with the nostrum that the best science is done openly, with results shared with everyone. It would be catastrophic, he believes, if someone else got their hands on this technology before the United States does, much like it would have been a crippling blow to U.S. military hegemony had another country figured out stealth bomber technology before we did. The United States, he argues, has to keep the bulk of its efforts secret, lest we allow any enemy, perceived or real, to take an advantage. Quantum computing would seem to fit into a category rule for legitimate secrets.

But science is irrepressible. Legions of scientists work openly on quantum computing efforts; rarely does an issue of *Nature* print without the report of some small advance. In 1994, mathematician Peter Shor published an algorithm that a quantum computer could use to break a cryptographic system whose key was based on the difficulty of factoring incredibly large prime numbers. That's well and good, because there is no computer capable of employing it yet.[10] Encryption systems that depend on large-number factoring are called asymmetric; the most common is the RSA public key,* which is central to the way the Internet encodes and transmits data packets.[11] Many banks and financial exchange mechanisms use

---

*RSA derives its name from the first initials of the three scientists who invented it.

public key cryptography to protect their control systems. According to a study for computer security firm SANS Institute, written by Bob Gourley, who would later serve as chief technology officer for the Defense Intelligence Agency, a working quantum computer in existence would suddenly mean that "encryption algorithms such as RSA which rely on the difficulty of factoring large primes will suddenly be obsolete, and everything ever encrypted by RSA will be at risk. If quantum computers become functional very little on the current day internet would be safe from cracking."[12]

Likewise, there is speculation that a quantum computer might be able to break Pretty Good Privacy (PGP) encryption. To put that in perspective, theoretically PGP could be bombarded with keys and ultimately penetrated. But even under the best, nonexistent, and likely impossible conditions, this would require constant bombardment for ten trillion years. That comes out roughly to "a thousand times the age of the known universe."[13] (The Utah Data Center, a secret facility run by the NSA, has a prototype quantum computer dubbed VESUVIUS, estimated to be capable of performing 100,000,000,000, 000,000,000,000,000,000,000,000 computations at once.)[14]

Such raw computing power is one reason most discussions of quantum computing focus on the cryptography issue. It's scary and interesting to think about all the information in the world suddenly flowing free. A country whose computers are enriched by quantum processing could overwhelm virtually every piece of defensive technology we employ, using unstoppable viruses to cripple financial markets and missile defense systems and power grids. Scary stuff, though we stress the conditional. This is the quantum world, where in order to be exploited the information bit must be as perfectly contained as possible. In classical physics, the moon is the moon—something tangible, solid, always there. In quantum physics, there is a tiny but nonzero chance that if you look up at the sky and look in the direction where the moon is supposed to be, you won't find it. That's because the indivisible bits of matter envisioned by scientists from Aristotle to Einstein are more aptly described as mathematical wave-function equations, where a certain something has at least some probability of being anywhere in the universe at a certain point, and might also be spookily entangled with something else that is farther away. But why do we see the moon if this is true? Because these fuzzy equations bump into each other and suddenly the bits of information decohere into things that much better approximate the solid stuff we're used to dealing with. This is an extremely simplified, largely misleading way of saying that anything suspended in a quantum state has to be free from error—that is, the chance that it will decohere has to be very low.

And so the first thing a working quantum computer will do, as Christopher Monroe, the Bice Zorn Professor of Physics at the University of Maryland's Joint Quantum Institute, put it to a curious senior Bush administration official in 2009, "is spend 99 percent of its time correcting errors and the other one percent of its time on computation."[15] Right now, scientists have managed to get the error rates down to about 0.1 percent. That sounds impressive, but in order for a quantum computer to work, scientists need to reduce the error to a level of $10^{-6}$, or 0.00006. "We have a ways to go," as Monroe put it. The next thing a quantum computer will do, one scientist working on the problem told the authors, is "build a better version of itself." That is, the first thing any smart person would want to do with a quantum computer is to use it to make a better one, because of all the computational time and energy spent building the first one.

Tether was at first very reluctant to talk to the authors about his quantum concerns. He said he did not want to reveal the degree to which the U.S government was worried about the problem. Here is his case for more secrecy: "Having something other than the United States get a quantum computer would be an enormously big deal," he says. While some of his colleagues liken the advent of quantum to the development of the nuclear bomb—its disruptive effects are that significant—Tether remembers back to the development of the solid state computer in the 1960s, which suddenly allowed millions of transistors to be placed on chips the size of a thumbnail (no more vacuum tubes). "People back then could not imagine the applications of an integrated circuit with billions of transistors in the chip."

For Tether, it is the economic impact of quantum that worries him the most. "Forget the cryptography. Imagine our ability to model things down at the atomic level and get back an answer in seconds. We could make a new metal, much stronger than steel, that is transparent and incredibly thin. You could solve all sorts of complex biochemistry equations and make new medicines. If we had a quantum computer in 1939, the atomic bomb could have been designed in a week." The United States, he insists, must be "first to market" with a quantum computer. "You really have to have two or three years' lead time in the market. That's all we're really talking about. You're not going to keep in front of anyone else forever. We need to have it so that we as a corporation can come up with new products and new solutions that we can sell on the world market that will increase our economic strength." Tether is advancing quite deliberately the model of a country as a corporation because, he says, that's how our rival nations look at themselves—especially China.

DARPA, its intelligence cousin IARPA, and the NSA refused to discuss quantum computing with the authors, as did Microsoft, which has a quantum research program under way behind locked doors at its Santa Barbara campus.

The government is working on a solution to a potentially nearer-time problem: it needs to develop a cryptographic system that would sustain a quantum assault. To that end, the NSA and other government laboratories are partnering with the private sector to rapidly understand the "major ramifications" that the ability to quickly factor prime numbers would have, according to a National Research Council white paper on the frontiers of quantum science.[16] In a vaultlike series of rooms at Stanford University's SRI International, mathematicians and engineers are trying to develop an impregnable form of what's known as elliptical curve cryptography, which serves as the basis for most U.S. government cryptographic research efforts today, and which is currently vulnerable to a quantum computer.[17]

There are classified and semiclassified DARPA and Army/Air Force/Navy Research Lab programs for the potential uses of quantum cryptography for a set of select defense technologies, including:

- The ability to design a perfect sensing laser for drones or satellites;
- The ability to decrypt, in real time, RSA-based public key systems (the NSA can usually begin real-time decryption as soon as it breaks a key or a code);
- The ability to design radar that can defeat counterstealth techniques the Chinese and Russians are working on;
- The ability to design coatings for aircraft that truly are stealth, owing to the exploitation of quantum fluid dynamics;

- Advances in acoustical detection technology;
- Nuclear weapon dispersal and damage simulations.

Quantum computing has its skeptics, including many scientists who believe that building an operating computer is impossible. The transition from a world of normal cryptography to a world of quantum cryptography would pose significant costs on the first country to try it, which is one counterpressure to the security concerns over mastering it. Even a basic system to use quantum encryption to encode, say, a message from the White House to NORAD in Cheyenne, Wyoming, would require a quantum repeater infrastructure that no one knows how to build.[18]

Most of what DARPA does is unclassified by design, owing to the principle that transparency and efficiency and collaboration will produce the best results. But Tether had a bad experience that leaves him worried about the future of a quantum free-for-all. He was the main driver of the Total Information Awareness (TIA) project, the first major DOD research effort to envision using bulk data collection and mining for counterterrorism purposes. In Tether's mind, there were two problems with the idea: that Vice Admiral John Poindexter, an Iran-Contra figure, was too controversial to tend to such a project that would itself become so controversial; and that he did not classify it from the start. "The reason for that program is that I watched the Twin Towers come down and I knew that we were going to find that we had all the data and had trouble connecting the dots—that type of thing. So we started the program to develop the technology and give the intelligence community a chance to do this better. I put John in charge, and he was a lightning rod. The program being unclassified meant that all of the privacy people had access to it. A couple of them became alarmed and started talking about it to reporters, and then someone went to William Safire, and that was the end of it." The *New York Times* columnist wrote about TIA in November 2002, casting DARPA's $200 million effort as a totalitarian effort to create psychographic "dossiers" on all American citizens. Congress got involved and held hearings, canceled the program, and prevented DOD from engaging in mass data mining.

The research programs that TIA funded were farmed out and put to use. One version of TIA migrated over to the NSA, where it was classified. (The DOD funding provision apparently had no effect on the NSA's bulk data collection mining program, in part because the armed services committees did not know about it.) TIA's technologies are ubiquitous now; every counterterrorism entity in the government uses social network analysis, evidence extraction and link discovery, instantaneous speech translation software, and more. "I assumed that no one would make a big fuss about it, said Poindexter. "We did all the right things. We brought people in. But I guess I was wrong. I thought we were at war, and when you're at war, everyone works together and plays by the rules."

If Tether were to do it over, he says, he would not have accepted the project's Orwellian name, would not have appointed Poindexter (not because Poindexter did a bad job, but rather because he had too much baggage), and "I would have classified it. There was a clear national security interest there. I actually think that the TIA thing made it much more difficult for these types of programs to be created with the type of privacy safeguards that we had. But we could never convince anyone that we never had any intentions of using these tools on Americans."

Tether is obviously defensive about the program, which is part of his legacy; the chronology he shares is not universally accepted, and civil libertarians who knew about the project say they objected to it precisely because safeguards were nonexistent.[19] He blames civil libertarians for the demise of another program that he thinks could have saved lives. It was called CITIES THAT SEE, and its purpose was to set up a networked series of rugged cameras in Baghdad that could track cars and trucks. The camera feeds would be recorded 24/7. "If we saw a car blow up, we could roll back the tape and see exactly where it came from. But Congress killed it after one year."

Why?

"I was told that, well, if you can do this in Baghdad, the Bush administration is going to figure out how to do it in the U.S., and we can't have that. Congress would have rather killed the baby in the crib. They were more concerned with unintended consequences of having this capability. They were more concerned about the rights of a private citizen than they were about capturing a terrorist."

Tether sets up a neat dichotomy with his critics, and both are correct. Eventually, versions of the technology he had seen *did* wind up being used to find the makers of bombs in Iraq, while it *also* crept its way into local law enforcement pilot projects in the United States. As much as Tether may disagree, DARPA's—and science's—predilection for transparency did not completely curtail the use of promising technology. But to Tether's point, some degree of discretion might have helped those technologies save lives earlier than they did.

No technology is born classified; it took the government a long time to figure out it needed to put controls on the transmission of information about nuclear weapons, and it was probably too late in doing so, at least from the perspective of wanting to preserve the strategic advantage of building the bomb. Today, the U.S. Patent Office will automatically assume that something related to a cryptoanalytic or cryptographic technique ought to be classified unless the government says otherwise; the same rule now applies to nuclear weapons technology. In 2001, the Department of Energy forced an Australian company working in the United States to classify a promising technology to use lasers to separate isotopes for uranium enrichment—only the second time since the dawn of the nuclear age that the government used an obscure power to retroactively classify a technology.[20] As of 2011, GE was on the verge of using the technology to develop a much more efficient process to enrich uranium at a plant in Delaware.[21] GE insists it developed the technology to facilitate its civilian nuclear power research, but in the wrong hands, it could help a country like Iran more quickly develop enough highly enriched uranium to pack into the core of a nuclear bomb. The government is so sensitive about the spread of uncontrolled information that it once tried to classify a student's research dissertation.

George Washington University's Sean Gorman culled information from both open and unclassified sources to map the nation's technological infrastructure. The government, when it became aware of the project, saw two things: the secret concerning America's hosting transit communications for many other nations, and the frailty of the fiber optic network that underlay America's digital commerce. "Burn it," said Richard Clarke, the decidedly not conservative former senior National Security Council hero, to the *Washington Post*. In the end, the university caved: it agreed to keep the paper under lock and key.[22]

But eventually, as these things do, the paper got out there, somehow.

# Shooting at Ahmadinejad

In late September 2006, President George W. Bush attended the 61st United Nations General Assembly in New York. Each morning, the president is given a highly classified newspaper of sorts that summarizes the latest intelligence and events from around the world. The document is called the President's Daily Brief, and the most chilling item that morning was saved for last.

The item was three sentences long and marked Top Secret, and it scared the hell out of the dozen or so White House officials cleared to read it. According to one official, it began, "A U.S. Secret Service agent, in an apparent accident, discharged his shotgun as President Ahmadinejad was loading his motorcade at the Intercontinental Hotel yesterday."

At the time, the Bush administration was still weighing options for how best to deal with the Iranian nuclear weapons program. And here, a U.S. Secret Service agent had just given the president of Iran a massive and potentially devastating public relations coup. Mahmoud Ahmadinejad was certain to reveal the accident in some grand form on the world stage—before the whole of the United Nations. He might allege that the United States had tried to assassinate him, or scare him, or somehow send a grave message to the Middle East, and thus upend the entire conference.

"When I read that, I remember closing my eyes and saying, 'Three, two, one . . .'" recalls the official. But a quick scan of the morning newspapers revealed no word of the incident. The Secret Service, embarrassed and chastened, informed the White House that the agent had been pulled off the detail and that a full, secret investigation was under way.

It remains unclear to everyone why the incident never leaked. The agent had hopped into the armored follow-up Suburban and was adjusting the side-mounted shotgun when it discharged. The armor was strong enough to stop the slug, but every agent on the detail— and certainly the half dozen or so Iranian security agents escorting Ahmadinejad to his car—knew what that sound was.

"Everyone just stopped. The Iranians looked at us and we looked at the Iranians. The agent began to apologize. Ahmadinejad just turned his head and got into his car." And that was it.

The Iranians told no one. Not that day. Not to this day. And their silence—their helping the Bush administration to keep an embarrassing secret—led several White House aides, previously inclined to view Iran's leadership as being driven by the emotions of the moment, to begin to see Ahmadinejad and his circle of advisers in a new light. Here was evidence that maybe Iran was acting strategically, and therefore cautiously.


One of the more nuanced arguments against excessive secrecy (but not against secrecy itself) comes from Jennifer Sims, the director of intelligence studies at Georgetown University and a member of the Public Interest Declassification Board. She believes that the system protects irrelevant information almost by design and thus creates tensions that inevitably lead to leaks and conflict. Properly developed, secrets are valuable to policymakers choosing from among many difficult options. Those secrets make it easier to govern. But frivolous secrets generated by overclassification create conditions for massive counterintelligence problems. The more leaks there are, the less liaison cooperation the United States will get, and the more likely the enemy will perceive the U.S. national security system as vulnerable. Her solution is to radically reduce the number of things that are kept secret and to radically increase the protection accorded to those secrets. Here, Sims is describing one of the mechanisms that we've discussed throughout the book: that the bigger the system gets, the more difficult it becomes to manage, and the harder it is to properly assess and analyze secret information. Sims's board oversees the government's declassification efforts. She acknowledges that the rules now in place are at once necessary and impossibly burdensome.

"It was Pat Moynihan's fundamental insight that secrecy is a regulatory system just like any other," says John Podesta. "What really struck him were the cases where the more secrecy there was, the more likely something was to be unsuccessful."

Things marked Secret draw attention to themselves, and their importance is automatically elevated. The CIA was obsessed with the Soviet Union's nuclear arsenal and generated an enormous number of secrets about it. Meanwhile, it missed open source information about the USSR's demography that told a more reliable story about the challenges facing the country. The United States ignored suggestions in the Indian press that a nuclear weapon was about to be tested in 1998, because their secret reconnaissance told them that none was in the offing.

And sometimes the government uses secrecy to avoid doing its job. Podesta recalls a debate in the Clinton administration over chemical plants in the United States. A lot of plants were underregulated, but instead of rewriting rules to ensure that, say, a vat of chlorine wasn't left outside overnight, some members of the administration wanted to classify the locations of these plants and keep details about them secret.

Overclassification is the detritus of a self-perpetuating secrecy apparatus, the result of rapidly advancing technology, and the natural evolution of an entrenched national security state. But to focus on overclassification as the root of the problem is myopic. Absent an official and sustained push for reform from the top, overclassification will remain a problem in perpetuity.

And the state is showing its wear. General Bryan Douglas Brown, former commander of the U.S. Joint Special Operations Command and the U.S. Special Operations Command, says that secrecy "is just very expensive," which he means in terms of dollars spent maintaining the apparatus and opportunities lost by distracting intellectual resources from other, more important areas. Bulk declassification of very old historical records is pretty easy. But reviewing every document that's been classified in the past twenty-five years and has been marked with a "Do Not Declassify" caveat is impractical.

Selective declassification, on the other hand, is a workable start. During the Clinton administration, Al Gore was particularly keen to declassify such scientific data as telemetry from the nation's undersea surveillance system, which could help monitor climate change. The National Reconnaissance Office, as part of its fiftieth anniversary, gave historians a bonanza of data about some of its earlier reconnaissance systems. By comparison, the Obama administration has been cagey about major declassification efforts directed at documents from the 1980s and 1990s, as many of them might relate to counterterrorist activities still under way.

The intelligence community produces an enormous amount of collateral intelligence, because technology allows it to do so. The State Department, for example, is never *not* going to communicate via Secret cables, and so on. There are simply too many incentives to classify something at a higher level than necessary, and no incentive at all to underclassify.

The process to protest a classification decision within the government is rarely used. If minor, inconsequential information is being classified, the public isn't necessarily being deprived of critical information. And the enormous expense associated with any serious go at declassification is a deterrent, whatever the long-term financial gain.

Formal self-correcting mechanisms such as the Freedom of Information Act, the Public Interest Declassification Board, and the Interagency Security Classification Appeals Panel, combined with the informal mechanisms—dogged researchers like Thomas S. Blanton, Jeffrey Richelson, Steven Aftergood, and curious historians—are probably sufficient to ensure that historically relevant classified material is released, perhaps not in as timely a manner as it could be, but eventually. And an enlightening portrait of the deep state for all the public to see is the result.

Ironically, another informal hedge against overclassification is the growing number of people with access to classified information. The more people who have access to a secret, the greater the chances that it will leak.[1] This especially applies to immoral and illegal activities of the government. Whistleblowers will provide sunlight.

One reason for the "stamp and leak" culture is the institutional failure of the intelligence community to find an effective way of allowing people uncomfortable with certain secrets to protest them *without* leaking to the public. Channels that allow for proper and credible adjudication are essential. David Grannis, the staff director of the Senate Select Committee on Intelligence, says he is not aware of a single instance where a whistleblower from within the community successfully navigated the complex rules set up by agencies to handle complaints. And simply put, the people who work with secrets have little faith in the inspectors general, no matter how independent they are, and have every reason to believe, because they can read newspapers, that their whistleblowing will end their careers if done internally.

One reason the government has tended so poorly to the culture of secrecy is that the executive branch refuses to concede that any other branch of government (and certainly not the press) has the right or the duty to question classification decisions, to help determine what qualifies as national security information and how that information should be protected. Sometimes Congress can press the issue. The Senate, for example, forced the executive branch's hand in declassifying the existence of the National Reconnaissance Office in 1992; it was going to include line items in its unclassified authorization. (At any rate, the press had long since revealed it.)[2] But more often than not, the legislative branch abdicates its responsibility.

Congressional oversight of national security would be more effective if the same legal opinions that underlie executive decisions were given to the congressional committees, but the executive branch, citing its constitutional prerogative, will never consider that. The executive branch is self-defeating in another way: the public now more than ever knows how the government works. As a result, it grows skeptical when told that it can't access information, especially as society itself has begun reorganizing itself around openness and access. This is especially so when the government goes to excessive lengths to protect information that has a direct bearing on the national security debate. Very few people inside government consciously use secrecy as a means to sow fear and anxiety among Americans, and yet it fosters that anxiety and serves to recursively justify a permanent state of war and a massive military budget. (Government contractors are direct beneficiaries, as the independent journalist Tim Shorrock has documented.)[3]

Barton Gellman conceives the secrecy debate as a struggle between the government and the press for information, and the way that information ought to be presented and interpreted. It is a competition that is structured by, and limited by, a mutual understanding of each side's respective role in protecting American interests. The notion that journalists even *have* a role to play in the broader protection of American interests strikes some journalists as folly, because it implies jingoism at best and capture at worst. But Gellman, whose body of work disproves any such allegation against him, with a reputation for breaking stories that hold the government and powerful interests to account, never argues for surrender. He wants the executive branch (even informally if it must) to recognize that journalists have a significant degree of control over secrecy. He believes that trust between antagonists can be built, while appropriate oppositional roles can be maintained: "Hard questions about government secrecy involve a clash of core values. Call them self-preservation and self-government. Any answer that fails to take both of those values seriously, and address them both explicitly, has not even engaged the central problem."[4]

Suppose, he says, that we know that the "president lied about Iraq's nonconventional weapons and thereby took the nation to war in Iraq by a kind of fraud." This is the kind of thing that the public should know before they vote. Further suppose that the information proving this was released. "Opening files would resolve the mystery but undoubtedly carry high costs. It might put the safety of human sources at risk, reveal enough about intelligence methods to enable their defeat, compromise ongoing operations, or warn enemies of operations to come. Withholding the evidence, on the other hand, renders citizens unable to judge what may be the most consequential act of this presidency."

Who gets to make this judgment? What's the right decision? The press doesn't know enough to do so. The judicial branch will defer to the executive branch, in whose interest it is not to disclose the information. Congress probably won't have the information to begin with.

The answer, as Gellman sees it, is the status quo: "In practice, the flow of information is regulated by a process of struggle as the government tries to keep its secrets and people like me try to find them out. Intermediaries, with a variety of motives, perform the arbitrage. No one effectively exerts coercive authority at the boundary. And that's a good thing."[5]

The formal checks, such as oversight or an inspector general's process for whistleblowers, are insufficient. The informal checks, like the power of the press and the ubiquity of access to information, are potent and necessary, as are the informal negotiations that occur between the government and the press. Malfeasance, wrongdoing, cover-ups—there is simply no normative principle the government can use to defend secrecy in these cases. Someone must call the system to account.

To Gellman's prescription we would add a few more.

The government uses a vocabulary that Americans do not understand. For example, what does the U.S. government mean when it tells Americans that it has received a "specific," "credible but unconfirmed," or "uncorroborated" terrorist threat, as it did on September 10, 2011? Candidate Barack Obama and President-Elect Barack Obama decided as a matter of policy that the worst way to respond to a distinctive threat was to treat the country to a command performance by scary adults in suits, grimly conveying vague but ominous information to citizens. But that's precisely what President Obama has continued. So what happened? Even if Obama came to appreciate that the old style didn't actually incite panic, it did lead to an inevitable question for which there is no answer: what do we do with this "information" you have just given us?

When the intelligence community thinks something is "specific," what does that mean? At what point does John Brennan, counterterrorism adviser to the White House, consider a threat sufficiently "credible" that he checks his insurance policy? It's astonishing that in the millions of person-hours devoted to pondering strategic communication, no one has thought to tell Americans what the government means when it uses specific phrases. Doing so would not help terrorists. Rather, it would remove some of the Orwellian stigma associated with vague government warnings. It would foster a common sensibility about terrorism, and a more realistic view of what the law enforcement and intelligence communities can and cannot do to defuse potential threats.

Here is what the words actually mean.

A *specific threat* is one that includes details that are distinctive enough to allow the government to narrow the target set (what's supposed to blow up) and/or the identities of the terrorists (not just "two men," but "two guys who trained at terrorist camp X and who might have entered the United States on or around this specific date"). For the most part, timing doesn't factor into these considerations, because anniversaries of some particular event come up almost every day.

A *credible threat* refers to the source. What makes a source credible? Generally, if the source has in the past provided specific (see above) information that has turned out to be correct, then it is credible. Usually, a credible source is a foreign government, as was the case for the 9/10/11 threat, according to U.S. officials. Another source of credible information: a terrorist or bad guy recently apprehended, who may feel some incentive to provide accurate information to interrogators.

What about *uncorroborated* or *unconfirmed*? These terms are mostly interchangeable. It means that the government's massive global surveillance network has not intercepted or yet processed any information that correlates to the specific details provided by the source. That is to say, the National Security Agency has not intercepted a phone conversation that provides verification; liaison services haven't picked up the same information; a cursory link analysis of names, financial transactions, transits to and from the United States, and other data searched with reference to the terms associated with the specific threat has not resulted in any pattern than would corroborate the threat. Or as a senior FBI agent who works counterterrorism cases told the authors, "We call something *uncorroborated* when it meets other thresholds but we haven't proven it to be false."

Why the government can't—or won't—explain this is not obvious. It may be that counterterrorism specialists simply don't know how to effectively communicate often sophisticated information in an accessible manner. It may be that some within the intelligence community believe that providing even such basic definitions would compromise sources and methods. (If that's the reason, then only the president can change the communication posture.)

A major source of post-9/11 tension between the FBI and the New York Police Department has been the NYPD's decision to better communicate with New Yorkers about threats. The FBI wants to be general. Ray Kelly, commissioner of the NYPD, and Michael Bloomberg, the mayor of New York, want to be specific. This is one reason the NYPD wants the FBI to have a presence at its press conferences, but also a reason the FBI rarely gives a statement.

To the Obama administration's credit, when word of the September 10 threat first leaked (and a government official says that there was no plan to divulge the information precisely because there was nothing that Americans could do with it), the Department of Homeland Security released a very short statement confirming the threat. The spokesman used the aforementioned confusing set of words, but he also tried to put them into context, pointing out that as "we always do before important dates like the anniversary of 9/11, we will undoubtedly get more reporting in the coming days. Sometimes this reporting is credible and warrants intense focus; other times it lacks credibility and is highly unlikely to be reflective of real plots under way."

Transparency is generally a good thing. And it is very difficult to keep the existence of a credible threat from the American people, which is also a good thing. Part of our implicit bargain between the government and the governed is the state's responsibility to treat us as adults when it comes to the level of danger we face going about our daily lives.

Complicating matters, in the post-9/11 rush to share information, plenty of inaccurate details got out. Bad information adds to the collective anxiety we all feel when cable networks flash their "Breaking News" banners. Just as bad is a slow trickle of *accurate* details, which can compromise an active investigation. (Special agents don't necessarily want potential attackers to know how close an arrest looms.)

When it comes to real potential terrorist threats, it is reasonable to expect the government—the people who know as much as there is to know—to keep some things secret, and it is reasonable for us to allow them the discretion to do so. That's the public's end of the bargain. But the government is obliged to present a case with due diligence and to make sure that when it does communicate, whether to clarify leaks or simply to inform, that it makes a good-faith effort to ensure that the end result is a shared understanding.

When he became the principal deputy director of national intelligence (PDDNI),* David Gompert set out to institute precisely this approach. He believed that the intelligence community had to keep faith with the public, which had granted the secret world an enormous amount of power. He wanted the national security establishment to incorporate among its procedures the requirement to share as much information with the American people as possible. It is *their* intelligence agencies, after all. It's their values that are reflected in intelligence community operations. But Gompert received no support from his colleagues, and his ideas died.[6]

Still, that forward thinkers like Gompert can make it to the highest echelons of government suggests that the national security establishment is beginning to understand the value of effective communication with the public. That it is far better to preempt irresponsible activists like WikiLeaks, and easier to co-opt (from their perspective) the responsible ones, like the *New York Times*. The only way for the government to keep secrets from being stolen is to proactively give them away.

The press, which gets a bad reputation among the majority of high-level secret keepers, is due for a reckoning. The generation of Americans who will produce the judges who decide secrecy cases twenty years from now will not remember Watergate. They will not see national security journalists as serving a special, if informal, function, because newspapers—even highly respected ones—will be as ancient as papyrus scrolls. Already, this generation actively mistrusts the press.[7] They will likely be less willing to allow broad interpretations of normative concepts, which means that partisan politics will certainly intrude on secrecy cases in the future.

Journalists of today share their craft with the likes of WikiLeaks. They compete with WikiLeaks for the same information. We can use words like *reputation* and *quality* and *context* ad infinitum, but there is no useful (or legal) way to distinguish between what WikiLeaks does and what Dana Priest does. Presently, most

---

*Pronounced "P-Didney." Really.

Americans intuitively understand that Priest is performing a public service, whereas WikiLeaks is—well, we're still not sure.

Julian Assange understands this changing world. As we've demonstrated, WikiLeaks took advantage of the *New York Times's* access to the government as a way to negotiate and bargain and claim legitimacy. He knew that the world wasn't ready for unmediated information, and that the institutions of old still matter. In the future, this may change.

Another powerful check on secrecy is the budget cuts to the national security establishment. (Perhaps "cuts" isn't the right word, as it implies a pair of scissors. Economic and political forces are so aligning as to suggest a harvester.) The intelligence community will have to justify everything it does, and not just to Congress. The National Reconnaissance Office (NRO) decided on its fiftieth anniversary to open the barn door and give journalists an unprecedented briefing about its programs and some of its special projects. Of course there were things that NRO didn't disclose, but they have invited more scrutiny—respectful and orderly scrutiny—that may redound to their benefit, and to ours.

Yet another check we've discovered is that the reputation of a national security entity rests on how well its policies work and how they are presented. As we've noted, it may well have been necessary for the NSA to create its special programs after the attacks on September 11, 2001, but it did so at the cost of reputation. It remains to be seen how rapidly the agency adapts to its next big mission: to protect the country from massive, crippling cyber attacks.

Openness is coming. Whether it's a press demonstration at NRO headquarters in Chantilly or curious tourists in Dam Neck, it's coming. The implicit bargain between the government and the governed will have certain terms renegotiated. The hidden hand that controls secrecy policy is really one side of a handshake, and trust is the essential condition.

# ACKNOWLEDGMENTS

A number of officials agreed to be interviewed on the record, including James Clapper, Director of National Intelligence; Michael Morrell, Deputy Director of the Central Intelligence Agency; and Bill Leonard, Director of the Information Security Oversight Office. To them, and to the one-hundred-plus current and former government officials who worked with us—including several sitting cabinet members, military flag and general officers, and outside consultants—thank you for your time and encouragement.

Many public affairs officers were as helpful as they could be, given the subject matter. We appreciate those who balance a duty to their oaths and a responsibility to history and to truth. They include Preston Golson and his colleagues at the Central Intelligence Agency Office of Public Affairs; Lt. Col. James Gregory, the spokesperson for the Under Secretary of Defense for Intelligence; Col. Tim Nye and Kenneth McGraw of U.S. Special Operations Command; Todd Breasseale, George Little, Doug Wilson, Carl Woog, and Rear Admiral John Kirby in the Office of the Secretary of Defense.

Michael Allen, staff director for the House Permanent Select Committee on Intelligence, put together an unclassified briefing for us on the intelligence budget, which proved quite helpful. David Grannis, the staff director for the Senate Select Committee on Intelligence, patiently answered many questions about process and procedure.

The White House was no help at all. We acknowledge their silence, despite our numerous attempts to discuss a range of issues, both sensitive and mundane, about secrecy.

Bill Arkin was collecting information about government secrecy before we were born. All writers in this field stand on his shoulders. His most recent work, *Top Secret America*, written with Dana Priest, draws different conclusions than we do, but it proved extremely helpful, as did Arkin's 2005 opus, *Code Names*. We found many useful documents on such websites as Cryptome, PublicIntelligence.net, Cryptocomb, and Government Attic. John Young, Deborah Natsios, Michael Ravnitzky, and their peers provide an invaluable service.

We can't overstate the insight, help, and guidance offered by Julian Sanchez of the Cato Institute, Gabriel Schoenfeld, Richard Gid Powers, Jon Eisenberg, Amy Zegart, Yochi Dreazen, Barton Gellman, Dafna Linzer, Matthew Aid, Shane Harris, Jennifer Sims, David Gomez, Matthew A. Miller, Kris Gallagher, John Gresham, Bob Gourley, Lewis Shepherd, James Lewis, Frank Blanco, Robert Chesney, Ben Wittes, Ken Gude, Mieke Eoyang, Chris Jordan, Michele Malvesti, and the staff of the National Security Archive at George Washington University.

This book benefitted tremendously from the supreme research skills of Adam Rawnsley. His encyclopedic knowledge of the subject matter, and meticulous methods and information-gathering added significant value to the book.

At FinePrint Literary Management, Janet Reid took us from a one-paragraph concept to a completed manuscript. We are grateful for her insight and guidance. At John Wiley & Sons, Eric Nelson sharpened arguments, challenged assertions, and turned the manuscript into a book. It was our great fortune to work alongside him for over a year. Lisa Burstiner and her team, who copy edited this and *The Command: Deep Inside the President's Secret Army*, have our sincerest thanks.

The Fund for Investigative Journalism provided a grant that helped make this book possible. Thank you for assisting us, and for all the things you do to bring the truth to light, and make the world a more just place.

# NOTES

## Introduction: Asleep under Fire

1. Kenneth R. Mayer, *With the Stroke of a Pen: Executive Orders and Presidential Power* (Princeton: Princeton University Press, 2001), 146.
2. Report of the Commission on Protecting and Reducing Government Secrecy, Hearing before the Committee on Governmental Affairs, United States Senate, 105th Congress, First Session, May 7, 1997, p. 20, Testimony of David Wise, Washington, DC.
3. Daniel Patrick Moynihan, *Secrecy: The American Experience* (New Haven: Yale University Press, 1998), 216–217.
4. Chris Lawrence and Padma Rama, "Pentagon Destroys Thousands of Copies of Army Officer's Memoir," CNN, September 28, 2010, http://www.cnn.com/2010/US/09/25/books.destroyed/index.html.
5. Meredith Chaiken, "Poll: Americans Say WikiLeaks Harmed Public Interest; Most Want Assange Arrested," *Washington Post*, December 14, 2010, http://www.washingtonpost.com/wp-dyn/content/article/2010/12/14/AR2010121401650.html.
6. Michael Sheridan, "Julian Assange: WikiLeaks 'Insurance' File Could Unleash Secrets Should Website Get Taken Down," *New York Daily News*, December 5, 2010, http://articles.nydailynews.com/2010-12-05/news/27083351_1_wikileaks-new-servers-fox-news.
7. Adam Levine, "Top Military Official: WikiLeaks Founder May Have 'Blood' on His Hands," CNN, July 29, 2010, http://articles.cnn.com/2010-07-29/us/wikileaks.mullen.gates_1_julian-assange-leak-defense-robert-gates?_s=PM:US.
8. David Foster Wallace, *Infinite Jest: A Novel* (Boston: Little, Brown, 1996), 478.

## 1. Need to Know

1. Gabriel Schoenfeld, *Necessary Secrets: National Security, the Media, and the Rule of Law* (New York: Norton, 2010), 109.
2. Ibid.
3. Herbert O. Yardley, *The American Black Chamber* (Annapolis: Naval Institute Press, 1931), 20.
4. Patrick Radden Keefe, *Chatter: Dispatches from the Secret World of Global Eavesdropping* (New York: Random House, 2006), 10.
5. Michael Smith, *MI6: The Real James Bonds 1909–1939* (London: Dialogue, 2011).
6. John Earl Haynes and Harvey Klehr, *Venona: Decoding Soviet Espionage in America* (New Haven: Yale University Press, 1999), 15–16.
7. Matthew M. Aid, *The Secret Sentry: The Untold History of the National Security Agency* (New York: Bloomsbury, 2009), 26–27.
8. Ibid., 33.
9. National Security Council Intelligence Directive No. 9, "Communications Intelligence," December 29, 1952.
10. T. M. Hannah, "The Many Lives of Herbert O. Yardley," *Cryptologic Spectrum* (Fort George G. Meade, Maryland: National Security Agency, 1981), 26.
11. Todd S. Purdum, "Clinton Ends Ban on Security Clearance for Gay Workers," *New York Times*, August 5, 1995.
12. James Risen, "CIA to Issue Guidelines on Hiring Foreign Agents," *Los Angeles Times*, June 20, 1995.
13. John Deutch and Jeffrey Smith, "Smarter Intelligence," *Foreign Policy*, February 2002.
14. Douglas Jehl, "Abundance of Caution and Years of Budget Cuts Are Seen to Limit C.I.A.," *New York Times*, May 11, 2004.
15. Dana Priest and William Arkin, "A Hidden World, Growing beyond Control," *Washington Post*, July 19, 2010.
16. Government Accountability Office, "Personnel Security Clearances," May 19, 2009, http://www.gao.gov/products/GAO-09-488.
17. Ibid.

## 2. The Curious Case of Primoris Era

1. U.S. Office of Personnel Management, Questionnaire for National Security Positions (Standard Form 86), December 2010.
2. Spencer Ackerman, "Unfollowed: How a (Possible) Social Network Spy Came Undone," *Wired*, August 28, 2011, http://www.wired.com/dangerroom/2011/04/unfollowed-how-a-possible-social-network-spy-came-undone/all/1.
3. Naadir Jeewa, "An Update: The Company behind the Twitter Spies," *Random Variable*, April 30, 2011, http://www.randomvariable.co.uk/blog/2011/04/30/an-update-the-company-behind-the-twitter-spies/.
4. Marc Ambinder had a conversation with the sailor, who asked that his name be withheld; the author independently verified his identity.
5. Thomas Ryan, "Getting in Bed with Robin Sage," 2010, http://www.privacywonk.net/download/BlackHat-USA-2010-Ryan-Getting-In-Bed-With-Robin-Sage-v1.0.pdf, 2.
6. Ibid.

7. Ibid., 3.

8. Ibid., 4.

9. Shaun Waterman, "Fictitious Femme Fatale Fooled Cybersecurity," *Washington Times*, July 18, 2010, http://www.washingtontimes.com/news/2010/jul/18/fictitious-femme-fatale-fooled-cybersecurity/?page=1.

10. Ryan, "Getting in Bed with Robin Sage," 5.

11. Archived screenshots of http://www.twitter.com/PrimorisEra.

12. Jeffrey Rosen, "The Web Means the End of Forgetting," *New York Times Sunday Magazine*, July 21, 2010, MM30.

13. Laura Emmett, "WikiLeaks Revelations Only Tip of Iceberg—Assange," *RT*, May 2, 2011, http://rt.com/news/wikileaks-revelations-assange-interview/.

14. Matt Raymond, "How Tweet It Is!: Library Acquires Entire Twitter Archive," Library of Congress, April 14, 2010, http://blogs.loc.gov/loc/2010/04/how-tweet-it-is-library-acquires-entire-twitter-archive/.

15. Rosen, "The Web Means the End of Forgetting."

16. Marine Administrative Message, "Immediate Ban of Internet Social Networking Sites (SNS) on Marine Corps Enterprise Network (MCEN) NIPRNET," U.S. Marine Corps, August 9, 2009, http://www.marines.mil/news/messages/Pages/MARADMIN0458-09.aspx.

17. William Lynn, Deputy Secretary of Defense Memorandum, "Directive-Type Memorandum (DTM) 09-026—Responsible and Effective Use of Internet-Based Capabilities," February 25, 2010, http://www.defense.gov/NEWS/DTM%2009-026.pdf.

18. Nancy Gohring, "U.S. Defense Department OKs Social Networking," *PC World*, March 1, 2010.

19. Personal email to Marc Ambinder, February 23, 2012.

20. Adam Rawnsley, "Hidden Bases, Secret Raids: WikiLeaks Reveals CIA's Iraq Ops," *Wired*, October 27, 2010, http://www.wired.com/dangerroom/2010/10/hidden-bases-secret-raids-wikileaks-reveals-cias-iraq-ops/.

## 3. From Inception to Eternity

1. John Maxwell Hamilton, *Journalism's Roving Eye: A History of American Foreign Reporting* (Baton Rouge: Louisiana State University Press, 2009), 151.

2. Ibid.

3. Daniel Patrick Moynihan, *Secrecy: The American Experience* (New Haven: Yale University Press, 1998), 133.

4. Philip H. Melanson, *Secrecy Wars: National Security, Privacy, and the Public's Right to Know* (Washington, DC: Brassey's, 2001), 173.

5. Charlie Savage, "Cheney Says He Urged Bush to Bomb Syria in '07," *New York Times*, August 25, 2011, A18.

6. Kevin Poulsen and Kim Zetter, "'I Can't Believe What I'm Confessing to You': The Wikileaks Chats," *Wired*, June 10, 2010, http://www.wired.com/threatlevel/2010/06/wikileaks-chat/.

7. D. M. Thomas Jr., Memorandum for Commander, "Combatant Status Review Tribal Input and Recommendation for Continued Detention under DOD Control (CD) for Guantanamo Detainee, ISN: US9KU-010024DP (S)," Headquarters Joint Task Force Guantanamo, December 8, 2006.

8. Jennifer K. Elsea, "Criminal Prohibitions on the Disclosure of Classified Information," Congressional Research Service, September, 2011, 19–24.

9. Gabriel Schoenfeld, "Has the *New York Times* Violated the Espionage Act?," *Commentary*, March 2006; this article was the genesis for his well-argued book on the subject.

10. Background on the court rulings can be found in Elsea, "Criminal Prohibitions on the Disclosure of Classified Information," 22–24.

11. John N. Nassikas III, Kate B. Briscoe, et al., *Memorandum of Law in Support of Defendants Steven J. Rosen's and Keith Weissman's Motion to Dismiss the Superseding Indictment*, U.S. District Court for the Eastern District of Virginia, Alexandria Division, January 19, 2006, http://www.fas.org/sgp/jud/rosen011906.pdf.

12. *United States v. Samuel Morison*, 844 F.2d 1057 (4th Cir. 1988).

13. Michael Kinsley, "Secrets and Spies," *Slate*, June 9, 2006.

14. Dan Morain, "Davis Defends Warning of Bridge Attack," *Los Angeles Times*, November 3, 2001, http://articles.latimes.com/2001/nov/03/local/me-65203/2.

15. Library of Congress, *James Madison and the Federal Constitutional Convention of 1787*, http://memory.loc.gov/ammem/collections/madison_papers/mjmconst.html.

## 4. Fairly Modest

1. WikiLeaks, "Collateral Murder," April 5, 2010, http://www.collateralmurder.com/.

2. Bill Keller, "Dealing with Assange and the WikiLeaks Secrets," *New York Times*, January 30, 2011, MM32.

3. Tim Hsia, "Reaction on Military Blogs to the WikiLeaks Video," *New York Times*, April 7, 2010, http://atwar.blogs.nytimes.com/2010/04/07/reaction-on-military-blogs-to-the-wikileaks-video/.

4. Ibid.

5. Michael Hastings, "Julian Assange: The Rolling Stone Interview," *Rolling Stone*, January 18, 2012, http://www.rollingstone.com/politics/news/julian-assange-the-rolling-stone-interview-20120118.

6. "190946: Interior Secretary Provides Terms of A. Q. Khan's Modified Detention," http://www.cablegatesearch.net/cable.php?id=09ISLAMABAD280.

7. "F-16 Security Notes: Request for Two Specific Changes That Will Benefit Coalition Operations," http://www.cablegatesearch.net/cable.php?id=07ISLAMABAD2794.

8. "VFM Chun Young-woo on Sino–North Korean Relations," http://www.cablegatesearch.net/cable.php?id=10SEOUL272.

9. "Google Update: PRC Role in Attacks and Response Strategy," http://www.cablegatesearch.net/cable.php?id=10BEIJING207.

10. "Al-Masri Case—Chancellery Aware of USG Concerns," http://www.cablegatesearch.net/cable.php?id=07BERLIN242&version=1314919461.

11. "Saudi King Abdullah and Senior Princes on Saudi Policy Toward Iraq," http://www.cablegatesearch.net/cable.php?id=08RIYADH649.

12. "General Petraeus with King Hamad: Iraq, Afghanistan, Iran, NATO AWACS, Energy," http://www.cablegatesearch.net/cable.php?id=09MANAMA642.

13. "Yemen's Counter Terrorism Unit Stretched Thin by War against Houthis," http://www.cablegatesearch.net/cable.php?id=09SANAA2230.

14. "Syrian Intelligence Chief Attends CT Dialogue with S/CT Benjamin," http://www.cablegatesearch.net/cable.php?id=10DAMASCUS159.

15. "Spain Details Its Strategy to Combat the Russian Mafia," http://www.cablegate search.net/cable.php?id=10MADRID154.
16. "Medvedev's Address and Tandem Politics," http://www.cablegatesearch.net/cable .php?id=08MOSCOW3343.
17. "DOD News Briefing with Secretary Gates and Adm. Mullen from the Pentagon," U.S. Department of Defense, Office of the Assistant Secretary of Defense (Public Affairs), News Transcript, November 30, 2010, http://www.fas.org/sgp/ news/2010/11/dod113010.html.
18. Scott Neuman, "Clinton: WikiLeaks 'Tear at Fabric' of Government," NPR, November 29, 2010, http://www.npr.org/2010/11/29/131668950/white-house-aims-to-limit-wikileaks-damage.
19. Thomas Jefferson, *The Writings of Thomas Jefferson*, vol. 8 (Thomas Jefferson Memorial Association, 1904), 92–93.
20. David Newsom, *The Public Dimension of Foreign Policy* (Bloomington: Indiana University Press, 1996), 33.
21. "WikiSecrets: Julian Assange Interview Transcript," *Frontline*, April 4, 2011, http:// www.pbs.org/wgbh/pages/frontline/wikileaks/interviews/julian-assange.html.
22. "Wikileaks U.S. Diplomatic Cables: Key Pakistan Issues," BBC, December 1, 2010, http://www.bbc.co.uk/news/world-south-asia-11886512.
23. Peter Wright, *Spycatcher: The Candid Autobiography of a Senior Intelligence Officer* (New York: Viking, 1987).

## 5. Vital Information

1. Dwight D. Eisenhower, *Mandate for Change, 1953–1956* (New York: Doubleday, 1963), 90.
2. Ralph E. Weber, *Spymasters: Ten CIA Officers in Their Own Words* (Wilmington, DE: Scholarly Resources, 1999), 117.
3. D. K. R. Crosswell, *Beetle: The Life of General Walter Bedell Smith* (Lexington: University Press of Kentucky, 2010), 48.
4. Ibid.
5. Tim Weiner, *Legacy of Ashes: The History of the CIA* (New York: Doubleday, 2007), 80.
6. Ibid., 76.
7. Roger Z. George and Robert D. Kline, eds., *Intelligence and the National Security Strategist: Enduring Issues and Challenges* (Lanham, MD: Rowman & Littlefield, 2005), 437.
8. Ibid.; David M. Barrett, *The CIA and Congress: The Untold Story from Truman to Kennedy* (Lawrence: University Press of Kansas, 2005), 380.
9. Christopher Andrew, *For the President's Eyes Only: Secret Intelligence and the American Presidency from Washington to Bush* (New York: HarperPerennial, 1996), 222.
10. Barrett, *The CIA and Congress*, 385.
11. Clarence R. Wyatt, *Paper Soldiers: The American Press and the Vietnam War* (Chicago: University of Chicago Press, 1995), 20.
12. Ronald Kessler, *The CIA at War* (New York: St. Martin's, 2003), 67.
13. Ibid.
14. Barrett, *The CIA and Congress*, 381–382.
15. Ibid., 386.
16. Kessler, *The CIA at War*, 68.

17. Barrett, *The CIA and Congress*, 416.
18. Donald Rumsfeld, memorandum to Steve Cambone, September 12, 2003.
19. General Wayne Downing, memorandum for the Secretary of Defense and Chairman of the Joint Chiefs of Staff, Special Operations Force Assessment, November 9, 2005. http://library.rumsfeld.com/doclib/sp/413/2005-11-09%20from%20General%20Wayne%20Downing%20re%20Special%20Operations%20Force%20Assesment.pdf.

## 6. The Horrors Book

1. Memorandum of Conversation, the Oval Office, the White House, January 4, 1975, Allegations of CIA Domestic Activities, Gerald R. Ford Library.
2. Memorandum for the File, United States Government, January 3, 1975, CIA Matters, Gerald R. Ford Library.
3. Memorandum of Conversation, Secretary Kissinger's Office, the White House, February 20, 1975, Investigation of Allegations of CIA Domestic Activities, Gerald R. Ford Library.
4. Richard Gid Powers, *Broken: The Troubled Past and Uncertain Future of the FBI* (New York: Free Press/Macmillan, 2004), 271–272.
5. Ronald Kessler, *The Bureau: The Secret History of the FBI* (New York: St. Martin's, 2003), 107.
6. Tad Szulc, "The Politics of Assassination," *New York*, June 23, 1975,
7. United States Senate, Select Committee to Study Governmental Operations with Respect to Intelligence Activities, *The Investigation of the Assassination of President John F. Kennedy: Performance of the Intelligence Agencies*, Book V, *Final Report of the Select Committee to Study Governmental Operations with Respect to Intelligence Activities*, April 23, 1976.
8. Ibid.
9. Ibid.
10. Ibid.
11. L. Britt Snider, "Unlucky SHAMROCK," CIA Center for the Study of Intelligence, April 14, 2007, https://www.cia.gov/library/center-for-the-study-of-intelligence/csi-publications/csi-studies/studies/winter99-00/art4.html.
12. Ibid.
13. Ibid.
14. James Bamford, *The Puzzle Palace: Inside the National Security Agency, America's Most Secret Intelligence Organization* (New York: Penguin, 1987), 306.
15. Ibid., 307.
16. U.S. Army Intelligence and Security Command History Office, *On the Trail of Military Intelligence History: A Guide to the Washington, D.C. Area*, 2004, 16.
17. Bamford, *The Puzzle Palace*, 76.
18. Ibid., 317.
19. Ibid., 319.
20. Ibid., 314, 322.
21. Ibid., 315, 336
22. Tim Weiner, *Legacy of Ashes: The History of the CIA* (New York: Doubleday, 2007), 186, 313–314.
23. Shane Harris, *The Watchers: The Rise of America's Surveillance State* (New York: Penguin Press, 2010), 332.

24. George W. Calhoun, Prosecutive Summary, United States Government Memorandum, March 4, 1977, 4.
25. Ibid., 8.
26. National Security Council Intelligence Directive No. 9, Communications Intelligence, Washington, DC, March 10, 1950.
27. Calhoun, Prosecutive Summary, 13, 14.
28. William Egan Colby and Peter Forbath, *Honorable Men: My Life in the CIA* (New York: Simon & Schuster, 1978), 14, 15.
29. James S. Van Wagenen, "A Review of Congressional Oversight: Critics and Defenders," CIA Center for the Study of Intelligence, 1997, https://www.cia .gov/library/center-for-the-study-of-intelligence/csi-publications/csi-studies/ studies/97unclass/wagenen.html.
30. 22 U.S.C. § 2422, Public Law 93-559, Section 662, December 30, 1974.
31. Alfred Cumming, "Gang of Four," Congressional Intelligence Notifications, Congressional Research Service, January 29, 2010, http://assets.opencrs.com/rpts/ R40698_20100129.pdf.
32. 22 U.S.C. § 2422, Public Law 93-559, Section 662, December 30, 1974.
33. Van Wagenen, "A Review of Congressional Oversight."
34. Philip Taubman, "Senate Approves Bill for Oversight on Intelligence," *New York Times*, June 4, 1980; Loch K. Johnson, "Controlling the Quiet Option," *Foreign Policy* 39 (Summer 1980). Note: Representative Les Aspin cast doubt on the CIA's claim that this resulted in briefings for more than two hundred members and staff, telling the *New York Times* that only three committees conducted routine covert action reviews and that the full membership of the remaining five committees did not receive notifications. Loch K. Johnson, a former staff director of the House Subcommittee on Intelligence Oversight, estimated the actual numbers to be forty-six members and seventeen staff.
35. Cumming, "Gang of Four."
36. James Risen, "Ex-Spy Alleges Effort to Discredit Bush Critic," *New York Times*, June 16, 2011, A1.
37. Sarah Belal and Christopher Rogers, "Bagram Prison Inmates Deserve Clear Answers about Their Fates," *Daily Beast*, April 29, 2012, http://www.thedailybeast .com/articles/2012/04/29/bagram-prison-inmates-deserve-clear-answers-about-their-fates.html.

## 7. Conspiracies

1. Tim Weiner, *Enemies: A History of the FBI* (New York: Random House, 2012), 608.
2. Max Hastings, *Retribution: The Battle for Japan, 1944–1945* (New York: Alfred A. Knopf, 2007), 448–499.
3. Ibid., 456–457.
4. Richard E. Neustadt and Ernest R. May, *Thinking in Time: The Uses of History for Decision Makers* (New York: Free Press, 1986), 140–155. See http://www.amazon .com/Thinking-Time-Uses-History-Decision-Makers/dp/0029227917.
5. Ibid., 142–143.
6. Jack Pfeiffer, *Official History of the Bay of Pigs Invasion, Vol. I and II*, Central Intelligence Agency, accessed from the National Security Archive, http://www.gwu .edu/~nsarchiv/bayofpigs; see also Peter Kornbluh, ed., *Bay of Pigs Declassified: The Secret CIA Report on the Invasion of Cuba* (New York: New Press, 1998).

7. United States Senate, Select Committee to Study Governmental Operations with Respect to Intelligence Activities, *The Investigation of the Assassination of President John F. Kennedy: Performance of the Intelligence Agencies*, Book V, *Final Report of the Select Committee to Study Governmental Operations with Respect to Intelligence Activities*, April 23, 1976.
8. Richard Gid Powers, *Broken: The Troubled Past and Uncertain Future of the FBI* (New York: Free Press/Macmillan, 2004), 263.
9. Select Committee to Study Governmental Operations with Respect to Intelligence Activities, *Investigation of the Assassination of President John F. Kennedy*.
10. Joseph Trento, *The Secret History of the CIA* (Roseville, CA: Forum, 2001), 269.
11. Vincent Bugliosi, *Reclaiming History: The Assassination of President John F. Kennedy* (New York: Norton, 2007), 338 fn.
12. Ibid., 158–159.
13. Ibid., 1213, fn1.

## 8. Inside the Enclave

1. Thornton D. Barnes, *Roadrunners Internationale*, http://www.roadrunnersinternationale.com/roadrunner_blog/; Trevor Paglen, *I Could Tell You but Then You Would Have to Be Destroyed by Me* (Brooklyn, NY: Melville House, 2010).
2. United States Air Force, *Airport Diagrams: Russia and CIS*, October 2010, http://www.checksix-fr.com/Files/DCS/A-10C/Doc/chart.pdf.
3. John Pike, "Area 51—Groom Lake, NV," Federation of American Scientists, April 2000, http://www.fas.org/irp/overhead/groom.htm.
4. William J. Broad, "Snooping's Not Just for Spies Any More," April 23, 2000, *New York Times*. http://www.nytimes.com/library/review/043200satellite-review.html
5. U.S. Air Force, Rapid Capabilities Office Fact Sheet, September 2, 2009, http://www.af.mil/information/factsheets/factsheet.asp?id=3466. The term *Big Safari* refers to the acknowledged special access program under which these aircraft are budgeted. See Department of Defense Inspector General, *Audit Report: Allegations Relating to the Security Controls on Two Air Force Programs*, December 16, 1999, http://www.dodig.mil/Audit/reports/fy00/00-059.pdf.
6. Keith Rogers, "Area 51 'Camo Dudes' on Strike," December 11, 2001, *Las Vegas Review-Journal*; Keith Rogers, "Security Guards for 'Nowhere' Strike for Contract, Higher Pay," *Las Vegas Review-Journal*, December 12, 2001. The figure of 350 security officers is from an EG&G job posting seeking candidates for a security manager at a "TS/SCI Air Operations" facility in Nevada.
7. Email exchange with Tim Farrell, former commander of the 99th Security Forces Squadron.
8. Nellis Air Force Base, Wing Infrastructure Development Outlook (WINDO): Final Environmental Assessment, June 2006, p. 32, http://www.nellis.af.mil/shared/media/document/AFD-060619-037.pdf; Bill Murphy, "Tonopah Test Range Open for Business," *Sandia Lab News*, March 2010, http://www.lazygranch.com/ttr.htm#area52_area54.
9. Threat Systems Management Office, August 24, 2011, http://www.peostri.army.mil/PM-ITTS/TSMO/.
10. U.S. Air Force, "U.S. Air Force Declassifies Elite Aggressor Program," November 13, 2006, http://forum.keypublishing.co.uk/archive/index.php?t-64908.html.

11. Trevor Paglen, *Blank Spots on the Map: The Dark Geography of the Pentagon's Secret World* (New York: Dutton, 2009), 32–48.

## 9. The Tip of the Spear

1. Joint Special Operations Command, "United States Special Operations Command," http://www.socom.mil/Pages/JointSpecialOperationsCommand.aspx.
2. Congressional modification of 1991 to Section 503(e) of the National Security Act of 1947.

## 10. Necessary Secrets

1. U.S. Department of State, *Foreign Affairs Handbook*, vol. 5, handbook 3, p. 1, http://www.state.gov/documents/organization/89254.pdf.
2. Barack Obama, Executive Order 13526, 2009.
3. Daniel Patrick Moynihan, *Secrecy* (New Haven: Yale University Press, 1998), 73.
4. Mark Bowden, *Black Hawk Down* (New York: Signet, 2002), 33–34.
5. Based on correspondence with Colonel Guidry.
6. Chris Monty, "SEAL Commander Told to 'Get the Hell Out' of the Media," Blippitt, February 8, 2012, http://www.blippitt.com/seal-commander-told-to-get-the-hell-out-of-the-media-video/.
7. Based on interviews with firsthand participants.
8. Charlie A. Beckwith and Donald Knox, *Delta Force: The Army's Elite Counterterrorist Unit* (New York: Avon, 2000), 331.
9. Christopher J. Lamb and Evan Munsing, *Secret Weapon: High-Value Target Teams as an Organizational Innovation* (Washington, DC: National Defense University, 2011), 11.
10. Dana Priest and William M. Arkin, *Top Secret America: The Rise of the New American Security State* (New York: Little, Brown, 2011), 223, iPad edition; Sean D. Naylor, "Years of Detective Work Led to Al-Qaeda Target," *Army Times*, November 21, 2011.
11. Based on interviews with firsthand participants.
12. From the author's brief interview with Richard Holbrooke, the special envoy to Afghanistan and Pakistan, shortly before his death.

## 11. The Tools for the Job

1. Avery Plaw, "The Legality of Targeted Killing as an Instrument of War: The Case of Qaed Salim Sinan al-Harethi," 5th Global Conference on War, Virtual War and Human Security, Budapest, 2008, pp. 3–4, http://www.inter-disciplinary.net/ptb/www/wvw5/Plaw%20paper.pdf.
2. Annie Jacobsen, *Area 51: An Uncensored History of America's Top Secret Military Base* (New York: Little, Brown, 2011), 352.
3. Phillip Smucker, "The Intrigue Behind the Drone Strike," *Christian Science Monitor*, November 12, 2002.
4. Michael Smith, *Killer Elite: The Inside Story of America's Most Secret Special Operations Team* (New York: St. Martin's Griffin, 2008), 247.
5. Interview with a Marine who was part of a mission in Yemen.

6. Stanford International Human Rights & Conflict Resolution Clinic, Living Under Drones, http://livingunderdrones.org/numbers/
7. Interview with a former senior intelligence official who worked with Blair.
8. Lorenzo Franceschi-Bicchierai, Revealed: 64 Drone Bases on American Soil, Wired, June 13, 2012, http://www.wired.com/dangerroom/2012/06/64-drone-bases-on-us-soil/.
9. National Research Council Committee on Experimentation and Rapid Prototyping in Support of Counterterrorism, *Experimentation and Rapid Prototyping in Support of Counterterrorism* (Washington, DC: National Academies Press, 2009), 72.
10. Ibid., 24.
11. Dana Priest and William M. Arkin, *Top Secret America: The Rise of the New American Security State* (New York: Little, Brown, 2011), 222.
12. National Research Council Committee on Experimentation and Rapid Prototyping in Support of Counterterrorism, *Experimentation and Rapid Prototyping in Support of Counterterrorism*, 20.
13. Interview with a former DIA official.
14. Henry Kenyon, "A Mandate to Innovate in Intelligence Analysis," *Federal Computer Week*, March 28, 2011, http://fcw.com/Articles/2011/03/28/FEATURE-Di-Leonardo-Al-Special-Operations.aspx?Page=2.
15. Gareth Porter, "How McChrystal and Petraeus Built an Indiscriminate 'Killing Machine,'" *Truthout*, September 26, 2011, http://www.truthout.org/how-mcchrystal-and-petraeus-built-indiscriminate-killing-machine/1317052524.
16. An oblique outline of this dispute can be found in Flynn's unauthorized essay for the Center for New American Security in January 2010, "Fixing Intel: A Blueprint for Making Intelligence Relevant in Afghanistan," http://www.cnas.org/files/documents/publications/AfghanIntel_Flynn_Jan2010_code507_voices.pdf.
17. Based on interviews with firsthand participants.

## 12. The Known Unknowns

1. Author's interview with Michael Leiter.
2. Based on interviews with firsthand participants.
3. Christopher J. Lamb and Evan Munsing, *Secret Weapon: High-Value Target Teams as an Organizational Innovation* (Washington, DC: National Defense University, 2011).
4. "U.S. Military Offers Sheep in Exchange for Afghanistan Deaths," *Christian Science Monitor*, April 8, 2010, http://www.csmonitor.com/World/Asia-South-Central/2010/0408/US-military-offers-sheep-in-apology-for-Afghanistan-deaths.
5. Memorandum to the Deputy Under Secretary for Policy, from Frank Carlucci, secretary of defense, May 26, 1982, accessed from the National Security Archive website, http://www.gwu.edu/~nsarchiv/NSAEBB/NSAEBB46/document7.pdf.
6. Sean D. Naylor, "Years of Detective Work Led to Al-Qaeda Target," *Army Times*, November 21, 2011.
7. John Gresham, "The Year in Special Operations," interview with General Doug Brown (ret.), *Defense Media Network*, 2010.

## 13. The Structure of Secrecy

1. Robert M. Pallitto and William G. Weaver, *Presidential Secrecy and the Law* (Baltimore: Johns Hopkins University Press, 2007), 71.

2. John F. Sullivan, *Gatekeeper: Memoirs of a CIA Polygraph Examiner* (Washington, DC: Potomac Books, 2007), 12.
3. Ibid., 211–212.
4. The best official government primer on the poly is *Educing Information: Interrogation: The Art and Science*, compiled by the Intelligence Science Board in 2006. See chapter 4, "Mechanical Detection of Deception: A Short Review," by Kristen E. Heckman and Mark D. Happell.
5. Intelligence Community Authorized Classification and Control Markings, Register and Manual, Volume 5, Edition 1, Controlled Access Program Coordination Office, March 30, 2012, pp. 54–57.
6. William E. Burrows, *Deep Black* (New York: Random House, 1986), 22–23.
7. Jeffrey Smith, *Redefining Security: A Report to the Secretary of Defense and the Director of Central Intelligence*, Joint Security Commission, February 28, 1994, p. 1, http://www.fas.org/sgp/library/jsc/.
8. Testimony of Senator Daniel Patrick Moynihan, Committee on Governmental Affairs, United States Senate, Hearing on Government Secrecy, May 7, 1997, http://www.fas.org/sgp/congress/hr050797/moynihan.html#3.
9. Joint Security Commission, Redefining Security: A Report to the Secretary of Defense and the Director of Central Intelligence, February 28, 1994, Chapter 2: Classification Management, http://www.fas.org/sgp/library/jsc/chap2.html.
10. Dick Cheney, *In My Time: A Personal and Political Memoir* (New York: Threshold Editions, 2011), 140.
11. Ibid., 141.
12. Joseph Wilson, "What I Didn't Find in Africa," *New York Times*, July 6, 2003.
13. Government Exhibit 2A, Bates Number 001746, p. 62, *Washington Post*, http://media.washingtonpost.com/wp-srv/politics/special/plame/GX2A.pdf.
14. Peter Baker, "Cheney Defiant on Classified Material," *Washington Post*, June 22, 2007, http://www.washingtonpost.com/wp-dyn/content/article/2007/06/21/AR2007062102309.html.
15. David Addington, Letter to John F. Kerry, June 26, 2007, http://www.fas.org/sgp/news/2007/06/ovp062607.pdf; White House Office of the Press Secretary, Press Briefing by Dana Perino, June 22, 2007, http://georgewbush-whitehouse.archives.gov/news/releases/2007/06/20070622-4.html
16. Kevin Bogardus and Rebecca Brown, "Cheney Gets Last Laugh," *The Hill*, June 19, 2008, http://thehill.com/homenews/news/15345-cheney-gets-last-laugh.
17. Richard Sale, *Clinton's Secret Wars: The Evolution of a Commander in Chief* (New York: Thomas Dunne, 2009).
18. Jeffrey T. Richelson, Lifting the Veil on NRO Satellite Systems and Ground Stations, The National Security Archive, October 4, 2012, http://www.gwu.edu/~nsarchiv/NSAEBB/NSAEBB392/.

## 14. Partisan Transparency

1. Dennis Merrill and Thomas Paterson, *Major Problems in American Foreign Relations, Volume II, Since 1914* (Boston: Wadsworth, 2009), 291.
2. Norman Friedman, *The Fifty-Year War: Conflict and Strategy in the Cold War* (Annapolis: Naval Institute Press, 2007), 238–239.
3. Ibid.
4. "Defense: The Missile Gap Flap," *Time*, February 17, 1961, http://www.time.com/time/magazine/article/0,9171,826840-1,00.html.

5. Richard Reeves, *President Kennedy: Profile of Power* (New York: Simon & Schuster, 1994), 58–59.
6. Stephen E. Ambrose, *Eisenhower: Soldier and President* (New York: Simon & Schuster, 1991), 501.
7. Christopher Preble, "Ike Reconsidered," *Washington Monthly*, March/April 2011, http://www.washingtonmonthly.com/features/2011/1103.preble.html.
8. David Barno and Travis Sharp, "The Right Cuts," *Foreign Policy*, January 7, 2011, http://www.foreignpolicy.com/articles/2011/01/07/the_right_cuts.
9. Dwight D. Eisenhower, Farewell Address (January 17, 1961), American Rhetoric, http://www.americanrhetoric.com/speeches/dwightdeisenhowerfarewell.html.
10. Gregg F. Herken, *Counsels of War* (New York: Knopf, 1985), 140.
11. Thomas Fingar, "Reducing Uncertainty: Intelligence and National Security Using Intelligence to Anticipate Opportunities and Shape the Future," Lecture, October 21, 2009, http://iis-db.stanford.edu/evnts/5859/lecture_text.pdf.
12. Office of the Director of National Intelligence, *National Intelligence Estimate: Iran: Nuclear Intentions and Capabilities*, November 2007, http://www.dni.gov/press_releases/20071203_release.pdf.
13. Trevor Paglen, *Blank Spots on the Map: The Dark Geography of the Pentagon's Secret World* (New York: Dutton, 2009), 222.
14. Frederick P. Hitz, *Why Spy? Espionage in an Age of Uncertainty* (New York: Thomas Dunne, 2008), 120.
15. President George W. Bush, Memorandum, "Disclosures to the Congress," October 5, 2001.
16. National Commission on Terrorist Attacks Upon the United States, *The 9/11 Commission Report: Final Report of the National Commission on Terrorist Attacks Upon the United States* (New York: Norton, 2004), 127.
17. Patrick Radden Keefe, "Cat-and-Mouse Games," *New York Review of Books* 52, no. 9 (May 26, 2005).
18. Joby Warrick and Dan Eggen, "Hill Briefed on Waterboarding in 2002," *Washington Post*, December 9, 2007.

## 15. Open Source Strikes Back

1. Noah Shachtman, "Listen: Secret Libya Psyops, Caught by Online Sleuths," *Wired*, March 20, 2011, http://www.wired.com/dangerroom/2011/03/secret-libya-psyops.
2. David Cenciotti, "The White FEST C-32 to Andrews AFB Using an FBI Callsign on a 'Black' Mission?," May 15, 2011, http://cencio4.wordpress.com/tag/foreign-emergency-support-team/.
3. Andrew Orlowski, "PayPal Restores Cryptome for Real," *Register*, March 11, 2010, http://www.theregister.co.uk/2010/03/11/paypal_cryptome/.
4. Osama bin Laden Compound Raid Mock-up, Cryptome, October 9, 2012, http://cryptome.org/2012-info/obl-raid-mockup/obl-raid-mockup.htm.
5. Microsoft Online Services Global Criminal Compliance Handbook, March 2008, http://www.scribd.com/doc/27394899/Microsoft-Spy.

## 16. Resistance

1. U.S. Attorney's Office, District of Oregon, "U.S. Branch of Al-Haramain Islamic Foundation and Two Officers Indicted for Conspiring to Defraud

U.S. Government," February 17, 2005, http://www.justice.gov/usao/or/PressReleases/20050217_al_haramain.htm; Department of the Treasury, Office of Foreign Assets Control, *Specially Designated Nationals and Blocked Persons List*, September 22, 2011, http://www.treasury.gov/ofac/downloads/t11sdn.pdf.

2. American Civil Liberties Union, "ACLU v. NSA: The Challenge to Illegal Spying," http://www.aclu.org/national-security/aclu-v-nsa-challenge-illegal-spying.

3. Bobby Chesney, "State Secrets and the Limits of National Security Litigation," Selected Works, August 2007, http://works.bepress.com/cgi/viewcontent.cgi?article=1001&context=robert_chesney.

4. Ibid.

5. Jerry Markon, Lawsuit against CIA Is Dismissed, May 19, 2006, *Washington Post*, http://www.washingtonpost.com/wp-dyn/content/article/2006/05/18/AR200605180 2107.html. See also El-Masri v. United States, 479 F.3d 296 (4th Cir. 2007), cert. denied, No. 06-1613, 2007 WL. 1646914 (U.S. Oct. 9, 2007).

6. Interviews with three former national security officials; interview with Greg Stone, University of Chicago law professor and friend of President Obama.

7. United States Court of Appeals for the Ninth Circuit, No. 08-15693, *Mohamed v. Jeppesen Dataplan*, Opinion, September 8, 2010, http://www.ca9.uscourts.gov/datastore/opinions/2010/09/07/08-15693.pdf; interview with Holder aide.

8. President Barack Obama, "Ten Questions: Warrantless Wiretaps, Video," August 1, 2007, http://www.youtube.com/watch?v=B6fnfVJzZT4.

9. John Schwartz, "Obama Backs Off a Reversal on Secrets," *New York Times*, February 10, 2009, A12.

10. Glenn Greenwald, Obama's Efforts to Block a Judicial Ruling on Bush's Illegal Eavesdropping, Salon, February 28, 2009, http://www.salon.com/2009/02/28/al_haramain_3/.

11. Interview with Frank Blanco, former executive director, NSA and U.S. representative to the Five Eyes treaty board.

12. John Bingham, "Hillary Clinton Made Security Help 'Threat' to David Miliband over Binyam Mohamed Case," *The Telegraph*, July 29, 2009, http://www.telegraph.co.uk/news/uknews/law-and-order/5934016/Hillary-Clinton-made-security-help-threat-to-David-Miliband-over-Binyam-Mohamed-case.html.

13. https://www.eff.org/node/57955. The case is compelling. For a full list of all the transcripts, motions and related documents, see https://www.eff.org/cases/al-haramain.

14. For a full account of their rivalry on national security matters, see Klaidman, Daniel, *Kill or Capture: The War on Terror and the Soul of Obama's Presidency* (New York: Houghton Mifflin Harcourt, 2012).

15. Tara Mckelvey, "Inside the Killing Machine," *Daily Beast*, February 13, 2011, http://www.thedailybeast.com/newsweek/2011/02/13/inside-the-killing-machine.html.

16. Ronald Brownstein, *The Second Civil War: How Extreme Partisanship Has Paralyzed Washington and Polarized America* (New York: Penguin Press, 2007), 20.

## 17. The Flicker of a Piercing Eye

1. Kurt Eichenwald, *500 Days: Secrets and Lies in the Terror Wars* (New York: Touchstone, 2012), 98.

2. Ibid, 96.

3. National Security Agency, "American Cryptography during the Cold War 1945–1989," declassified February 13, 2006.
4. Matthew M. Aid, *The Secret Sentry: The Untold History of the National Security Agency* (New York: Bloomsbury, 2009), 196.
5. Interview with former senior intelligence official.
6. James Bamford, *Body of Secrets: Anatomy of the Ultra-Secret National Security Agency* (New York: Doubleday, 2001), 458.
7. Michael V. Hayden, USAF, Director, National Security Agency, Address to Kennedy Political Union of American University, 17 February 2000, http://www.fas.org/irp/news/2000/02/dir021700.htm.
8. CryptoKids: America's Future Codemakers & Codebreakers, National Security Agency, http://www.nsa.gov/kids/home.shtml.
9. Interview with a former senior official in the Justice Department, June 2011.
10. Correspondence with General Michael Hayden.
11. Interview with a government official who works on the program.
12. Ellen Nakashima, "A Surveillance Story," *Washington Post*, November 7, 2007; Barton Gellman, Dafna Linzer, and Carol D. Leonnig, "Surveillance Net Yields Few Suspects," *Washington Post*, February 5, 2006.
13. United States Signals Intelligence Directive 18; Executive Order 12333.
14. Dahlia Lithwick, "Secrets and Lies," *Slate*, August 29, 2002, http://www.slate.com/id/2070287/; United States Foreign Intelligence Surveillance Court, Memorandum Opinion, May 17, 2002, http://www.washingtonpost.com/wp-srv/onpolitics/transcripts/fisa_opinion.pdf
15. A good description of the nexus of law enforcement cooperation with the telecom companies can be found in Susan Landau, *Surveillance or Security* (Cambridge: MIT Press, 2010), 80–95.
16. A good guess at how the NSA does this part of the mission can be found in *IXmpas: Intereactively Mapping NSA Surveillance Points in the Internet "Cloud,"* http://ixmaps.ca/documents/interactively_mapping_paper.pdf.
17. Barton Gellman, *Angler: The Cheney Vice Presidency* (New York: Penguin Press, 2008), pp. 144–145.
18. Unclassified Report on the President's Surveillance Program, Office of the Inspectors General of the Department of Defense, Department of Justice, Central Intelligence Agency, National Security Agency, Office of the Director of National Intelligence, 19–20, http://www.fas.org/irp/eprint/psp.pdf.
19. 50 USC Chapter 36—Foreign Intelligence Surveillance, Sec.1803(c)
20. Requirements for the TRAILBLAZER and THINTHREAD Systems, Deputy Inspector General for Intelligence, 28, 107, http://www.fas.org/irp/agency/dod/ig-thinthread.pdf.
21. Siobahn Gorman, "NSA Killed System That Sifted Phone Data Legally," *Baltimore Sun*, May 18, 2006.
22. USC Title 50, Chapter 36, Subchapter I, § 1802. Electronic Surveillance Authorization without Court Order; Certification by Attorney General; Reports to Congressional Committees; Transmittal under Seal; Duties and Compensation of Communication Common Carrier; Applications; Jurisdiction of Court, http://www.law.cornell.edu/uscode/html/uscode50/usc_sec_50_00001802—000-.html#a_1_A.
23. Ibid.

24. "Spying on the Home Front," *Frontline*, May 15, 2007, http://www.pbs.org/wgbh/pages/frontline/homefront/interviews/yoo.html.

25. Interview with a former senior intelligence official, August 9, 2011.

26. James Bamford, *The Shadow Factory* (New York: Anchor Books), 117–118.

27. Interview with a former senior intelligence official, August 9, 2011.

28. Michael Isikoff, "The Fed Who Blew the Whistle," *Newsweek*, December 12, 2008.

29. TeleGeography, Global Internet Map 2011, http://www.telegeography.com/telecom-resources/map-gallery/global-internet-map-2011/; interview with Alan Mauldin, August 8, 2011.

30. James Bamford, *The Shadow Factory*, 208–211.

31. Ibid.

32. Interview with a consultant for the National Security Agency.

33. Rus Shuler, *How Does the Internet Work*, 2002, http://www.theshulers.com/white papers/internet_whitepaper/index.html

34. Interview with Matthew Aid, September 2010.

35. Aid, *The Secret Sentry*, 287.

36. Ibid.

37. Tash Hepting, Gregory Hicks, Carolyn Jewel, and Erik Knutzen, on Behalf of Themselves and All Others Similarly Situated, v. AT&T Corp., et al., Exhibits A–K, Q–T, and V–Y to Declaration of J. Scott Marcus in Support of Plaintiffs' Motion for Preliminary Injunction, June 8, 2006, https://www.eff.org/sites/default/files/filenode/att/marcusa-k.pdf.

38. Unclassified Report on the President's Surveillance Program, Office of the Inspectors General of the Department of Defense, Department of Justice, Central Intelligence Agency, National Security Agency, Office of the Director of National Intelligence, 22, http://www.fas.org/irp/eprint/psp.pdf.

39. USC Title 18, Part I, Chapter 121, § 2702. Voluntary Disclosure of Customer Communications or Records, http://www.law.cornell.edu/uscode/18/usc_sec_18_00002702—000-.html.

40. An account confirmed by two who were present.

41. Thomas Hennessey and Claire Thomas, *Spooks: The Unofficial History of MI5* (Stroud, UK: Amberley, 2011), 233.

42. Interviews with several Bush Justice Department officials and one White House colleague of Gonzales who spoke with the president after the Comey incident.

43. Barton Gellman, "In New Memoir, Dick Cheney Tries to Rewrite History," *Time*, August 29, 2011, http://swampland.time.com/2011/08/29/in-new-memoir-dick-cheney-tries-to-rewrite-history/#ixzz1WfMmWiow.

44. Television: "Cavuto," Fox Business, July 7, 2007.

45. Marc Ambinder, "Pentagon Wants to Secure Dot-Com Domains of Contractors," *The Atlantic*, August 13, 2010, http://www.theatlantic.com/politics/archive/2010/08/pentagon-wants-to-secure-dot-com-domains-of-contractors/61456/.

46. Congressional Record, August 3, 2007 (Senate), S10866, https://www.fas.org/irp/congress/2007_cr/s080307.html; Public Law 110–55, August 5, 2007, Protect America Act of 2007; Hugh D'Andrade, New NSA Whistleblowers Say NSA Spied on US Service Members and Aid Workers, Electronic Frontier Foundation, October 10, 2008, https://www.eff.org/deeplinks/2008/10/new-nsa-whistleblowers.

47. James Risen and Eric Lichtblau, "E-Mail Surveillance Renews Concerns in Congress," *New York Times*, June 17, 2009, A1, http://www.nytimes .com/2009/06/17/us/17nsa.html?_r=2&hp=&pagewanted=all; Interview with current National Security Agency official.
48. Tim Weiner, *Enemies: A History of the FBI* (New York: Random House, 2012), 420–422; interviews with current and former FBI officials.
49. Interview with a current National Security Agency official.
50. E-mail from Vannee M. Vines, NSA spokesperson, October 15, 2012.
51. Much of the information about the types of data associated with the database names comes from LinkedIn and by cross-referencing the résumés of analysts, the job functions they had, and the database they say they used at the time. The names of the databases are not classified.
52. David Kaplan, "Nuclear Monitoring of Muslims Done without Search Warrants," *U.S. News & World Report*, December 22, 2005, http://www.usnews.com/usnews/ news/articles/nest/051222nest.htm.
53. *A Review of the Federal Bureau of Investigation's Use of Exigent Letters and Other Informal Requests for Telephone Records*, Oversight and Review Division Office of the Inspector General, January 2010, 63; interview with a current Federal Bureau of Investigation official.
54. Federal Bureau of Investigation, *Domestic Investigations and Operations Guide*, December 16, 2008, 56
55. Federal Bureau of Investigation, *Domestic Investigations and Operations Guide*, December 16, 2008, 74.
56. Tim Fought and Nedra Pickler, "Mohamed Osman Mohamud Arrested in Portland Car Bomb Plot," *Huffington Post*, November 27, 2010, http://www.huffingtonpost .com/2010/11/27/mohamed-osman-mohamud-portland-car-bomb_n_788695.html.
57. Interview with a senior U.S. counterterrorism official in Washington, D.C.
58. Dave Gilson et al., "Terror Trials by the Numbers," *Mother Jones*, September/ October 2011, 36–37.

## 18. Olympic Games

1. CNN, The Situation Room, Transcript, June 6, 2012, http://www.cnn.com/ TRANSCRIPTS/1206/06/sitroom.02.html.
2. Dylan Byers, "Kerry Questions NYT Decision to Run Stories," *Politico*, June 12, 2012, http://www.politico.com/blogs/media/2012/06/kerry-questions-nyt-decision-to-run-stories-125498.html.
3. Michael Joseph Gross, "A Declaration of Cyber-War," *Vanity Fair*, April 2011, http://www.vanityfair.com/culture/features/2011/04/stuxnet-201104.
4. Kim Zetter, "How Digital Detectives Deciphered Stuxnet, the Most Menacing Malware in History," *Wired*, July 11, 2011, http://www.wired.com/ threatlevel/2011/07/how-digital-detectives-deciphered-stuxnet/all/1.
5. "Cyber Attacks Linked: Security Experts," *Daily Telegraph*, June 12, 2012, http://www.windsorstar.com/technology/Cyber+attacks+linked+Security+ex perts/6767097/story.html.
6. Portions of this chapter were first published online in a blog post for the *Atlantic*'s website: Marc Ambinder, "Did America's Cyber Attack on Iran Make Us More Vulnerable?," June 5, 2012, http://www.theatlantic.com/national/archive/2012/06/ did-americas-cyber-attack-on-iran-make-us-more-vulnerable/258120/.

7. Richard Helms and William Hood, *A Look over My Shoulder: A Life in the Central Intelligence Agency* (New York: Random House, 2003), 184.

8. Marcus Eyth, "The CIA and Covert Operations: To Disclose or Not to Disclose—That Is the Question," Brigahm Young University Law School, http://www.law2.byu.edu/jpl/Vol%2017.1/Eyth-pdf.pdf.

9. Tabassum Zakaria, "CIA Gets 'New Leeway' to Destroy bin Laden Covertly," *Middle East Times*, October 26, 2001, http://www.metimes.com/2K1/issue2001-43/reg/cia_gets_new.htm.

## 19. The Next Battlespace

1. Siobhan Gorman, August Cole, and Yochi Dreazen, "Computer Spies Breach Fighter-Jet Project," *Wall Street Journal*, April 21, 2009, A1.

2. Robert Westervelt, "White House Declassifies CNCI Summary, Lifts Veil on Security Initiatives," *Security Search*, March 2, 2010, http://search security.techtarget.com/news/1407888/White-House-declassifies-CNCI-summary-lifts-veil-on-security-initiatives.

3. Siobhan Gorman, "Details of 'Einstein' Cyber Shield Disclosed by White House," *Wall Street Journal*, March 2, 2010, http://blogs.wsj.com/digits/2010/03/02/"einstein"-program-disclosed-as-us-cyber-shield/?blog_id=100&post_id=11601.

4. Marc Ambinder, "Pentagon Wants to Secure Dot-Com Domains of Contractors," *Atlantic*, August 13, 2010, http://www.theatlantic.com/politics/archive/2010/08/pentagon-wants-to-secure-dot-com-domains-of-contractors/61456/; Ellen Nakashima, "NSA Allies with Internet Carriers to Thwart Cyber Attacks against Defense Firms," *Washington Post*, June 16, 2011, http://www.washingtonpost.com/national/major-internet-service-providers-cooperating-with-nsa-on-monitoring-traffic/2011/06/07/AG2dukXH_story.html.

5. Joseph Marks, "Industry Urges Better Cooperation from Government on Cyber Threats," *NextGov*, April 15, 2011, http://www.nextgov.com/nextgov/ng_20110415_2482.php.

6. CBS News, "Cyber War: Sabotaging the System," June 15, 2010, http://www.cbsnews.com/stories/2009/11/06/60minutes/main5555565.shtml.

7. Chris Reed, "Taking Sides on Technology Neutrality," *Scripted*, 2007, http://www.law.ed.ac.uk/ahrc/script-ed/vol4-3/reed.asp. Note the term "tech indifference."

8. Susan Landau, *Surveillance or Security?: The Risks Posed by New Wiretapping Technologies* (Cambridge: The MIT Press, 2011), 247.

9. "Ten years after its founding," an observation from Georgetown University terrorism scholar Bruce Hoffmann, speaking at the Woodrow Wilson Center, September 12, 2011.

10. Matthew Hayward, "Quantum Computing and Shor's Algorithm," April 26, 2008.

11. RSA Laboratories, "What Is Public-Key Cryptography," 2011, http://www.rsa.com/rsalabs/node.asp?id=2165.

12. Bob Gourley, "Quantum Encryption vs Quantum Computing: Will the Defense or Offense Dominate," SANS *Security Essentials GSEC Practical Assignment Version 1.2e*, July 15, 2001, http://www.sans.org/reading_room/whitepapers/vpns/quantum-encryption-quantum-computing-defense-offense-dominate_720.

13. Pgp.net FAQ, "Chapter 3: Security Questions," http://www.pgp.net/pgpnet/pgp-faq/pgp-faq-security-questions.html#security-against-brute-force.

14. Alexander Higgins, "Building a $2 Billion Quantum Computer Artificial Intelligence Spy Center," March 18, 2012, http://blog.alexanderhiggins .com/2012/03/18/nsa-building-a-2-billion-quantum-computer-spy-center-98341/.

15. Email from Christopher Monroe to Steve Fetter, Office of Science and Technology Policy, June 27, 2009, from an FOIA obtained by the authors.

16. "The Growth of Cryptography," *MIT Video*, February 8, 2011, http://video.mit .edu/watch/the-growth-of-cryptography-9655/.

17. Jodie Eicher and Yaw Opoku, "Using the Quantum Computer to Break Elliptic Curve Cryptosystems," July 29, 1997, http://www.mathcs.richmond.edu/~jad/sum merwork/ellipticcurvequantum.pdf.

18. R. Sakthi Vignesh, S. Sudharssun, and K. J. Jegadish Kumar, "Limitations of Quantum and the Versatility of Classical Cryptography: A Comparative Study," *Proceeding ICECS '09, Proceedings of the 2009 Second International Conference on Environmental and Computer Science,* 2009, http://dl.acm.org/citation .cfm?id=1726307.

19. Shane Harris, *The Watchers: The Rise of America's Surveillance State* (New York: Penguin Press, 2010), 237–238. This book contains the best history of the TIA affair.

20. Steven Aftergood, "A Correction on Nuclear Secrecy," *Secrecy News*, August 25, 2011, http://www.fas.org/blog/secrecy/2011/08/correction_nuclear.html; Department of Energy, "Record of Decision to Classify Certain Elements of the SILEX Process as Privately Generated Restricted Data," *Federal Register* 26, no. 123 (June 26, 2001), http://www.fas.org/sgp/othergov/doe/silex.html.

21. William J. Broad, "Laser Advances in Nuclear Fuel Stir Terror Fear," *New York Times*, August 21, 2011, A1.

22. Laura Blumenfeld, "Dissertation Could Be Security Threat," *Washington Post*, July 8, 2003, A1.

## Conclusion: Shooting at Ahmadinejad

1. Interagency Security Classification Appeals Panel, Information Security Oversight Office, http://www.archives.gov/isoo/oversight-groups/iscap/index.html; Mandatory Declassification Review Appeals, Information Security Oversight Office, http:// www.archives.gov/isoo/oversight-groups/iscap/mdr-appeals.html; National Security Archive, http://www.gwu.edu/~nsarchiv/index.html.

2. Office of the Director, National Reconnaissance Office, Memorandum, Subject: "Changing the National Reconnaissance Office (NRO) to an Overt Organization," July 30, 1992, http://www.gwu.edu/~nsarchiv/NSAEBB/NSAEBB35/17-01.htm.

3. Tim Shorrock, "Out of Service," Mother Jones, September-October 2009, http:// www.motherjones.com/politics/2009/09/out-service.

4. Barton Gellman, "Revealing a Reporter's Relationship with Secrecy and Sources," excerpts from lectures, http://www.nieman.harvard.edu/reportsitem .aspx?id=100824.

5. Ibid.

6. Interview with David Gompert, April 2011.

7. Lymari Morales, "Americans Regain Some Confidence in Newspapers, TV News," Gallup, June 27, 2011, http://www.gallup.com/poll/148250/americans-regain-confi dence-newspapers-news.aspx. Note: eighteen- to twenty-nine-year-olds have seen a ten-point drop in year-to-year confidence in newspapers.

# INDEX

Abdullah (king of Saudi Arabia), 57
Abdul-Rahman al-Iraqi, Abu, 148
Abramson, Jill, 56, 239
Ackerman, Spencer, 23
"active defense," 268
Adams, John, 60
Addington, David, 169–172, 214, 223–
   224, 226–229, 238, 239, 240, 242
Afghanistan War
  Cross Functional Teams, 132
  executive power and, 90
  Flynn and, 143
  JSOC role in, 152
  NSA and, 214, 229, 232, 233, 234n,
    241, 243
  "Salt Pit," 42–43, 55
  social media used by soldiers, 28–29
Ahmadinejad, Mahmoud, 280–281
Aid, Matthew, 15, 229
Air Force One, 122, 190
American Black Chamber, 12–13, 17–18
*American Black Chamber, The* (Yardley),
  17
American Civil Liberties Union, 175, 195,
  210
American Israel Public Affairs Committee
  (AIPAC), 45–46

Amory, Robert, 68
Area 51, 101–109
Areeda, Phillip, 80, 81
Arkin, William, 19, 141, 162–163
Armed Forces Security Agency (AFSA),
  14–15, 84
Asad, Bashar, al-, 58
Ashcroft, John, 238
A-Space, 182
Assange, Julian, 8–10, 27–28, 48, 59,
  289–290
AT&T, 222
Awlaki, Abdulrahman, al, 121, 209–210
Awlaki, Anwar, al, 121, 209–210

Babbin, Jed, 184
Baginski, Maureen, 224
Baker, James, 62
Baldwin, Hanson, 68
*Baltimore Sun*, 226n
Bamford, James, 83, 215
Bash, Jeremy, 2
Bazari, Haj al-, 148
Beckwith, Charlie, 114, 130
BellSouth, 222
Ben Ali, Zine El Abidine, 48–49
Benjamin, Daniel, 58

311

partisan transparency, 184–186
press and, 39
Special Capabilities Office and, 160
*See also* Operation Neptune's Spear;
Qaeda, al-
SF-86 security clearance, 18, 22
Shabbab, al-, 252
Shachtman, Noah, 256
Shils, Edward, 168
Shor, Peter, 273
Shorrock, Tim, 285
Siemens, 255
signals intelligence (SIGINT), 13,
92, 203, 215–216, 229–234, 246,
265
Sims, Jennifer, 281–282
Single Scope Background Investigation,
163
"Site Post Assignment Log," 33–36
SKOPE (National Geospatial-Intelligence
Agency), 141, 142
Smith, Walter Bedell, 16–17, 67–68
social media
civil liberties threatened by, 27–28,
247–248
open source websites and security
breaches, 189–190
Primoris Era, 21–23, 25, 29–32
"Robin Sage" incident, 24–26
U.S. soldiers in war zones, 28–29
Somalia
JSOC missions in, 154–155, 156
NSA and, 214, 249, 252
Soviet Union
cryptography, 14–15
Eisenhower and, 68–69, 70
Kennedy on "missile gap," 176–177,
178–179
Oswald and, 96, 98
press and confidential information, 37
*See also* Russia
Space Imaging, 104
Sparks, William Sidney, 83
special access programs (SAPs), 166–167
Special Air Service (SAS) (Britain), 75
Special Capabilities Office (SCO),
159–162
Special Intelligence (SI), 165

Special Operations Command
(SOCOM), 116, 118, 129, 140–146,
154, 156–158
specific threat, defined, 287
*Spiegel, Der* (Germany), 51, 52
SRI International, Stanford University, 276
STA-6400 Semantic Traffic Analyzers,
222n
state secrets privilege, 194–212
drone program, 209–211
Foreign Intelligence Surveillance Act,
198–199, 201, 206
Al-Haramain case, 194–195, 200–207
El-Masri case, 197–198
*Mohamed et al. v. Jeppesen Dataplan,*
200
torture of detainees, 207–209
*United States v. Reynolds,* 195–196
Status of Forces Agreement (SOFA), 151
Stavridis, James, 25
Stephanopoulos, George, 36
Stevenson, Adlai, 37
Stimson, Henry, 13, 94
Stonestreet, Eric, 36
Stored Communications Act of 1986
(SCA), 235, 237
Stuxnet, 254–260
Sulzberger, Arthur Hays, 68
Swope, Herbert, 37
Symantec, 255
Symington, Stuart, 176–177, 178–179
Syria
nuclear weapon program of, 182–184
WikiLeaks on, 58

Talent-Keyhole (TK), 165
Tamm, Terrence, 240
*Task Force Black* (Urban), 73
Task Force 9-14 (Task Force North), 149
Taubman, Phil, 239
telecommunications industry
cell phone technology and, 141–142,
161, 230
cyber security and, 267–268
domestic surveillance and, 82–85, 217,
220, 222, 241
*See also* National Security Agency
(NSA)